MW01492385

THE CALCUTTA QURAN PETITION

The Calcutta Quran Petition

compiled with an introduction by
SITA RAM GOEL

VOICE OF INDIA
New Delhi

First edition, 1986
Second enlarged edition, 1987
Third revised and enlarged edition, 1999
Third reprint of revised and enlarged edition, 2018

ISBN 978-81-85990-58-3

website: www.voiceofin.com

Published by Voice of India, 2/18, Ansari Road, New Delhi – 110 002.
Printed and bound in India by Replika Press Pvt. Ltd.

Contents

Preface to Third Edition

The first two editions of this book were published in quick succession — July 1986 and July 1987 — because it was received with great interest and appreciation by the Hindu intelligentsia at large, in this country and abroad. But the present (third) edition has been delayed inordinately in spite of persistent demand after the second edition went out of print in 1988. A reprint of the second edition was not brought out because I wanted to include in a new edition the copious materials which I had collected in the meanwhile from orthodox collections of Hadis and which I thought worth presenting to the readers. But that was not to be.

I had finished reading the six authentic Hadis collections — Bukhari, Muslim, Tirmizi, Ibn Majah, Ibn Daud, Nasaii — which an orthodox Muslim organization had published in several volumes each, with Arabic text and Urdu translation. I had marked in the margins of several thousand pages the relevant references pertaining to the five pillars of Islam, the character of the Muslim *Ummah*, and the doctrine of *jihād*. I had noted many stories which provide the context in which particular *sūrahs* and *āyats* of the Quran were "revealed"; they made it more than clear as to how Allah of the Quran had functioned as a mouthpiece of the Prophet and even some of his companions. But as I started sorting out the references and putting them together under particular themes, I suffered a prolonged spell of illness which persists even as I write these lines. So I wait and hope that I will be able to resume the work at some future date.

Some of the material included in the present edition had gone into the computer in the winter of 1990-91. But a lot of new material has been added during 1999. As this edition stands now, I think the reader will find it better arranged and more informative.

The book is still divided into two sections. The second section stands as it did in the earlier editions except that it has been renamed as 'The Petition and the Judgment' instead of 'Court Documents'. The first section, however, has not only been renamed as 'Introduction' instead of 'Preface', but also carries new insertions, reflections and formulations which have added as many as 50 more pages to it. Many new footnotes have been added, and several new publications cited as the Bibliography at the end goes to show.

The Second Preface to the second edition has been retained intact except that now it stands renamed as, 'Preface to Second Edition'. But sections of the First Preface to the second edition have been rearranged as chapters, most of which have been revised, enlarged and renamed. Chapter 4, 'The Prophet sets the Pattern', is entirely new. It is a summary of the first orthodox biography of the Prophet, and provides a background to the chapters that follow. Chapter 5, 'The Orthodox Exposition of *Jihād*', has been enlarged with extensive passages from *Tuhfat-ul-Mujahideen*, a sixteen century (CE) treatise on *jihad* composed at Bijapur and carrying many citations from orthodox collections of Hadis. In a way, this part of the chapter fulfils to a certain extent my plan to present Hadis materials vis-à-vis *jihād*. Chapter 6, '*Jihād* in India's History', now includes *jihāds* waged by Sher Shah Sur, Akbar the Great Mughal, and Ahmad Shah Abdali. Many myths have been floated about the 'secularism' of Sher Shah and Akbar by Muslim and Stalinist "historians" in recent times. Pandit Jawaharlal Nehru, the architect of India's 'secularism', has gone to the extent of hailing Akbar as "the father of Indian nationalism" who "deliberately placed the ideal of a common Indian nationhood above the claims of separatist religion".[1] I hope the readers will draw their own conclusions.

II

This book is going to the press while the *jihād* in Kargil is raging, and the end is not yet in sight. The Hindu intelligentsia in India in general and the present-day Hindu leadership in particular, has yet to show any sign that they have learnt any lesson from what is essentially a renewed contest between Islamic imperialism and Indian nationalism. On the other hand, a realization seems to be dawning in the West, particularly the USA, that Pakistan has become the foremost citadel of what they (the West) prefer to describe as Islamic fundamentalism and terrorism. I wish to point out that Pakistan has not invented the Islam it is practising; it has always been there in India (which is now known as Indo-Pak Subcontinent or South Asia, but which is the same as the Bhāratavarṣa of hoary history) since the eighth century CE. Let it be realized by everybody concerned that India has always been and remains, the citadel of the most bigoted and bloodthirsty zealotry of Islam. The historical reasons for why it is so, are many. I do not have the time to detail them here. The main reason may be told. Islam in India has been what it has been because India has continued to stare at Islam as its greatest failure. Islam in India has never been able to relax, as it could do in countries which it converted completely. And it will not relax till Hindus learn to knock out its ideological fangs which are rooted in the Quran.

New Delhi   **Sita Ram Goel**
10 July 1999

---

[1] *Glimpses of World History*, Fourth Impression, OUP, 1982, p. 306. I have examined the 'myth of Akbar' in *The Story of Islamic Imperialism in India*, Second Revised Edition, Voice of India, New Delhi, 1994, pp. 99-103.

Preface to Second Edition

Soon after the first edition of this book was published in July 1986, a significant judgment on some *āyats* of the Quran was pronounced by Z.S. Lohat, metropolitan magistrate of Delhi. As most of these *āyats* and others of a similar sort figure in the Calcutta Quran Petition of Chandmal Chopra, we thought it relevant to reproduce the impugned poster in which the *āyats* were cited. Operative portion of the judgment is also being reproduced in order to give a glimpse of the arguments for and against.

The poster had been published on behalf of the Hindu Raksha Dal, Delhi, by its President, Indra Sain Sharma, and Secretary, Rajkumar Arya. Both of them had been arrested under Sections 153A and 295A of the Indian Penal Code. These are the same sections which were invoked by Chandmal Chopra in his petition for prohibiting publication of the Quran.

The publishers of the poster had cited 24 *āyats* of the Quran under the caption, *Why riots take place in the country*. They had added the comment that these *āyats* "command the believers (Musalmans) to fight against followers of other faiths" and that "so long as these *āyats* are not removed [from the Quran], riots in the country cannot be prevented".

The case acquired considerable weight when it came before the court because Indra Sain Sharma happened to be Vice-President of the All India Hindu Mahasabha at that time. The prosecution seemed to be convinced that it had caught a big fish. But the magistrate thought otherwise. He found that the prosecution had failed to provide sufficient grounds such as could enable him to frame charges. He discharged both the accused with the observation that "With due regard to the holy book of 'Quran Majeed', a close perusal of the 'Aytes' shows that the same *are harmful and teach hatred*, and are likely to create differences between Mohammedans on one hand and the remaining communities on the other" (emphasis added).

The poster was printed in Hindi. The *āyats* it cited were taken verbatim from an authentic edition of the Quran published by an orthodox Muslim organization, Maktaba al-Hasnāt of Rampur in Uttar Pradesh. The edition provides the Arabic text of the Quran together with Hindi and English translations in parallel columns. We are reproducing the English translation of the *āyats*.

II
THE POSTER

"Some *āyats* of the Quran Majid command the believers (Musalmans) to fight against followers of other faiths:

1. Then, when the sacred months have passed, slay the idolaters wherever ye find them, and take them (captive) and besiege them and prepare for them each ambush. But if they repent and establish worship and pay the poor due, then leave their way. Lo! Allah is Forgiving, Merciful. (*Sūrah* 9, *āyat* 5)

2. O ye who believe! The idolaters only are unclean... (9.28)

3. In truth the disbelievers are an open enemy to you. (4.101)

4. O ye who believe! Fight those of the disbelievers who are near to you and let them find harshness in you... (9.123)

5. Lo! Those who disbelieve our revelations, We shall expose them to the Fire. As often as their skins are consumed We shall exchange them for fresh skins that they may taste the torment. Lo! Allah is ever Mighty, Wise. (4.56)

6. O ye who believe! Choose not your father nor your brethren for friends if they take pleasure in disbelief rather than faith. Whoso of you taketh them for friends such are wrongdoers. (9.23)

7. Allah guideth not the disbelieving folk. (9.37)

8. O ye who believe! Choose not for friends People of the Book and of the disbelievers. But keep your duty to Allah if ye are true believers. (5.57)

9. Accursed, they will be seized wherever found and slain with a (fierce) slaughter. (33.61)

10. Lo! Ye (idolaters) and that which ye worship beside Allah are fuel of hell. Thereunto ye will come. (21.98)

11. And who doth greater wrong than he who is reminded of the revelations of his Lord, then turneth from them. Lo! We shall requite the guilty. (32.22)

12. Allah promiseth you much booty that ye will capture. (48.20)

13. Now enjoy what ye have won as lawful and good. (8.69)

14. O Prophet! Strive against the disbelievers and the hypocrites, and be stern with them. Hell will be their home, a hapless journey's end. (66.9)

15. But verily We shall cause those who disbelieve to taste an awful doom and verily We shall requite them the worst of what they used to do. (41.27)

16. That is the reward of Allah's enemies: the Fire. Therein is their immortal home, payment for as much as they denied Our revelations. (41.28)

17. Lo! Allah hath bought from the believers their lives and their wealth because the Garden will be theirs. They shall fight in the way of Allah and shall slay and be slain... (9.111)

18. Allah promiseth hypocrites, both men and women, and the disbelievers fire of hell for their abode. It will suffice them. Allah curseth them and theirs is lasting torment. (9.58)

19. O Prophet! Exhort the believers to fight. If there be of you twenty steadfast they shall overcome two hundred, and if there be of you a hundred steadfast they shall overcome a thousand of those who disbelieve because they (the

disbelievers) are a folk without intelligence. (8.65)

20. O ye who believe! Take not the Jews and Christians for friends. They are friends one to another. He among you who taketh them for friends is (one) of them. Lo! Allah guideth not wrongdoing folk. (5.51)

21. Fight against such of those who have been given the scripture as believe not in Allah nor the Last Day, and forbid not that which Allah hath forbidden by His messenger and follow not the religion of truth, until they pay the tribute readily, being brought low. (9.29)

22. Therefore, We have stirred up enmity and hatred among them till the day of Resurrection, when Allah will inform them of their handiwork. (5.14)

23. They long that ye should disbelieve even as they disbelieve that ye may be upon a level (with them). So choose not friends from them till they forsake their homes in the way of Allah. If they turn back (to enmity) then take them and kill them wherever ye find them, and choose not friend nor helper from among them. (4.89)

24. Fight them! Allah will chastise them at your hands, and He will lay them low and give you victory over them, and He will heal the breasts of folk who are believers. (9.14)

"There are numerous (other) *āyats* of the same sort. Here we have cited only twenty-four *āyats*. Obviously, these *āyats* carry commandments which promote enmity, ill-will, hatred, deception, fraud, strife, robbery and murder. That is why riots take place between Muslims and non-Muslims, in this country as well as [the rest of] the world.

"In the above-mentioned twenty-four *āyats* of the Quran Majid, Musalmans are commanded to fight against followers of other faiths. So long as these *āyats* are not removed [from the Quran], riots in the country cannot be prevented."

Defects in English Translation

On comparing the Hindi and English translations of the *āyats* under reference, we find that at places the English rendering does

not follow the Hindi version very faithfully. We think it worth-
while to point out as to where the English translation has failed to
convey the full meaning in keeping with the Arabic text and the
spirit of Islamic theology initiated by the Prophet and elaborated
by orthodox schools in subsequent centuries.

For instance, the Hindi translation of *āyat* 8.69 cited under
No. 13 of the poster uses the words *"ghanīmat kā māl"*. This is in
keeping with the original Arabic term. But the English rendering,
"what you have won", is a very weak version of what is sought
to be conveyed. A closer rendering would be "war booty" or
"plunder acquired through war". In the Quran, Allah promises
plenty of plunder to the believers, again and again. The Prophet
also claimed that one of the six points of his superiority over
earlier prophets was that while plunder was not lawful for them,
Allah had made it so for him. He also laid down the rule according
to which one-fifth of the plunder belonged to Allah and his
Prophet, while the remaining four-fifth was to be divided among
those who took part in the war which brought the plunder. This
"sacred one-fifth" came to be known as *khams* which became in
later times one of the four main sources of revenue for the Islamic
state, the other three being *kharāj* (land revenue from the
conquered peasantry), *jizyah* (poll tax from the People of the Book
and others who were accepted as *zimmis*) and *zakāt* (charity from
the faithful).

Similarly, the English word "strive" in *āyat* 66.9 at No. 14 of the
poster is too innocuous to convey the ringing militancy of *"jihād
karo"* which is used in the Hindi translation. It is true that literally
the Arabic word *"jihād"* means "to strive". But in the mouth of the
Prophet as also in latter-day Islamic theology, *jihād* is not a mere
word like any other. It has become a whole institution, namely,
aggressive war for the spread of the "only true faith" till the *kāfirs*
get converted, or humble themselves by agreeing to become
zimmis, or are killed *en masse*. The Prophet minces no words in
making *jihād* an obligatory duty for every Muslim. Allah himself
harangues the faithful to vie with each other in spending their

wealth and staking their lives "in the way of Allah" which is only a euphemism for *jihād*. *Āyats* cited at Nos. 1, 4, 17, 19 and 21 of the poster make the message from Allah more than clear. This aggressive war was held up by the Prophet as superior to all other meritorious deeds such as prayer, fasting, pilgrimage, etc. The believer who kills *kāfirs* in a *jihād* is honoured as a *ghāzi* and enjoys a higher status in the Muslim *Ummah*. The believer who gets killed in a *jihād* becomes a *shahīd* (martyr) and goes straight to the Quranic paradise without having to wait for the Day of Judgment like the rest of the believers.

Again, while the Hindi word "*yātanā* " in 41.27 at No. 15 of the poster is quite close to the Arabic word "*azāb*", the English rendering, "awful doom", hardly conveys what is meant. The word "doom" carries a sense of finality, however awful. It happens and the story ends for all time to come. But the torments with which Allah threatens the unbelievers, again and again, are far more formidable. It is a continuous process in which the victims are subjected to ever more terrible modes and doses of torture. *Āyats* 4.56, 21.98, 41.28 and 9.58 cited in Nos. 5, 10, 16, and 18 of the poster tell something of the type of torment which awaits the unbelievers. "Terrible and everlasting torment" would have been a more faithful translation of the Arabic term.

Lastly, the English word "Garden" in 9.111 at No. 17 of the poster is a poor rendering of the Arabic word "*jannat*" which has been used as such in the Hindi translation. "Paradise" would be a more precise English rendering. After all, the paradise which Allah promises to the believers is no mere garden, however green, well-watered and full of fruit trees as well as fresh breezes it may be. What has made it particularly alluring for the faithful throughout the ages is something else, namely, the bevy of beautiful virgins who never grow old or lose their charms, and who never tire of providing newer and ever more plentiful pleasures to those who have lived or died for the faith. Lusty and lurid descriptions of paradise comprise a whole corpus of Islamic lore starting with the Quran and the Hadis.

III
The Judgment

"I have heard learned APP [Assistant Public Prosecutor] for the state and counsel of the accused and have gone through the relevant record on the file. The main thrust of the prosecution is that the above words[1] in the disputed poster tend to create communal disharmony and [the comment] is an act with deliberate and malicious intention of outraging the religious feelings of a particular class of citizens of India and is an attempt to insult the religion or the religious belief of the said class. It is also submitted that 'Aytes' in the form published in the poster are not available or are the distorted version of the same...

"There is a dispute that the 24 'Aytes' published in the poster have not been taken from the 'Quran Majeed' translated by Mohammedan writer. It is found that they are reproduced in the same form as are translated in the said 'Quran Majeed'. In my opinion the writer by writing the above words has expressed his opinion or suggestion and at the most it can be branded as a fair criticism of what is contained in the holy book of Mohammedans. By no stretch of imagination the opinion expressed by the writer that unless these 'Aytes' are removed from holy book of 'Quran Majeed' there will be no hope of stopping the communal disturbances in different parts of India, can be said to promote and attempt to promote feeling of enmity or hatred between different classes of citizens of India. In my opinion it is a sort of suggestion to the readers or at the most a fair criticism and by publishing such suggestion or criticism, the writer or publisher has not in any way outraged or attempted to outrage the religious feelings of Mohammedan community nor it tends to create communal disharmony or hatred between two classes. With due regard to the holy book of 'Quran Majeed', a close perusal of the 'Aytes' shows

---

[1]Reference is to comments in the poster regarding the consequences of the Quran's teachings.

that the same are harmful and teach hatred and are likely to create differences between Mohammedans on one hand and the remaining communities on the other.

"I have personally compared the disputed 'Aytes' with 'Quran Majeed' translated in Hindi with notes by one Mohd. Farookh Khan and have found that most of the 'Aytes' have been reproduced in the poster in its original form as is available in the 'Quran Majeed'...

"The close reading of all the 'Aytes' published in the poster and read from the book do not in any way give different meanings nor suggest anything that the same were published with malicious intention. Therefore, I do not agree with the contention of the learned APP that 'Aytes' Nos. 2, 5, 9, 11 to 19 and 22 are either not available in 'Quran Majeed' or they are distorted version of the said 'Aytes'...

"In view of the above discussion, I am therefore of the view that there is no prima facie case against the accused as offences alleged against the accused do not fall prima facie within the four corners of Sections 153-A/295-A and hence both of the accused are discharged.

"dated 31st July, 1986 Sd/ Z.S. Lohat"

The portions of the judgment we have left out relate to technicalities such as case law on the subject or the correctness of certain terms used in the Hindi translation for conveying the spirit of the original in Arabic. We thought that while they are not likely to be of much interest to the lay reader, they mar the smooth flow of the magistrate's observations. Moreover, the magistrate has summed up in his judgment the substance of arguments advanced by the prosecution.[2]

---

[2]For full text of the case, see *Freedom of Expression: Secular Theocracy Versus Liberal Democracy*, Voice of India, New Delhi, 1998, pp. 1-9.

IV
Banning of Books is Counter-Productive

When we published for the first time (1986) the documents relating to the Calcutta Quran Petition, we should have made it absolutely clear that we do not stand for a ban on the publication of the Quran. We take this opportunity to state unambiguously that we regard banning of books, religious or otherwise, as counter-productive. In the case of the Quran, we believe and advocate that more and more non-Muslims should read it so that they know first hand the quality of its teachings.

Our only intention in publishing the court documents of the Calcutta Quran Petition and providing a long preface to it, was to promote a public discussion of Islam as a religion, particularly its claim that every bit of the Quran and the Hadis has a divine source. This claim is used at present to prevent a close examination of what the book contains and what message Islam has for mankind at large. While all other religions have been subjected to such an examination, Islam has so far managed to remain a closed book. Our plea in the Preface to the first edition was that if such commandments as we find in the Quran emanate from what is proclaimed as a divine source, then the character of that source should also invite questions. Our rational faculties and moral sensibilities should not stop functioning the moment Allah's name is mentioned. The character of Allah as revealed in the Quran also invites a close examination.

March 20, 1987   **Sita Ram Goel**

Section I

INTRODUCTION

Chapter 1

A Government in Panic

Muslims in India have often sought shelter under Sections 153A and 295A of the Indian Penal Code (I.P.C.) for preventing every public discussion of their creed in general and of their prophet in particular.[1] Quite a few publications which examine critically the sayings and doings of the Prophet or other idolized personalities of Islam, have been proscribed under Section 95 of the Criminal Procedure Code (Cr.P.C.) as a result of pressure exerted by vociferous, very often violent Muslim protests. Little did they suspect that the same provisions of the law could be invoked for seeking a ban on their holy book, the Quran.

The credit for this turning of tables goes to Chandmal Chopra of Calcutta. It was he who filed a Writ Petition in the Calcutta High Court on 29 March 1985 stating that publication of the Quran attracts Sections 153A and 295A of the I.P.C. because it "incites violence, disturbs public tranquility, promotes, on ground of religion, feelings of enmity, hatred and ill-will between different religious communities, and insults other religions or religious beliefs of other communities in India". He also prayed for a rule nisi on the Government of West Bengal "to show cause as to why

---

[1]The latest instance is provided by Syed Shahabuddin's letter dated 20th August 1993 written to P.M. Sayeed, Minister of State in the Ministry of Home Affairs, demanding a ban "under the law of the land" on Ram Swarup's *Hindu View of Christianity and Islam*, published by Voice of India, New Delhi, 1993.

a writ of mandamus be not issued to it directing it to declare each copy of Quran whether in the original Arabic or in any of the languages as forfeited to the Government" in terms of Section 95 of the Cr.P.C.

The case had caused considerable excitement among the "believers" (*Mu'mins*) and interest among the "infidels" (*Kāfirs*) in April-May, 1985. The press in India and abroad gave many headlines to what was rightly regarded as an unprecedented event in the history of religion. It was the first time that a Pagan had questioned the character of a document hailed as the very Word of God by a People of the Book. The roles now stood reversed. So far it had been the privilege of the Peoples of the Book to ban and burn the sacred literature of the Pagans.

The Petition was disallowed by the High Court. But the issues raised by the Petition remain pertinent. No law court can deny to "infidels" the right to know what treatment the Quran prescribes for them at the hands of the "believers".

Law has its limitations, particularly in a country where its main corpus continues to be what alien regimes, Islamic and British, had devised for their own imperialist purposes. Moreover, a law court is hardly the forum for framing final judgments on matters of grave moral and spiritual import. A free and forthright discussion of the Quran cannot and should not come to a stop simply because the existing law is not competent to take cognisance of its contents.

The *sūrahs* and *āyats* of the Quran which Chandmal Chopra had cited in support of his plea, received scant or no attention at all in the heat of the controversy whether a book regarded as sacred by a large number of people can be the subject of a lawsuit. Those who have not read the Calcutta Quran Petition, as it came to be known, cannot envisage the quantum and quality of evidence marshalled by Chopra. Our people are entitled to know exactly the issues that were involved. It is only a properly informed public opinion which can decide in the long run whether a book qualifies — rationally, morally, and spiritually — or not as a religious scripture. This is the end we have in view while publishing verbatim the Petition as well as other papers relating to it.

1256

A brief history of the case will help in placing the Petition in its proper perspective. Most people do not know why the Petition was presented. They also do not know how the case was politicised form the very outset and what powerful pressures were brought into play even before the High Court had a chance to consider whether the Petition could be admitted for adjudication.

Himangshu Kishore Chakraborty takes the Initiative

Before Chandmal Chopra came into the picture, Himangshu Kishore Chakraborty, also of Calcutta, had written a letter on July 20, 1984 to the Secretary, Department of Home, Government of West Bengal, pointing out that the Quran contains matter which makes its publication an offence under Sections 153A and 295A of the I.P.C. In three Annexures to his letter, he had cited quite a few sayings of the Quran — 37 sayings which "preach cruelty, incite violence and disturb public peace"; 17 sayings which "promote, on ground of religion, feelings of enmity, hatred and ill-will between different religious communities in India"; and 31 sayings which "insult other religions as also the religious beliefs of other communities". He had requested that all copies of the Quran in the original Arabic as well as in translations be forfeited forthwith to the Government in terms of Section 95 of the Cr.P.C.

Citations made by Chakraborty showed that he had made a painstaking study of the Quran. He had reason to do so. As a former resident of East Bengal (now Bangladesh) which became a province of Pakistan in August 1947, he had witnessed at the time of Partition as well as later on, a peculiar pattern in the behaviour of the Muslim majority towards the Hindu minority. He had also known how the renowned religious leaders of East Bengal Muslims had approved of that behaviour pattern as in keeping with the highest tenets of Islam. Ever since, he had been searching for the belief system which inspired this behaviour pattern. He felt sure that he had found the primary source of that belief system when he studied the Quran.

The Secretary of the West Bengal Home Department, however, did not even acknowledge Chakraborty's letter. He, therefore, wrote a reminder on 14 August 1984, enclosing a copy of his first letter along with the Annexures. But six months passed and there was no response. It was during this interval that he met Chandmal Chopra who also had been studying the Quran in order to understand why the Hindus in Bangladesh were being systematically uprooted from their ancestral homeland, even after India had made great sacrifices for securing freedom for Bangladesh.

Chandmal Chopra is an adherent of the ancient Jain tradition which has all along stood for the five principal virtues prescribed by all schools of Sanatana Dharma — non-violence, truthfulness, non-stealing, chastity and non-covetousness. It was a puzzle for him as to how adherents of another religion could persist in practices to the contrary and that, too, with a good conscience. His question stood as if answered when he came to the Quran. He was in a position to confirm that the conclusions reached by Chakraborty were correct.

Chandmal Chopra now felt reinforced to do something about what he thought to be a matter of major public interest. So he wrote a letter on March 16, 1985 to the same Secretary in the Government of West Bengal, drawing the latter's attention to the contents of the Quran and referring to the demand made earlier by Chakraborty. He requested that his letter be treated as "notice demanding justice" and made it clear that unless necessary steps were taken by the Government of West Bengal within 7 days from the receipt of his letter, he would take "such steps as may be advised to us".

Chopra's letter also remained unacknowledged. He, therefore, filed on March 29, 1985 his famous Writ Petition in the Calcutta High Court under Article 226 of the Indian Constitution. Sital Singh, another public-spirited citizen, joined him as a co-petitioner. The grounds the Petition gave for seeking action from the Government of West Bengal were the same as provided earlier by Chakraborty. But now they were couched in appropriate legal language and presented according to the correct legal procedure.

The Writ Petition came up before Mrs. Justice Padma Khastgir on April 1, 1985. She directed that the matter would appear in her list on April 8. There were, however, two postponements before the matter could appear on April 12. On that date, the learned judge gave directions for filing of affidavit-in-opposition by the Respondent (State of West Bengal) by May 3, 1985, and affidavit-in-reply by the Petitioners by May 17, 1985. The matter then stood adjourned to May 27, 1985.

The affidavit-in-reply was duly filed by the Government of West Bengal stating that "as the Holy Quran is a Divine Book, no earthly power can sit upon judgment on it and no court of law has jurisdiction to adjudicate it" and that "from the time of the British Rule and since Independence, inspite of the Indian Penal Code being in existence, there had never been such an application in any Court in India". But for reasons unknown, Justice Khastgir released the matter from her list on May 2. On May 7, the Advocate-General of West Bengal requested the Chief Justice of the Calcutta High Court to assign the matter to another bench. Finally, on May 10, the Chief Justice chose Mr. Justice Bimal Chandra Basak for hearing the Writ Petition.

The Union Government becomes Panicky

Meanwhile, all hell had broken loose. *The Telegraph* of Calcutta dated May 9 carried a UNI report date-lined New Delhi, May 8. "The Union Government," the report said, "has decided to intervene in the writ petition in the Calcutta high court praying for a ban on the Quran. According to an official release, the law minister [Ashoke Sen] is proceeding to Calcutta immediately for giving the necessary instructions. The government has decided to seek the outright dismissal of the petition, the release added. It is also understood that the attorney-general [of the Government of India] is being briefed to appear in the case."

A Staff Reporter of *The Telegraph* added: "Justice Khastgir had asked the state government and the Union government to show cause as to why the Quran should not be banned. The order created considerable resentment at the Bar Association [in Calcutta] where Muslim lawyers had called an extraordinary meeting and moved a motion for condemning Justice Khastgir for having admitted the case. The motion was, however, defeated as the lawyers moving the motion could not muster enough votes."

The Telegraph dated May 10 reported that the same sort of pressure was being mounted by the Government of West Bengal: "The Chief Minister, Mr. Jyoti Basu," it wrote, "today [May 9] described the writ petition filed in the Calcutta High Court challenging certain portions of the Quran a 'despicable act.' Mr. Basu who was replying to the Forward Block MLA, Mr. Anil Mukherjee, in the state Assembly also felt that the court should have dismissed the petition outright as the subject matter pertains to religion. According to him, the Union government has already contacted the state authorities who had sought the former's help in resolving the issue. 'I have also told the advocate general to talk to the chief justice of Calcutta high court in this regard,' Mr. Basu added." It did not occur to Jyoti Basu that the matter being subjudice, he was committing contempt of court. Nor did the court reprimand him for this breach of law.

The matter was also raised in the Lok Sabha at New Delhi on May 10 by two MPs, one belonging to the Congress(I) and the other to the CPI (M). According to *The Statesman* dated May 11, "The speaker, Mr. Balram Jakhar, agreed with them that this was a serious matter. There was, he noted, enough trouble in the country and there was no need to add anything which would stir up another conflagration." What bothered Balram Jakhar was the fear of trouble and not the right or wrong involved in the case. In fact, he was inviting Muslim mobs to take to the streets, and create trouble. In his reply to the MPs, the Minister of State for Law, H.R. Bhardwaj, said that "when the writ petition had come to the Government's notice, the Government had immediately considered measures to counter it" and that "the Government was deputing the Attorney-General to Calcutta to seek dismissal of the writ petition".

The Government and politicians of Pakistan, however, were not impressed by the Government of India's efforts to protect the

Quran. *The Telegraph* dated May 14 carried a PTI report datelined Islamabad, May 13: "Pakistan's minister of state for religious and minority affairs, Mr. Maqbool Ahmed Khan, said today that the petition against the Quran moved in the Calcutta high court was the 'worst example of religious intolerance.' The Pakistan President. Gen. Zia-ul-Haq, was quoted by an Urdu daily as saying that the facts of the case were being ascertained. Mr. Khan alleged that religion and life and property of minorities were unsafe in India and urged the Indian government to 'follow the example of Pakistan' in ensuring freedom of religion. He said 'if the Quran had been banned in the name of secularism, the religious books of Hindus should also be banned.' Maulana Kausar Niazi, a pro-Zia politician, asked the Organisation of Islamic Conference chairman, Mr. Sharifuddin Pirzada, to draw the attention of the Muslim world to 'react against this heinous act.' He asked the government to make an official complaint to India and appealed to the Pakistani religious leaders to observe Friday as a protest day." Thus the theocratic state of Pakistan made it an occasion for delivering lectures to Indians on the subject of religious freedom and the rights of minorities. Nobody who was anybody in India at that time is known to have reacted to this assault from an Islamic state which had driven out most of its Hindu minority, and was treating the rest as non-citizens.

Contradiction in the Government's Stand

The governments of India and West Bengal had panicked because of their presumption that the Writ Petition had been admitted by Justice Padma Khastgir. But this was by no means certain. *The Telegraph* of May 10 carried a report of the controversy which was raging in Calcutta round this point. "There is a serious difference of opinion," it wrote, "between Chief Justice Satish Chandra and Justice Padma Khastgir on the one hand and the advocate-general Mr. Snehangshu Acharya and a large number of lawyers on the other, on whether Justice Khastgir had admitted a writ petition demanding the banning of the Quran.

Justice Chandra and Khastgir maintain that the petition moved by Chandmal Chopra and Sital Singh was not admitted in the court. However, the advocate-general and a large number of lawyers, are convinced that the petition was admitted by Justice Khastgir. The significant fact is that the controversy has acquired a serious dimension only because Justice Khastgir 'entertained' the mischievous petition, instead of dismissing it outright. Justice Khastgir told *The Telegraph* that she issued directions on the petition as she would not turn down any petitioner. Meanwhile, the registrar of the high court has informed *The Telegraph* that he has been directed to state that the petition under Article 226 had not been admitted by Justice Khastgir." The accomplices of Islamic imperialism in India — Communists, Socialists, Nehruvian Secularists, Gandhians — were throwing all judicial proprieties and procedures to the winds in defence of Islam which they viewed as the most effective weapon against their common enemy — Hindu society and culture.

Spokesmen for the State and the Union governments could not or did not want to see the contradiction involved in their stand. If, as they affirmed, the petition had been admitted, the matter was subjudice and their comments on it constituted contempt of court. But if it had not been admitted, they should have waited for Justice Khastgir's ruling regarding its admissibility. Obviously, the panic created by mounting Muslim protests had paralysed all rational faculties in certain quarters. According to *The Tele-graph* dated May 10, "The Union law minister, Mr. Ashoke Sen, informed the advocate-general that the Union government would make itself a party to the case as it would affect the Muslim community all over the country and that the case would have international ramifications." Political considerations thus came to override legal proprieties.

A Mean Move

What was still more reprehensible, the Government of West Bengal set in motion its Intelligence Branch for digging up some information which could be used for a smear campaign against the Petitioners. *The Telegraph* dated May 10 reported: "According to an intelligence report Chandmal Chopra and Sital Singh are not permanent residents of the addresses given by them. Chandmal Chopra, who said he resided in 25 Burtolla Street, does not stay there. According to the report, Chandmal aged 55 has a room in his name at the above-mentioned premises... The 50 year old Sital Singh is an ex-army man and resident of Hyderabad. He occasionally comes to the city and stays at 1 Sadruddin Street in north Calcutta in Jorasanko area which is actually an Arya Samaj mandir. Both of them did not have any police records nor were their names on the special branch files." Obviously, police files had been rummaged in order to locate something which could compromise the character of Chandmal Chopra and Sital Singh. No one from India's public life stood up to ask the simple question whether checking the police record of someone was legal or legitimate just because that person had filed a Writ Petition in a High Court.

Muslim Mobs on the Warpath

The panic on the part of the State and Union governments could not but produce some more unsavoury results. Muslim mobs in India and elsewhere had been incited by all those who mattered in India, Pakistan and Bangladesh. They started taking to the streets and turning violent. *The Statesman* dated May 13 published the following news date-lined Dhaka, May 12: "At least 12 people were killed and 100 wounded when Bangladesh police fired on a demonstration yesterday in the border town of Chepal Nawabgunj, 320 km. from here. Some 1000 demonstrators, belonging to the fundamentalist Jamaat-i-Islami, were protesting against a case filed by two Indian civilians in Calcutta High Court calling for a ban on the Quran in India. The town chief administrator said today that the police opened fire in self-defence when the demonstrators went on a rampage throwing missiles and setting ablaze government property. Yesterday's incident followed a demonstration by at least 20,000 Jamaat-i-Islami supporters in the capital on Friday {May 10}." The demonstrators in Dhaka, according to other reports, were trying to storm the office of India's High Commission when they were stopped by the police.

The Statesman dated May 14 carried a report dated May 13 from Ranchi in Bihar: "Agitated over the writ petition concerning the Koran, Muslims here marched in protest for the second day on the main thoroughfare. The marchers carried banners and black flags and shouted anti-Government slogans. Yesterday some processionists threw stones at a few shops on the main road while asking the shopkeepers to pull their shutters down. Following yesterday's incidents, most of the shopkeepers today preferred to keep their establishments closed when the procession was taken out."

On the same day, widespread violence was staged by Muslim mobs in Srinagar in the Kashmir Valley which was to become a centre of widespread Islamic terrorism four years later when V.P. Singh, an unashamed champion of Islamic imperialism, became India's Prime Minister. *The Telegraph* dated May 14 reported: "The police fired to disperse a mob which ransacked the CPI headquarters in Srinagar today in protest against the petition seeking to ban the Quran. An attempt was made to set fire to a bridge. There was violence in other parts of the city and demonstrators carrying black and green flags stoned the police. Shops and cinema halls were closed and as a precaution the authorities shut down all educational establishments. Slogans were raised against the West Bengal government." There could be no greater irony that the Communist Party of India (CPI), a consistent defender of all Islamic causes, had been bracketed with 'Hindu communalists' by Muslim mobs. But mobs are mobs, and the responsibility for what they do rests on those who mobilize them ever so often.

It was in the midst of this mob fury that *The Times of India* published three articles by Dr. Rafiq Zakaria in praise of the Quran. It was one of the many efforts being made by concerned authorities to mollify the Muslims. According to knowledgeable circles, the articles were a command performance.[2]

A High Court in a Hurry

The developments that took place in the Calcutta High Court were no less dramatic. As stated earlier, Justice Khastgir had directed Chandmal Chopra to file his affidavit-in-reply by May 17. He was busy preparing it when he received a message on the midnight of May 12-13 that the matter would appear "to be mentioned" on May 13 before Justice Bimal Chandra Basak. Next day, when Chopra appeared in the court, Justice Basak recalled the earlier court directions regarding filing of affidavits and directed him to move the Writ application afresh as a Court Application. Chopra had no alternative and had to do what he was told to do by an august authority.

On the other hand, the Attorney-General of India and the Advocate-General of West Bengal had come to the court fully prepared as was obvious from the fat volumes they had brought with them. Chopra requested for an adjournment on the ground that he had received notice only for "to be mentioned". But his request was rejected. The Advocate-General of West Bengal and the Attorney-General of the Government of India were directed to proceed with their arguments against the Writ Petition, which they did with considerable confidence. Ill-prepared as he was, Chopra tried his best to counter the arguments. Justice Basak then dismissed the Writ Petition and reserved his judgement for a later date.

The judgment which Justice Basak delivered on May 17 is a lengthy document. It quotes copiously from criminal and constitutional case law. It also contains some passage about the profundities of Islam and India's philosophy of Secularism. In

---

[2]Some of us approached Girilal Jain, Chief Editor of the daily at that time, and asked him if a rebuttal of Zakaria's white-washing of the Quran would be acceptable for publication in the same columns. He regretted his inability to do so for reasons, he said, he could not reveal.

between, there are some observations about the eternal, the unknowable, the transcendental, and so on. A layman's summary, were are afraid, may mar the majesty of the learned judge's performance. Readers will do well to read the full document in Section II of this publication.

Sequel to the Judgment

There was, however, one point in the judgment which had a sequel even after the Calcutta High Court considered the matter as closed. Justice Basak had criticised Justice Padma Khastgir for having admitted the Writ Petition. He had pronounced : "The application was entertained and admitted without going into the question of prima facie case and the jurisdiction and power of the Court to entertain this petition. In spite of the same, directions were given for filing of affidavits. This by itself amounts to holding that there is a prima facie case though this question was not gone into. The Court should be circumspect in such kind of matters and be very cautions about the same. Otherwise though it might attract cheap publicity but may cause untold misery and disruption of religious harmony. The petition should have been rejected forthwith and in limen as unworthy of its consideration as soon as it was moved."

Some Muslim leaders pounced on this point to demand action against Justice Padma Khastgir. A notable example was G.M. Shah, the Chief Minister of Jammu and Kashmir. He had returned from abroad on May 20 after a month's stay in the U.S.A. On the same day, he addressed a mass rally at Iqbal Park in Srinagar. According to a PTI report reproduced by *Navabharat Times*, New Delhi, dated May 22, Shah said that "action should be taken against the judge who permitted the petition to be filed".

The mass rally itself was the climax of continued violence in the Kashmir Valley even after the Writ Petition had been dismissed on May 13. Leaders of the Muslim community in Kashmir had widened their protest against the Writ Petition for voicing some permanent Muslim "grievances". *The Statesman* dated May 18 had carried a news date-lined Srinagar, May 17: "One person was killed and at least three persons were seriously injured when the police fired and exploded tear-gas shells to disperse a stone-throwing mob at Fateh Kadal in Srinagar today, according to police sources, report UNI and PTI. Srinagar and other parts of the Kashmir Valley today observed a bandh in response to a one-day hartal called by Mirwaiz Maulvi Farooq, chairman of the Awami Action Committee and other leaders. Shops and commercial establishments were closed in the city and other towns of the Valley and vehicular traffic came to a standstill. Banks and Government offices were open, but schools and colleges were closed for the day. The hartal is being observed in protest against the 'conspiracies against the Koran, interference in Muslim personal law, communal riots and the increasing cult of violence in the country,' according to a police spokesman."

Another sequel to Justice Basak's judgment may be mentioned briefly. Chandmal Chopra filed a Review Petition on June 18, 1985 stating that the premises on which the judgment was based were not sound. He gave eight grounds on which the judgement could be reviewed. In violation of the normal judicial procedure, the Review Petition also came up before Justice Basak on June 21. He dismissed it the same day for purely technical reasons without going into the grounds. The only concession he made was that some of the grounds "may or may not be grounds for appeal". Papers relating to the Review Petition are also being published verbatim in Section II.

Chapter 2

The Judgment misses the Main Point

It is not for laymen like us to discuss the correctness or otherwise of a High Court judgment. It should better be left to those who are conversant with the law and can enter into the intricacies of interpretation and logical construction. For all we know, it is perhaps impossible to impugn a book under the existing law, if it is assumed at the very outset that the book is a sacred scripture cherished as such by a certain community.

It must, however, be said to the credit of Justice Basak that he took considerable pains to establish such an assumption in respect of the Quran. He cited authorities like the *Encyclopaedia Britannica* in order to certify that the Quran is the basic textbook of Islam. He did not stint in using his own stock of literary and philosophical flourishes for fortifying the fundamental Muslim belief that the Quran has a divine source.

But the Writ Petition had not contested the point that Muslims revere the Quran as divine revelation. In fact, the Petition had stated quite clearly that "the Quran, particularly in its Arabic original, moves Muslims to tears and ecstasy" — a sign of extreme devotion. The real issue raised by the Petition was not what Muslims believe about the Quran but what behaviour pattern the Quran inculcates in its votaries vis-à-vis the unbelievers.

We find that Justice Basak neither faced this issue squarely nor ignored it completely in his judgment. He was not required to face it after he had constructed the legal concept that the Quran is a sacred scripture. He could have cited the relevant law which exempts scriptures from legal review, and gone straight ahead to draw the logical conclusion that no court in India can sit in judgment on the contents of the Quran. He, however, chose to make three observations which, though brief, are significant.

Firstly, in para 24 of his judgment, he observed, "In the faith of Muslims, and according to the theory propounded in the book itself, the Koran is the revealed word of God. This postulates God, and indeed the kind of God who has something to say to us and who takes the initiative in saying it. Religion in this view is not a human searching after God; it is God who acts, and is known because and in sofar as, and only as, he chooses to disclose himself." The same view of the Quran is repeated and further elaborated by him in paras 25 and 26 which follow.

Secondly, he said in para 29 of his judgment that "Some passages containing interpretations of some chapters of the Koran quoted out of context cannot be allowed to dominate or influence the main aim and object of the book". The Advocate-General of Bengal and the Attorney-General of India had also made the allegation that the Writ Petition had quoted some passages of the Quran out of context, though they had not said that these passages were "interpretations of some chapters of the Koran".

Thirdly, Justice Basak concluded in para 37 of his judgment that "This book is not prejudicial to maintenance of religious harmony". He added that "Because of the Koran no public tranquility has been disturbed upto now and there is no reason to apprehend any likelihood of such disturbance in future".

The third observation is of too general a nature to be discussed properly till we have a clear picture of Islamic theology propounded by Muslim scholars on the basis of Quranic pronouncements. We shall take it up at a later stage. For the present we shall confine ourselves to the first two observations, namely, that the Quran is the word of God, and that the Writ Petition had quoted some passages containing interpretations of some chapters of the Quran out of context. The two points conveyed in these observations are interrelated.

The passages which the Writ Petition has quoted from the Quran are not "interpretations" but the very words of Allah conveyed through the Prophet. They have been translated into English by a translator viewed as competent by Muslims, and published by an orthodox Muslim publishing house.

Nor have these passages been culled at random from different chapters of the Quran with a view to making the book sound sinister. On the contrary, they provide an almost exhaustive list of Allah's sayings on a subject of great significance, namely, what the believers should believe about and do to the unbelievers. The fact that these saying are scattered over as many as 30 chapters is explained by the peculiar manner in which the Quran has been compiled. Most chapters in it happen to combine "revelations" received by the Prophet on different dates at different places, and regarding varied subjects.

There is no question of these passages dominating or influencing the "main aim and object of the book". The Quran provides no other passages which abrogate or run counter to these passages. In fact, these passages embody, more or less completely, one of the two main themes of the Quran, the other theme being as to how Muslims should become a militant brotherhood (*ummah*) on the basis of uniform beliefs and behaviour.

As regards the observation that these passages have been quoted out of context, it would have carried weight if the legal luminaries had come out with what they knew or thought to be the proper context, at least for one passage as an illustration. In the absence of an illustration, one cannot help suspecting that the plea about "out of context" was no more than a stereotyped remark which is often made by those who run out of relevant arguments.

The observation sounds all the more astounding because finding the context of the passages cited in the Writ Petition, presents no problem. The meanest mullah in any village mosque can tell us as to when and in what situation the Prophet received which particular "revelation" from Allah. Islam is not a mythical religion, howsoever chock-full it may be of magic and miracles.

It is a historical creed which was floated less than fourteen hundred years ago. Moreover, the pious scholars of Islam have been more than meticulous in preserving a record of what "revelation" the Prophet received on which occasion. We have several orthodox biographies of the Prophet and as many as six authentic collections of the Prophet's Traditions (*Hadis*). Commentators on the Quran have used this wealth of first-hand historical material for connecting most of its verses to concrete situations in which the Prophet had received guidance from Allah in the form of "revelations". The oft-quoted authentic editions of the Quran, in original Arabic as well as translations, also carry detailed information about the context of every *sūrah* and *āyat* in it. And all this literature is available in English translations made by pious Muslim scholars or renowned Western Islamologists. The government lawyers could have consulted some of this literature and brought it to the notice of Justice Basak, if they were really interested in the context of Quranic passages.

Context is the Key to the Quran

Apart from the failure on the part of the concerned lawyers to provide the context, no one can quarrel with the proposition that passages from the Quran cannot be understood properly unless the context is known. Only we do not see our way to accepting the implied proposition in Justice Basak's observation that the context is likely to elevate in any manner the meaning of passages cited in the Writ Petition.

The language of the passages under reference is far from being ambiguous or allegorical. It is precise and plain in every instance. Nor do the passages embody any abstract principles. On the contrary, they contain concrete rules of conduct. There is plenty of evidence, as we shall see, that all imams and sufis and ulema and qazis have always stood for a literal and matter-of-fact acceptance of these passages. They have always frowned upon those who show a taste for allegorical interpretations (*ta'wīl*).

The Quran in Context

The Quran has 114 *sūrahs* (chapters) and more than 6,200 *āyats* (verses).[1] The bulk of the material in it consists of stories and doctrines borrowed bodily from the Bible and the Judeo-Christian lore floating around in Arabia in the Prophet's time. Many rituals and social forms as well as norms have been taken over from the Pagan Arab traditions, and transformed in a manner so that they look like original contributions of Allah. The only "revelations" which stand apart from this general mass, are those which Allah relays at certain critical junctures in the Prophet's career. As the Quran has been compiled neither in a chronological nor in a thematic order, these key "revelations" lie scattered (or secreted?) in many chapters. But biographers of the Prophet in the modern West have sorted them out, and connected them to the concrete contexts in Muhammad's life as a prophet spread over 23 (610-632 CE) years.[2]

We list below, in a chronological order, the occasions when Allah either commanded his prophet to do what the latter had already decided to do, or confirmed and justified what his prophet had already done:

1. *Allah's command to preach Islam publicly*: The Prophet had launched the Islamic brotherhood in Mecca as a secret society which converts to his creed were asked to join. They performed their new rituals either inside their homes, or outside the city limits of Mecca. This went on for three

---

[1]There are five different systems of numbering the verses which number 6,239 in Kūfah version, 6,204 in Basrah version, 6,225 in Shāmī version, 6,219 in Makkah version, and 6,211 in Madīnah version. It has 323,671, or according to other authorities, 338,606 *hurūf* or letters, and 77,934, or according to other authorities, 79,934 *kalimāt* or words (T.P. Hughes, *Dictionary of Islam*, 1885, New Delhi reprint, 1976, p. 489).

[2]We recommend two modern biographies of the Prophet which have been reprinted by Voice of India — *Mohammed and the Rise of Islam* by D.S. Margoliouth, New Delhi, 1985; and *The Life of Mahomet* by Sir William Muir, New Delhi, 1992.

years. Seeing that the number of converts had reached a certain number, and that some of the well-known desperados of Mecca had joined the secret society, he felt confident about proclaiming publicly what Islam stood for. Allah obliged him with appropriate "revelations" immediately (Quran, 74.1-3).

2. "Revelation" from Satan: But the Prophet had over-estimated his strength. It was not before long that the Pagans of Mecca started offering stiff resistance to his public preaching so that the spread of Islam got stopped and some of the converts started going back to the Pagan fold. The Meccans organised a boycott of the Prophet's clan, Banū Hāshim, and he found himself in a difficult situation. He felt dejected and yearned to be reconciled with his people. So Allah permitted him to proclaim that the ancient Goddesses of the Arab Pagans — al-Lāt, al-Manāt, and al-'Uzza — could also intercede for Allah's favours. This "revelation" is found in the Quran (53.1-23) except that the original verse 21 has been replaced with new verses (21-23). Allah had found his prophet in serious trouble with the latter's followers who had flocked to the fold of Islam because till then he had denounced these Goddesses as "false" and "filthy". Two orthodox Muslim biographers of the Prophet — Ibn Ishāq and at-Tabari — have narrated the incident, and preserved the original verse 21 which praises the three Goddesses as "exalted birds whose intercession Allah approves". Two more verses (22.52-53) were "revealed" by Allah at the same time in order to assure the Prophet and his flock that this was not the first occasion when Satan had succeeded in mixing his own "untruth" with Allah's "truth".

3. "Revelations" against the Jews: The Prophet had migrated to Medina because that city had a large population of Jews whom he expected to confirm his prophethood. Most of what he had been "revealing" so far, was derived from the Jewish scripture. But he discovered very soon that the Jews

had nothing but contempt for him and his creed. They made fun of him so that he was in danger of getting discredited even in the eyes of his own Muslims, not to speak of the Arab Pagans whom he was striving to convert. He became increasingly hostile to the Jews and thought of denouncing them as renegades who had fallen from the path blazed by Abraham. Allah obliged him by "revealing" a large number of verses (2.1-100; 3.111-12, 118-20) which mouthed the Prophet's new message to the Muslims and pronounced Abraham as the first Muslim. So far Muslims had prayed facing the Jewish Temple in Jerusalem. Allah changed the *qiblah* from Jerusalem to Ka'ba at Mecca (2.142-45, 149-50). Muslims were now commanded to fight the Jews, subjugate them (9.29) and harass them in every way.

4. *Formation of the Islamic Brotherhood*: The first brotherhood (*ummah*) which the Prophet had founded immediately after he settled down in Medina, consisted of converts to Islam from Mecca (*mūhājirūn*) and Medina (*anṣārs*) and the Jews of Medina. The text of the agreement between the Muslims and Jews for a defensive alliance against the common enemy — Meccan Pagans — is available in some biographies of the Prophet.[3] But he had to disown and denounce the Jews before long for reasons related in 3 above. Now the Prophet was out to form a new brotherhood consisting of Muslims alone. Accordingly, Allah sent down "revelations" commanding his prophet to form a Muslim *Ummah* (2.143; 3.110) which had inherited dominion over the whole earth from the earlier scriptuaries (7.128) — the Jews and the Christians — who had fallen

---

[3]This document was cited and the Muslim-Jewish alliance invoked by Maulana Abul Kalam Azad when he harangued the Muslims in India to join hands *with* the Hindus and *against* the British during the Khilafat agitation (1920-22) without informing anyone why the alliance had broken down soon after it was sealed. No other mullah came out with the truth. They were depending upon Hindu ignorance of the history of Islam, particularly of the Prophet.

from the true path shown by his earlier prophets. Henceforward, Muslims were the Chosen People (10.13-14) entrusted with the mission of spreading the "only true faith".

5. *Sword in the service of Allah*: The Prophet had decided to use the sword (*jihād bil saif*) when he saw that the Pagans of Mecca were refusing to come round and convert to his creed by means of "peaceful persuasion". He had sought help from Abyssinia and Ta'if, but failed. He was preaching to pilgrims from outside Mecca when some leading people from Medina met him at Aqaba, and rescued him from his plight by inviting him to their own city. During his early days in Medina, the Prophet apprehended attacks from the Quraish of Meeca. So he formed the Muslim-Jewish alliance as a defensive measure. Allah came forward with "revelations" (22.39-41) permitting the Prophet to fight in self-defence, and promising help. But no attacks came from Mecca so that the Prophet was left free to break his alliance with the Jews and form his own Muslim *Ummah*. Allah obliged immediately by converting the permission into a command (2.216; 4.76-77, 84, 8.39, 66-66). War against the Pagans now became obligatory on all Muslims. Muslims were to go out and attack the infidels in regular military formations (4.71; 8.15; 9.123; 61.4). As the Muslims succeeded in the raids on Arab settlements and caravans, the Prophet used the plunder obtained for building a formidable military machine at Medina. Lust for loot attracted to his fold desperados from all over Arabia; they joined the Muslim *Ummah* in droves. The Prophet went on elaborating this doctrine of "war in the way of Allah" (*jihād fī sabīlallah*) till it became a total and permanent war for establishing Islam all over the world. And Allah went on sending down appropriate "revelations" as and when the Prophet needed them in his campaign of slaughter and rapine till he died after giving a call for world conquest Allah had purchased the lives and properties of the

Muslims in exchange for dominion in this word and paradise hereafter (2.244-45; 9.111). Avoiding *jihād* became a great sin and violation of the covenant with Allah (2.218; 3.156; 4.74, 77, 95; 9.24, 38-39, 81.84). Becoming a martyr (*shahīd*) became the highest merit for every Muslim (2.154; 3.157, 169-70, 195, 198; 22.58; 33.16-17). It is significant that all these "revelations" about *jihād bil saif* were received by him after his migration to Medina.

6. *Bloodshed in the Sacred Months justified*: An expedition which the Prophet had sent to Nakhla was successful in obtaining some plunder, after the earlier ones he had sent elsewhere had failed in this respect. But the leader of this expedition which was mounted in the Sacred Month of Rajab killed a man from Medina, which was a serious violation of the ancient Arab tradition that no blood was to be shed in the four Sacred Months of which Rajab was the last. The incident invited not only strong comments from Arab Pagans everywhere but also murmurs of disapproval from the Muslims in Medina. The Prophet kept quiet for some time. But he had a justification up his sleeve. Allah confirmed his prophet's reasoning in a "revelation" (2.217) so that the plunder could be distributed among the Muslims and their murmurs silenced.

7. *Ransom for prisoners of war*: The Muslim army had captured a number of Pagans from Mecca in the Battle of Badr. The Prophet got two of them killed because they had mocked or otherwise insulted him after he proclaimed his prophethood in Mecca. About the rest of the prisoners, he faced a controversy as to whether they should be killed or released after exacting ransom from the Quraish. Abu Bakr was in favour of ransom, while 'Umar wanted them to be slaughtered. The Prophet decided to ransom them out but wanted to pacify 'Umar at the same time. Allah was quick to come to the rescue of his prophet. In a sudden "revelation" he reprimanded the Prophet for "not committing slaughter in the land" but pardoned him for accepting ransom (8.67-70) because he was in need of it.

8. *Division of plunder:* The Muslims who participated in the Battle of Badr, had collected a lot of plunder, particularly from the bodies of the enemies killed. They deposited every bit of it with the Prophet but kept on demanding that it should be distributed among them without delay. Their mouths were watering in expectation of a rich share. The Prophet was keen to keep a part of the plunder for himself but could not make up his mind about how to say it. Allah took him out of the tight corner by an appropriate "revelation" (8.1, 41) which established the Islamic institution of *khams*, "the sacred one-fifth". In times to come, as the Islamic empire expanded over large areas, *khams* became the principal source of revenue for every Islamic state.[4] Other sources of state revenue were tapped much later in the history of Islam.

9. *Expulsion of Banū Qaynuqa' Jews from Medina:* Success in the Battle of Badr encouraged the Prophet to implement a scheme which he had had in his mind ever since he turned against the Jews. He wanted to massacre the Jews of Medina and seize the rich properties they possessed in various forms in their three settlements around the city. But the Jews had allies among the Arab tribes of Medina, some of whom had converted to Islam while others had remained Pagans. So the Prophet decided to test the alliance by besieging one of the Jewish tribes — Banū Qaynuqa'. The Arab allies incited the Jews not to yield, but did not make any effort to raise the siege. The Jewish tribe was starved into surrender. The Prophet tried to do what he had in his mind. But at this point the Arab allies intervened, and saved the Jews from slaughter and rapine. The Prophet had to rest content with expelling the Banū Qaynuqa' from Medina. He had also to allow them to take away whatever movable properties they could. It was certainly a setback for him.

---

[1]K.S. Lal, *Theory and Practice of Muslim State in India*, Aditya Prakashan, New Delhi, 1999, pp. 95-110. Chapter IV of the book deals with Income of the Muslim State in medieval India. It has a section on *khams*.

But Allah was quick to approve the "compromise" in a new "revelation" (3.12-13, 19-20).

10. *Defeat suffered by Muslims at Uhud*: Another setback to the Prophet came soon after the "compromise" regarding Banū Qaynuqaʻ. An army of the Quraish from Medina defeated the Muslims at Uhud near Medina, killed some of their stalwarts like Hamza, and even wounded the Prophet himself. The Muslims had to run away from the battlefield to which they had gone in hope of victory and plunder. The Pagans and the Jews in Medina started making fun of him and his blind followers. The Prophet was now called upon not only to console his flock, but also to explain away their defeat in terms of their lack of firm faith. Allah sent down the appropriate "revelations" (93.139-57, 164-72).

11. *Cutting of date-palms and instituting Faiʻ*: A few months after defeat of the Muslims at Uhud, the Prophet got another opportunity to further unfold his scheme against the Jews of Medina and retrieve some of his reputation. The Jewish tribe of Banū Nazīr was accused by him of being in league with a tribe of Pagan Arabs who had massacred a party of Muslims sent by the Prophet in response to an invitation from the Pagans for converting them to Islam. He asked Banū Nazīr to leave Medina immediately. The Jews refused, and the Muslims led by the Prophet besieged their settlement. In order to force the Jews to surrender, the Prophet ordered his followers to cut down the date-palms around their settlement and burn the roots of the trees. The Jews appealed to the Prophet in the name of Moses who had forbidden cutting of date-palms. They thought that their appeal would have effect as the Prophet was in the habit of citing Moses every now and then and the Quran "revealed" so far was full of stories about Moses. But the Prophet received a "revelation" telling the Jews that the law of Moses had been violated in obedience to a specific order from Allah repudiating the disobedient ones (59.2-5). Banū Nazīr had to surrender and accept banishment from

Medina. But this time they had to leave their properties, the whole of which the Prophet appropriated for himself in obedience to a simultaneous "revelation" (59.6-8) in terms of which Allah ordained that plunder obtained without an armed conflict belonged solely to Allah and his prophet. The latter "revelation" established the institution of *fai'* which enriched many Muslim monarchs and commanders in the subsequent history of Islam.

12. *Marriage with Zainab*: The Prophet's first wife Khadija had presented to her husband a young slave, Zaid bin al-Hāris, whom he had freed, converted to Islam, and adopted as his son when he appointed himself a prophet in Mecca. Later on, he had married Zaid to a beautiful young girl, Zainab bint Jahsh. The couple had migrated to Medina along with the Muslims of Mecca, and lived in a house near those of the Prophet's other wives. One day, the Prophet went to see Zaid and found that the latter was not in his house. Zainab invited him inside. He saw her scantily clad, and her ravishing figure riveted his attention. He fell in love with her and pined for having her as his lawfully wedded wife. The Prophet's agony became known to Zaid who offered to divorce her so that she could enter the Prophet's harem. But the Prophet rejected the offer, somewhat angrily. According to a hallowed Arab tradition, the wife of a son, even if the son happened to be an adopted one, was to be treated as a daughter by the father, marriage with her being tantamount to incest. The Prophet's longing for her, however, remained unabated. Finally, Allah had to intervene with "revelations" (33.4-5, 59.37-40) which ordained that the Prophet should follow his heart's desire in matters of sex, and that Zaid was not *his* own son but the son of his (Zaid's) natural father. The dilemma stood resolved. Zaid divorced Zainab and the Prophet married her. He celebrated the occasion with a spectacular feast. It was, however, a great scandal, and tongues in Medina continued wagging for quite some time. 'A'isha got an

opportunity to mouth the scandal when someone accused the Prophet of concealing certain "revelations" which did not suit his convenience. Referring to verses regarding Zainab and Zaid, she is reported to have remarked, "If the Prophet had concealed anything of the revelation, it would have been those verses he ought to have hidden."[5] Incidentally, these "revelations" made adoption unlawful in Islam for all time to come.

13. *Renunciation of her 'day' by Saudah*: The Prophet had remained monogamous so long as his first wife, wealthy and influential Khadija, was alive. After her death, he had married Saudah, a widow of mature age, an year before his migration to Medina. In the next five years, he married five other women — 'A'isha, Hafsa, Zainab bint Khuzayma, Umm Salama, and Zainab bint Jahsh. He used to spend a day and night with each of his six wives. Thus every wife had her turn, and each of the six days was named after a wife — 'day of Saudah', day of 'A'isha, and so on. He was, however, getting tired of Saudah, and no more relished her company. He decided to divorce her and allot her 'day' to his favourite 'A'isha. Saudah offered to renounce her 'day' in favour of 'A'isha, and pleaded with the Prophet to let her remain his wedded wife. Allah "revealed" immediately (33.51) that the Prophet was free to do with his wives as he pleased. The Prophet did not divorce Saudah, and 'A'isha gained another 'day' to keep him company.

14. *'A'isha rescued from scandal*: In the same year that the Prophet married Zainab, there was another scandal which also became the talk of the town in Medina. 'A'isha had accompanied the Prophet in an expedition, but was left behind by mistake on the return march during the night. She had gone a little distance away from the army camp to

---

[5]Cited by Maxime Rodinson in *Mohammed*, Second (revised) edition, London, 1971, p. 207 with reference to Tirmidhī, *sahīh*, kitāb 44 ('tafsīr al-qurān), on sūrat al-azhāb, hadith 9a to 11 (ed. Cairo, 1292 H., vol. II, p. 209f).

answer the call of nature when she dropped her necklace somewhere. She went out again in search of the necklace but by the time she returned, she found that the army had broken camp and marched towards Medina. It was assumed by everyone concerned that she was inside her *howda* on her camel. She had to reach Medina next the morning riding on the camel of Safwan who was also in the same expedition but who too had been left behind searching for his camel which had wandered away in the night. Tongues in Medina started wagging again including those of a few prominent companions of the Prophet. It was suspected that the very young wife of an old man was involved in romance with a youth of her own age. The Prophet was in a fix; in fact, he shared the suspicion for a few days. But no evidence of 'A'isha's guilt was forthcoming from any quarter. Instead, Safwan had stabbed a person whom he found spreading the rumour. The Prophet was too fond of 'A'isha to be swayed by 'Ali's considered opinion that he should divorce her, and that there was no dearth of beautiful young women wanting to join his harem. Moreover, she was the daughter of 'Abu Bakr who had stood by him through thick and thin, and who ranked next to him in the hierarchy of the Muslim *Ummah*. So Allah had to be called in, and 'A'isha pronounced innocent (24.1-20). Allah also prescribed whipping for those found guilty of accusing married women of adultery without producing four eye-witnesses. These "revelations" have complicated the Islamic law regarding adultery, and it has become extremely difficult to settle cases involving this offence one way or the other.

15. *Massacre and plunder of Banū Qurayza Jews of Medina*: Of the three settlements of Jews in Medina, the Prophet had already dealt with two — Banū Qaynuqa' and Banū Nazīr. He was in search of an excuse for dealing with the third settlement, that of the Banū Qurayza. His opportunity came soon after he was finished with the Battle of the Trench in

which a Mecccan and allied army besieging Medina had been repelled. The Prophet and his flock were in a mood of triumph. Allah sent the angel Gabriel to them immediately, asking them not to lay down arms without finishing the Banū Qurayza who were reported to have had some negotiations with the foes from Mecca. So Banū Qurayza were besieged, and starved into surrender. Now the Prophet asked them as to the treatment they deserved. They named as arbitrator, Sa'd b. Mu'āz, leader of an Arab tribe of Medina which was allied to the Jews at one time but had converted to Islam in the meanwhile. Sa'd at this time was in a terrible temper because he had been mortally wounded in the Battle of the Trench. According the judgment he pronounced, all adult males of Banū Qurayza were to be put to death, their women and children sold into slavery, and their properties plundered. The Prophet issued orders accordingly. The market place in Medina was drenched in the blood of 900 Jews who were slaughtered non-stop during the night by the Prophet's stalwarts, particularly 'Ali and Zubayr; their women and children were sent to Egypt to be sold as slaves in exchange for horses and arms. The properties which the Prophet and his *Ummah* divided among themselves were quite rich. In addition, the Prophet acquired a beautiful Jewish girl, Rehāna, who agreed to become his concubine instead of converting to Islam and becoming one of his wives. Allah blessed the dreadful enterprise in "revelations" (33.13-14, 26-27) which descended without delay.

16. *Retreat from Hudaibiya*: In the sixth year of his migration to Medina (628 CE), the Prophet announced that he would proceed to Mecca in order to perform '*Umrah* i.e. the Lesser Pilgrimage. He was accompanied by a large number of Muslims. They carried no arms, only animals for sacrifice. The Prophet announced that he wanted to perform the ritual peacefully. The Muslims were all dressed like pilgrims. But the Meccans were not prepared

to trust the Prophet, and came out of the city prepared for battle. Muslims were encamped at Hudaibiya, a place a few miles outside Mecca. Finding the Meccans in a belligerent mood, they took a vow — the Pledge of the Tree — to die to the last man in defence of the Prophet. The Prophet, however, negotiated a treaty of peace with the Meccans and retreated to Medina with his flock. Muslims were greatly disappointed by this failure to enter Mecca. Some of them expressed their unhappiness rather loudly. But Allah pacified them with "revelations" which described the retreat from Hudaibiya as a real victory, promised to the Muslims greeter victories in near future, and assured that they would be enriched with plenty of plunder (48.1, 18-21, 24-27).

17. *Silencing the Prophet's clamorous wives*: The ruler of Egypt had presented to the Prophet a beautiful Coptic girl, Mary, whom the latter had made a concubine and kept in a garden house. As the Prophet started visiting Mary more and more frequently, he aroused great jealousy among his wives. The climax came when one day his wife Hafsa returned to her room unexpectedly from a visit to her father's (Umar's) house, and found the Prophet in her own bed with Mary. The scandal spread in the Prophet's harem, and his wives were up in arms. He tried to pacify them with the help of Abu Bakr and 'Umar, but failed. Finally, he got annoyed with them, started living separately, and did not visit any of them for 29 days. He, however, got tired of this self-imposed seclusion, and yearned for reconciliation with his wives. Allah obliged him immediately with the needed "revelations" (66.1-5), addressed to his wives, appealing to them to calm down or face a collective divorce. The poor wives had no choice except falling silent.

18. *Breach of pledge with Pagans*: The Prophet had performed *'Umrah* at Mecca in the year following the conquest of that city. But he had yet to perform *Hajj*. He avoided the ceremony next year because while performing *'Umrah*, he

had been pained to see crowds of Pagan Arabs inter-
mingling with Muslims around the Ka'ba and elsewhere in
Mecca. Conversions to Islam had increased by leaps and
bounds after his spectacular victories. But a large number
of Pagans had remained loyal to their ancestral faith, and
the Prophet was bound by the Treaty of Hudaibiya to
permit them to perform the traditional pilgrimage to their
holy city. This "sorry situation" had forced the Prophet to
postpone performing *Hajj* in the subsequent season. He had
sent Abu Bakr to lead the faithful in the pilgrimage. He
was, however, feeling uncomfortable with the treaty with
the Pagans, particularly after the submission of Ta'if which
had made him all- powerful over the whole of Arabia. So
Allah facilitated his breach of pledge with "revelations"
(9.1-5, 28-29) which "released" him from his treaty
obligations. He sent 'Ali to read Allah's commands to
the people, Muslims as well Pagans, gathered at Mecca.
Allah had allowed only four months to the Pagans to
"walk around in the land"; they were to he slaughtered by
the Muslims if seen anywhere after that period. The whole
of Arabia was reserved exclusively for Muslims, and so it
has remained till today.

This repeated coincidence between the Prophet's convenience
on the one hand and Allah's commands on the other, makes it
more than obvious that *Allah of the Quran is no other than the
Prophet himself*. Many people around the Prophet must have seen
through the game. But it needed a privileged person like 'A'isha to
expose it in so many words. When Allah approved of his wife
Sauda renouncing her 'day' in favour of 'A'isha (33.51), the latter
could not contain herself and quipped, "I find that Allah is prompt
to proclaim commandments in accordance with your desire (*main
dēkhtī hūṅ kē woh allah ta'la āp kī ārzū ke muwāfiq jald hukam
farmātā hai*).[6] The same comment by 'A'isha is recorded in a

---

[6]*Sahih Muslim Sharīf*, Arabic text with Urdu translation by Allama Wahid-uz-
Zaman, Aitqad Publishing House, Delhi, 1986, Volume IV, p. 80.

slightly different Urdu translation in another Hadis collection, "Allah excels even you in fulfilling your wish (*allah ta'la āp kī khwāhish pūrī karnē mēṅ āp sē bhī sabqat lē jātā hai*)."[7] We find far more clinching evidence to the same effect in biographies of the Prophet and Hadis collections. According to Ibn Ishāq, Muslims had constructed a hut for him to retire into at night on the eve of the Battle of Badr. Next morning, after he had "straightened the ranks", he returned to the hut and prayed, "O Allah! if this band [i.e. the Muslim army] perishes today Thou will be worshipped no more."[8] At-Tabari has a slightly longer passage in the same context. The Urdu translation we have before us, reads, "*Khudāwandā agar yēh mērī jamā't halāk hō gayī tō duniyā mēṅ phir tērā kōī parastār na rahēgā* (O Allah! if this band of *mine* perishes, then there will remain no worshipper of yours *in the world*)."[9] Here the "band" is defined specifically as "mine" and "the world" as a whole is supposed to stand threatened with the disappearance of Allah's worshippers. A modern writer has referred to the same passage without mentioning the source from which he has quoted it. According to him, "The Prophet's well-known remarks on the morning of the day of Badr were, 'Almighty Allah, if these *310* perish today, there would he none left to worship Thee on earth.'"[10] Thus he follows at-Tabari except for substituting the word "these" for "mine", and mentioning specifically the number of Muslim swordsmen who were present at Badr. Sir Muhammad Iqbal, the renowned poet of Islam in modern times, goes still further. In his famous poem, *Shikwah* (Grievance), he sings:

---

[7]*Sunan Ibn Mājah*, Arabic text with Urdu translation by Maulana Abdul Hakim Khan Akhtar Shahjahanpuri, Aitqad Publishing House, Delhi, 1986, Volume I, p. 557.

[8]Ibn Ishāq, *Sīrat Rasūl Allah*, translated by A. Gillaume, OUP, Karachi, Eighth Impression, 1987, p. 300.

[9]*Tārīkh-i-Tabari*, Volume I, *Sīrat an-Nabi*, Translated into Urdu by Saiyyad Muhammad Ibrahim, Nafis Academy, Karachi, n.d., p. 163. Emphasis added.

[10]Brigadier S.K. Malik, *The Quranic Concept of War*, Lahore, 1979, First Indian reprint, New Delhi, 1986, p. 81. Emphasis added.

tujhkō mā'lūm hai lētā thā kui nām tirā,
quwwat-i-bāzu-i-Muslim nē kiyā kām tirā.
(Did anyone mention your name before we [appeared on the scene]? It was the might of the Muslim muscle which made you click.)

I can multiply references to similar statements by stalwarts of Islam in medieval and modern times, particularly from the orthodox Hadis collections. We are thus led to the following conclusions:

1. No one in the whole world bothered about Allah before Islam appeared on the scene.
2. If the Muslim swordsmen who fought at Badr had been killed, Allah would have been worshipped no more anywhere in the world.
3. It was the might of the Muslim mailed fist which first established and later on maintained Allah's position.

Obviously, these claims are too tall or wild to be accepted. If Allah stands for God or some other name of the Divine, he was certainly known and worshipped by many people in all parts of the world since time immemorial. In fact, Allah was the name of the Great God whom the Pagan Arabs had known and worshipped, particularly at the Ka'ba in Mecca, for ages before Islam was born in 610 CE. Nor can it be conceded that Allah as God would have been forgotten if the handful of Muslim swordsmen at Badr had perished. A large part of the world has remained unconquered by the sword of Islam, and continues to worship the Divine known by numerous names. On the other hand, if Allah is the gangster known as Jehovah in the Bible which Prophet Muhammad made him mean after hijacking him from the Pagan Arab Pantheon, a large number of "revelations" in the Quran itself state loud and clear that he was known and worshipped ever since the first man, Adam, was created by him. All biblical prophets received "revelations" from him, and he had had the Jews and the Christians as his Chosen People at least for three thousand years before Prophet Muhammad tried to monopolize him for the Muslim *Ummah*. The Jews and Christians have continued to worship him till today, and taken together they exceed the number of Muslims in the world.

The three conclusions mentioned above should, therefore, be rewritten as follows:

1. No one in the whole world would have bothered about Prophet Muhammad if Muslim armies had not succeeded in imposing him first on Arabia and subsequently on other countries known as Islamic lands at present.
2. If the Muslim swordsmen who fought at Badr had perished, no one would have adored Prophet Muhammad any more.
3. It has been the might of the Muslim mailed fist which first established and then maintained Prophet Muhammad's position.

Authorship of the Quran

There is thus no substance at all in the Muslim belief or Justice Basaks' judgement that the Quran is the "word of God," unless God is another name for Prophet Muhammad. Allah of the Quran is no divine source of "revelations". On the contrary, the source of those "revelations" is wholly human. The Quran betrays, throughout its chapters and verses, the infirmities such as are native to ordinary and uncultivated human nature. The only difference which imparting a divine character to the Quran makes, is that it puts a heavenly stamp on monstrous monologues of an earthly person. What would have been dismissed out of hand as passing failure of normal human reason and natural moral sense, has thus acquired the authority of inviolable laws established for all time to come.

We should like to quote at some length from Maxime Rodinson, a modern biographer of the Prophet, who is well-known for being more than sympathetic to Islam and its institutions:

"May any Muslims who read these lines forgive my plain speaking. For them the Koran is the book of Allah and I respect their faith. But I do not share it and I do not wish to fall back, as many orientalists have done, on equivocal phrases to disguise my meaning. This may perhaps be of assistance in remaining on good terms with individuals and governments professing Islam; but I have no wish to deceive anyone.... *I do not believe that the Koran is the book of Allah.* If I did, I should be a Muslim. But the Koran is there, and since I, like many other non-Muslims, have interested myself in the study of it, I am naturally bound to express my views. For several centuries the explanation produced by Christians and rationalists has been that Muhammad was guilty of falsification, by deliberately attributing to Allah his own thoughts and instructions.

"We have seen that this theory is not tenable. The most likely one, as I have explained at length, is that Muhammad did really experience sensory phenomena translated into words and phrases and that he interpreted them as messages from the Supreme Being. He developed the habit of receiving these revelations in a particular way. His sincerity appears beyond a doubt, especially in Mecca when we see how Allah hustled, chastised and led him into steps that he was extremely unwilling to take. But it is said that in Medina, as Buhl has very aptly expressed it,

> When we see how his later revelations sometimes come to the aid of his less elevated inclinations, we observe how he becomes increasingly cautions in producing revelations to back him up, and how these, obviously enough, often contain conclusions at which he has himself arrived after reflection and meditation on the needs of the situation or even as a result of suggestions made by those close to him, it is very hard for us to believe that they appeared in the same innocent fashion as in the earlier period.

"Had the inspired visionary been transformed into an impostor, driven by necessity to produce convenient revelations at the appropriate moment and at no other, in the way that mediums have been known to resort to fraud in similar cases? 'A'isha certainly remarked sarcastically on one occasion on the Lord's readiness to answer her husband's wishes. There are a number of difficult occasions, when we find him hesitating to make up his mind, asking advice and thinking things over, before the revelation suddenly descends from heaven and solves the problem along lines of what human (*sometimes all too human*) cogitation might have suggested. 'Umar boasted innocently of having three times given advice which turned out miraculously to correspond with the dictates of heaven... Even Muslim tradition tells the story of a secretary of the Prophet's, Abdullāh ibn Sa'd, who was taking down the sayings of the Koran at his dictation. At one point, when the Prophet broke off, the secretary continued aloud to the end of the sentence as he thought it should read, and Muhammad absentmindedly incorporated 'Abdullāh's suggestion into the divine text. (A prey to doubts of the Prophet's inspiration, 'Abdullāh abjured Islam and fled to Mecca. When the city fell the Prophet wanted to kill him, but he finally escaped with his life after his foster brother 'Uthmān interceded for him.)

"All this is true, but does not necessarily imply deliberate deception. *Man's capacity for self-deception is infinite.* It is obvious to non-Muslims that the words which Muhammad heard, by which his experiences (in themselves almost inexpressible) were translated in so miraculously perfect a fashion, were dictated to him by his unconscious. He himself suspected it; he had doubted their source, he was afraid that human inspiration might have formed some part of it, and, as we have seen, he even admitted at a later stage that Satan himself had managed to insert his own orders.

"With success achieved, his own faith acknowledged, strengthened and confirmed by thousands of disciples, it was only natural that he should have fewer and fewer doubts about the promptings of his inner voice; and that these, too, should have conflicted less and less with the results of his conscious deliberations and with the urge of those strong instincts which were fostered by the comfort of his position, by the intoxicating influence of success and by the consciousness of power... There was nothing surprising in the fact that Allah should suddenly command him to take reasonable decisions which his own human reflections, or the advice of shrewd companions, had already urged. *Besides what could be more natural than that the Master's orders should correspond with the lawful wishes of his faithful servant?...*"[11]

The observation of Rodinson in the last line of the above citation is confirmed by a Tradition of the Prophet himself: "A Muslim saw in a dream that he met a person from a People of the Book [i.e. a Jew] who said, 'You would have been an excellent *ummah* if you had not practised idolatry and not said — what Allah pleases *and* Muhammad pleases.' He came to the Holy Prophet and reported the dream. The Prophet replied, 'By Allah! I also think alike. You should start saying — what Allah pleases, *then* Muhammad pleases.'"[12] But the Quran has retained verses which equate obedience to Allah with obedience to the Prophet, and promise reward and punishment accordingly (4.80; 5.92; 8, 1, 20, 46; 24.52, 56; 33.36, 71; 47.33; 49.14).

The Jew was commenting on the Islamic confession of faith (*Kalimah*) — There is no God but Allah and Muhammad is *the* Prophet of Allah. Mixing the name of Muhammad with that of Allah, must have sounded sacrilegious and a pollution of pure monotheism to the Jews — an idolization of Muhammad so to say. Their misgivings proved true. Islam started by substituting Muhammad for the idols of the Pagan Arabs, and that is what it has remained till our times.

Why Quran and Hadis are interchangeable

This identification of Allah with the Prophet alone can explain why orthodox Islam has placed the Quran, the word of Allah, on the same holy pedestal as the Hadis, the word of Muhammad. "The sources of Islam," observes Ram Swarup," are two: the Quran and the *Hadīs* (Sayings or 'Traditions'), usually called the *Sunnah* ('customs'), both having their centre in Muhammad. The Quran contains the Prophet's 'revelations' (*wahy*): the *Hadīs*, all

---

[11]Maxime Rodinson, *Mohammed*. Second (revised) edition, London, 1971, pp. 217-20. Emphasis added.

[12] *Sunan Ibn Mājah*, op. cit., p. 589.

that he did or said, or enjoined, forbade or did not forbid, approved or disapproved. Muslim theologians make no difference between the Quran and the *Hadīs*. To them, both are works of revelation or inspiration. The quality and degree of the revelation in both works are the same; only the mode of expression is different. To them, the *Hadīs* is Quran in action, revelation made concrete in the life of the Prophet. In the Quran, Allah speaks through Muhammad; in the *Sunnah*, he acts through him. Thus Muhammad's life is a visible expression of Allah's utterances in the Quran... No wonder that Muslim theologians regard the Quran and the *Hadīs* as being supplementary or even interchangeable. To them, the *Hadīs* is *wahy ghair matlū* ('unread revelation', that is, not read from the Heavenly Book like the Quran but inspired all the same); and the Quran is *hadīs mutwātir*, that is, the Tradition considered authentic and genuine by all Muslims from the beginning."[13]

It is this fixed and frozen image of the Prophet which is meant when a Muslim proclaims his *Dīn* (fundamental faith). In fact, the Prophet produced a "revelation" (33.21) presenting himself as the perfect model for those who look forward (with hope) for the Day of Judgment. For a pious Muslim, human life is lived best when it conforms to Muhammad's conduct even in minor matters such as defecating, urinating, brushing one's teeth, licking one's fingers after meals, combing one's hair, cutting one's beard to a specific size, and so on. Islam leaves no room at all for individual initiative or judgment, not to speak of innovation. In case of doubt, a pious Muslim must go to a *mufti* (jurisconsult) and obtain a *fatwa* about how the Prophet would have conducted himself in a situation which, according to all known sources, the Prophet is not known to have faced. The exercise is eulogized by Islamic scholars as *qiyās*, that is, laying down the law by analogy.

It is the same identification of Allah with the Prophet which has given currency to the patent Muslim slogan, "(you can) be reckless

---

[13]Ram Swarup, *Understanding Islam Through Hadīs:Faith or Fanaticism?*, published in the U.S.A., 1983, reprinted by Voice of India, New Delhi, 1984 and 1987, pp. vii-viii. This publication and its Hindi translation were banned by the Delhi Administration in 1990 and 1991.

(in your utterances) about Allah but when it comes to Muhammad, beware! (*bā khudā dīwānā bāsh o bā muhammad hoshiyār*)." Allah can be discussed, but Muhammad is a closed book. The only freedom of expression which one can exercise vis-à-vis Muhammad is the freedom to praise him.

Orthodox as well as liberal Muslims agree that Muhammad occupies the centre of Islam. "Urdu poetry," writes a liberal Muslim, "abounds in irreverent references to the Almighty. But there exists not a single couplet which takes similar liberties with Prophet Muhammad. Even scholars of Islam in the West, bar a few exceptions, have not quite understood the impact, over the centuries, of the Prophet of Islam on the Muslim mind... In 1985, the great scholar, Annemarie Schimmel published a classic entitled *And Muhammad is His Messenger: The Veneration of the Prophet in Islamic Poetry*. She drew not only on works of scholarship but also on poetry, music, folklore and literature to show the central place he has occupied in Muslim life and thinking since the down of Islam."[14]

The Judgement suffers from Syllolisation

Coming back to Justice Basak's judgement, we find that it is a syllogism which assumes arbitrarily in its major and minor premises what it has to prove in its conclusion. In other words, the conclusion has not been inferred from the evidence presented but deduced hypothetically.

The Writ Petition had placed before the court 85 *āyats* from the Quran which command Muslims to practise a particular behaviour pattern towards non-Muslims. The first point to be considered by

---

[14]A.G. Noorani in a review of *In Search of Muhammad* by Clinton Bennett, *The Statesman*, 24 May 1999. Noorani's credentials as a liberal Muslim are guaranteed by his quoting a length, in the same review, from Ziaduddin Sardar's *The Future of Muslim Civilisation*. Sardar attacks orthodox Muslims for interpreting Islamic injunctions mechanically and literally, thus losing "right of the individual freedom, the dynamic nature of many Islamic injunctions, and the creativity and innovation which Islam fosters within its framework".

the court was whether there was substance in the Petitioners' plea that the behaviour pattern prescribed by the Quran was inimical to public peace, communal harmony, and religious beliefs of those who did not subscribe to Islam. The belief system which produces that behaviour pattern should have been evaluated only after evaluating the behaviour pattern in terms of natural justice and common sense.

Justice Basak, however, chose to proceed the other way around. He started by accepting the Muslim claim that the Quran was the word of God. That was his major premise. His minor premise was that if the *āyats* sounded obnoxious, they must have been torn out of their proper context and interpreted to mean what they did not really mean. The conclusion he drew became unavoidable. How could a belief system based on the word of God prescribe an ungodly behaviour pattern? So the Quran and the creed embodied in it, posed no threat to public peace or communal harmony or to the religious beliefs of non-Muslims. *Quod erat demonstrandum.*

We have before us another case which came before the court of a metropolitan magistrate in Delhi in 1983 but the judgement on which was pronounced an year after Justice Basak pronounced his judgement in Calcutta on 17 May 1985. Two persons had been charged under Section 153A of the Indian Penal Code for publishing in a poster 24 *āyats* of the Quran and stating that riots in India cannot be stopped so long as those *āyats* remained in the Quran. All the 24 *āyats* are included in the Writ Petition which had been filed in the Calcutta High Court, and which Justice Basak had adjudged. The metropolitan magistrate, Shri Z.S. Lohat, however, drew a contrary conclusion. He pronounced on 31 July 1986, "With due regard, to the Holy Book of 'Quran Majeed', a close perusal of the Ayets shows that the same are harmful and teach hatred and are likely to create differences between Mohammedans on one hand and the remaining communities on the other."[15]

---

[15]For proceedings of the case in the court of Shri Z.S. Lohat, see *Freedom of Expressions: Secular Theocracy Versus Liberal Democracy*, compiled by Sita Ram Goel and published by Voice of India, New Delhi, 1998, pp. 1-9.

With due respect to the dignity of a High court judge, we find the procedure adopted by the metropolitan magistrate far more apt. Shri Lohat studied the *āyats* placed before him and inferred that what the accused had stated about the effect of those *āyats* on communal harmony was correct. He did not even mention the Muslim claim that the book containing those *āyats* was the word of God, though he referred to the Quran as "Holy Book".

Chapter 3

Entire Quran is a Manual on *Jihād*

Now we can take up the third observation in Justice Basak's judgement, namely, that "This book [The Quran] is not prejudicial to maintenance of religious harmony", and that "Because of the Koran no public tranquillity has been disturbed upto now and there is no reason to apprehend any likelihood of such disturbance in future". He has gone further and chosen to repeat the etymological exercise which we find in most of the books written by apologists of Islam in modern times. We are informed by Justice Basak that the word "*Muslim*" has been formed from the word "*Islām*" which in turn derives from "*as-salam*", meaning peace. The mission of Islam, we are assured by him, is the establishment of peace, and a Muslim is he who works wholeheartedly for this fulfilment. The argument is clever but not consistent either with what is advocated by the scriptures of Islam or with what we find in the recorded history of this creed spread over more than fourteen hundred years. Human history has known several movements which have used words to mean exactly the opposite of what those words stand for in common parlance. Christianity, Communism, and Nazism abound in such double-speak. So also Islam.

The Quran uses the words "*salam*", "*Islām*", and "*Muslim*" in some of its *āyats*, but the synonyms of these words — "*īmān*", "*Dīn*", and "*Mu'min*" — occur far more frequently. There is not a single *āyat*, however, in which these words or their synonyms stand or can be interpreted to stand for peace.

The word "*salam*" means literally "A contract involving an immediate payment of the price, and admitting delay in the delivery of the article purchased".[1] It has been used in the Quran (2.131, 3.20) to mean "bowing down before Allah" or "surrender to Allah". The word "*as-salām*" which has been derived from it is "One of the ninety-nine names or attributes of Allah" and means according to al-Baizāwī, "He who is free from all loss or harm."[2] Another word derived from it is "*taslīm*" which means "The benediction at the close of the usual form of prayer", that is, *namāz*.[3]

Similarly, the word "*Islām*" in the Quran means "doing homage to Allah" and "is said to be the religion of all the prophets" who preceded Muhammad, the Last Prophet.[4] According to 3.19, Islam is Allah's own religion, and those who reject Allah's revelations will be punished soon. According to 3.85, he who believes in a religion other than Islam will not be accepted, and will be a loser on the Last Day. According to 49.14, the Bedouins say that they have confessed *īmān* but they should say instead that they have confessed *Islām*.

Coming to the word "*Muslim*" it simply means "one who has received Islām".[5] We quote a few *ayāts* where the word occurs. At 2.132, the Quran says, "This is what Abraham and Issac bequeathed to their sons, 'Allah has chosen this religion for you. Die as Muslims.'" At 3.84, the Quran says, "We believe in what Allah has revealed to us. We are his Muslims", that is, obedient servants. At 22.78, the Quran says, "And wage war (*jihād*)... your religion is the religion of Abraham. He named you as Muslims." At 39.11-12, the Quran commands the believer to say, "I have been asked to worship Allah alone, and become a Muslim first of all."

---

[1]T.P. Hughes, *Dictionary of Islam*, op. cit., p. 561.
[2]Ibid.
[3]Ibid., p. 628.
[4]Ibid., p. 220.
[5]Ibid., p. 423.

Now we can take up the synonyms. The word "*īmān*" means "belief of the heart and confession of the lips to the truth of Muslim religion".[6] The word "*mu'min*" (pl. *mu'minūn*, popular *momin*) is "A term generally used for Muhammadans in the Quran and all Muslim books."[7] Two *sūrahs* of the Quran are named after this word. Sūrah 23, *Al-Mu'minūn*, gives a warning to those Meccans who argue with Muhammad and ask inconvenient questions, that they will burn in hell. And Sūrah 40, *Al-Mu'min*, describes the terrible torments of hell which are waiting for all unbelievers according to the "revelations" from Allah.

Finally, the word "*Dīn*" which occurs quite frequently in the Quran like the words "*īmān*" and "*mu'min*", is "The Arabic word for 'religion'," and "is used especially for the religion of the prophets and their inspired books".[8] Nowhere does it mean "peace" or "religion of peace". In fact, in some *āyats* (2.190-91; 8.39, 72; 9.19-22, 111), it is used for inviting the believers to engage in *jihād*.

Sir William Muir writes as follows about the earliest "revelations" received by Muhammad: "There is at this period hardly an allusion to Jewish and Christian Scripture or legend. The Kor'ān did not as yet rest its claim on the evidence of previous revelation and its correspondence therewith. But the peculiar phraseology of the new faith has already become fixed. The dispensation of Mohammad was distinguished as ISLĀM, that is, Surrender of the soul 'to Allah'; his followers as MUSALMĪN (those who *surrender themselves*), or as Believers; his opponents as KĀFIRĪN, that is, *those who reject the divine message*, or as MUSHRIKĪN, such as *associate* companions with Allah..."[9]

Maxime Rodinson defines the new creed in terms of Muhammad's feeling of "a sense of subjection to the terrible yet fascinating mysteries which surrounded him". He continues, "Many others besides him have had this feeling. But it manifested itself in a form which was peculiar to himself. The presence,

---

[6]Ibid., p. 204.
[7]Ibid., p. 419
[8]Ibid., p. 84.
[9]*Life of Mahamet*, op. cit., p. 79. Italics in the original.

Allah, was an almighty power which had no limits of any kind; a will which no bounds could contain... The only possible attitude towards this Allah was an infinite humility and total surrender (*islām*) in anticipation of a terrible judgment of which the outcome was wholly unpredictable."[10] This attempt to convert Muhammad into a philosopher and a mystic can be accepted only with a fistful of salt. Muhammad never claimed to be either; in fact, he had contempt for both. What is, however, quite clear again is that Islam has always stood for surrender to Allah, that is, Muhammad.

Margoliouth also has something to say on this subject. He writes, "Finally a name had to be given to the new sect, and either by accident or choice led to its being called the sect of the Muslims or *Hanifs*... no Arab seems to have known any thing about the Hanifs... and since in Hebrew the word means 'hypocrite' and in Syriac 'heathen', pious followers of Mohammed did not care to study its etymology. The other word, Muslim, naturally meant 'traitor,' and when the new sect came to be lampooned, it provided the satirists with a witticism; Mohammed showed some want of humour in adopting it but displayed great ingenuity in giving it an honourable meaning: *whereas it ordinarily signified one who handed over his friends to their enemies, it was glorified into meaning one who handed over his person to Allah*; and though, like Christian, it may conceivably have been first invented by enemies of the sect whom it designated, divine authority was presently adduced for the statement that Abraham coined the name."[11]

The reference here is obviously to Muhammad's Abyssinian connection.

The Abyssinian Connection

The Abyssinians who were Christians had invaded and occupied South Arabia in 525 CE. They had persecuted and

---

[10]*Mohammad*, op. cit., p. 235.
[11]*Mohammed and the Rise of Islam*, op. cit., pp. 116-17. Emphasis added.

oppressed the Pagan Arabs in various ways. An Abyssinian army had moved to Mecca also and threatened to destroy the Pagan Temple at Ka'ba in 570 CE, the same year in which Muhammad was born. The army had to retreat because of a plague which broke out soon after. But it had left a lasting hatred in the minds of the Meccans for both Abyssinia and Christianity. Abyssinia had continued to inspire fear also because it was a powerful kingdom as compared to Mecca which was a small city state.

It sounds strange that Muhammad should have thought of Abyssinia of all the places as soon as he met opposition at Mecca. But it is quite understandable once we grasp the psychology of those who get alienated from their own society and culture. They take little time in ganging up with the enemy. Small wonder that Muhammad sent some of his new converts to the court of Negus, the king of Abyssinia. The move caused considerable commotion in Mecca. His clansmen, the Quraish, hurried an embassy of their own to the same court in order to counter Muhammad's move.

Muhammad's biographers have presented the Muslim migrants to Abyssinia as refugees from persecution at Mecca. But they have concealed the true story. Margoliouth reveals: "On the analogy of similar scenes we should suppose that *the envoys of Mohammed urged the Negus to take an active part in suppressing paganism*, reminding him of the Abyssinian rule in South Arabia, a fact which gave him some sort of title to the country; and that the idea of regaining this ancient possession was what led him to favour the Meccan insurgents."[12] It was, therefore, natural for the Meccans to describe as "Muslims" the followers of a man who was inviting a ruthless enemy to slaughter and enslave his compatriots.

Curses and Street Brawls

In any case, Islam could not have sounded anything like a message of peace to Muhammad's contemporaries. He started by cursing that his clansmen who did not concede his claim, would

---

[12]Ibid., pp. 161-62. Emphasis added.

cook in the fire of hell for all time to come. The list included his indulgent uncle and protector, Abu Tālib. Before long, he would consign his dead mother also to the same dreadful place. The curses were soon backed by street brawls which his boisterous Muslims managed to provoke. He had a real tough lot on his side, apart from his ideology which animated the lowest passions in human nature. Margoliouth says: "The persons whose accession to Islam was most welcomed were men of physical strength, and much actual fighting must have taken place at Meccah before the Flight; else the readiness with which the Moslems after the Flight could produce form their number tried champions would be inexplicable. A tried champion must have been tried somewhere: and no external fights are recorded or are even the subject of an allusion for this period. The Prophet himself is said on one occasion after reciting Surah xxxvi to have flung dust on the heads of his opponents... *The growth of the new religion tended to spread discord between families and so keep the city in a state of turmoil and confusion.* Those who for any reason felt aggrieved with their condition could gratify their ill-will by joining Mohammed; and some probably did this in momentary pique. *Desperadoes of whom the whole city was ashamed seem to have been received into the fold of Islam; they could then on the strength of their faith claim to be better than their neighbours.*"[13]

Wars waged by the Prophet

Soon after Muhammad migrated to Medina, he started organising surprise raids on unsuspecting caravans and tribal settlements. He slaughtered quite a few of his clansmen at Badr. Waging war on his own countrymen became his main occupation during the succeeding years. Slaughter of those he viewed as his enemies not only satisfied his inflated ego but also brought to him much plunder. He also enriched himself by plundering the prosperous Jews of Medina. It is reported that his lieutenant,

---

[13]Ibid., pp. 154-55. Emphasis added.

'Umar, had counselled him to wear silk, and live in luxury. Muhammad had replied curtly that it was far better to spend the plunder on buying arms and horses. He acquired these sinews of war even by selling women and children captured in war and reduced to slavery. Biographers of Muhammad have listed as many as eighty-two expeditions which he mounted against various tribes of Arabia and the neighbouring lands, in a brief span of ten years between his migration to Medina in 622 CE and his death in 632 CE. The average comes to two expeditions every three months. Twenty-six of these, we are told, were led by him in person. After he had reduced Mecca and the rest of Arabia, he started planning expeditions against the Byzantine and the Persian empires. It was only his death which stopped him from waging more wars.

One, therefore, finds it difficult to believe that the word "*Islām*" could have meant peace in Muhammad's life-time, either to his votaries or to his unwary victims. Nor did it do so for a long time afterwards, as the sword of Islam swept east and west spreading death, devastation and dark terror over many lands. Muslim historians of those terrible times have not tried to hide what their "heroes" did to the "infidels" of all sorts, everywhere. In fact, they gloat over those gory scenes with unashamed glee. Hindus have known for more than thirteen hundred years what Islam stands for. It was not very long ago that Islam made rivers of blood flow on both sides of the borders of what remains of India today. Justice Basak's exercise in etymology cannot wipe out national memories and put the stamp of peace on an essentially violent creed. Islam was born as an ideology of totalitarian terror, and so it has remained till today. The key to understanding Islam is not in modern apologetics but in the life of the Prophet.

The Prophet's life-pattern becomes a Theology

The wars waged by Muhammad in his own life-time turn out to be no more than minor skirmishes when compared with even the not-so-famous conflicts of human history. They would have been forgotten before long but for the labours of Islamic theologians who transfigured the triumphant march of Muslim armies into the unfoldment of a divine plan. The seeds of this theology were already there in the Quran (33.21) and Muhammad's sayings in his normal moments, that is, when he did not speak in a state of trance (*wahy*). They flowered into full-fledged faith when fortune continued to smile on the Muslim military machine for two long centuries.

Perhaps the men who mattered after Muhammad's death were awe-struck at their own victories which followed in quick succession, and could not help looking at them as a series of miracles. Or, perhaps, that was what they could sell more easily to their followers who had become wide-eyed with wonder. In any case, it was in this darkroom of miracle-mongering that the portrait of the Prophet was enlarged to a fabulous size and painted in superhuman colours. Even the least little detail of his life, public and private, was invested with infallibility.

Finally, as the imams and the sufis stood face to face with the finished product, they were moved irresistibly to the conclusion that the Prophet's mode of living (*Sunnah*) was not a personal and passing phenomenon but a divinely designed pattern of universal and permanent validity. All men, everywhere and for all time to come, were now expected to fashion themselves after that pattern, voluntarily and willingly. The "infidels" who demurred were to be forced into this fixed mould for their own good, here and hereafter.

Place of War in Islam

Islam would have been a harmless fossil so far as the non-Muslims are concerned, if waging of aggressive wars for the spread of the faith had not occupied the pride of place in the petrified image of the Prophet. Presenting this persistent sabre-rattling as *jihād* or "exertion in the way of Allah", does not change the situation. Nor does the translation of this term as "holy war" help matters in any manner. We have to face the fact that violence and war-mongering have become essential and major ingredients of the Muslim psyche through the medium of the Prophet's *Sunnah*.

The *Mujāhid*

The Quran (9.10) makes the point quite clear. The *mujāhid* (Muslim who engages in *jihād*) is presented as far superior to the mere *mu'min* (person who affirms that there is no God but Allah and that Muhammad is *the* Prophet of Allah). Allah asks the Prophet (Quran, 9.19), "Do you make the givers of drink to pilgrims or the maintainers of Scared Mosques equal to the believers in Allah and Last Day, and the crusaders (*mujāhids*) in the cause of Allah?" He himself provides the answer in the same verse. "They are not," he announces, "comparable in the sight of Allah. And Allah guides not those who do wrong."

The *Sahih Muslim* is the second most important collection of Hadis. It reports the Prophet as saying: "Whoever cheerfully accepts Allah as his Lord, Islam as his religion and Muhammad as his Apostle is necessarily entitled to enter paradise... (yet) there is another act which elevates the position of a man in paradise to a grade one hundred (higher), and the elevation between one grade and the other is equal to the height of the heaven from the earth... What is that act? *Jihād* in the way of Allah! *Jihād* in the way of Allah !"[14]

The *Ghāzi*

A still higher grade goes to the *ghāzi*, that is, one who slays an "infidel" with his own hands. That is why this appellation was flaunted by all Muslim sultans who invaded or thrived in India at one time or the other. Babur became a *ghāzi* by raising tower after tower of severed Hindu heads in the wake of his victory over Maharana Sangram Singh of Mewar. Akbar also earned the rank

---

[14]Cited in Ram Swarup, *Understanding Islam Through Hadis*, op. cit., pp. 126-27.

when as a boy of only thirteen years, he was made to cut off the head of a defeated and half-dead Hindu king, Himu, after the Second Battle of Panipat. The Later Mughals, some of whom never went anywhere near a battlefield, claimed that they had inherited the title from their more renowned ancestors.

The *Shahīd*

It is, however, the *shahīd* (martyr) who gets the highest grade in the Islamic roll of honour. The *mujāhid* who gets killed in a *jihād* becomes a *shahīd* and goes straight to *jannat* (paradise) without having to wait for the Day of Judgment like the rest of the *mu'mins*. Muhammad did not believe in rebirth, nor in traffic between heaven and earth. But he forgot his own teaching when he tried to glorify a martyr. A martyr, he proclaimed, "will desire to return to this world and be killed ten times for the sake of the great honour that is bestowed upon him."[15]

If one is really interested in getting at the core of the Quran, one should go to the original sources rather than read the modern apologists who sell only sweet tales in the name of Islam. The earlier imams and sufis were far more honest and straight-forward in stating what the Quran stands for. They had no use for twentieth-century humanist notions which the apologists have been trying to foist on Allah and his Prophet.

Modern Islamic Apologetics

The Apologetics that presents Islam as a mission of peace, human brotherhood, social equality and the rest, is a recent development in the history of Islam. Till the last quarter of the nineteenth century, Islam had in its armoury only two weapons which have been wielded by all aggressively imperialistic and totalitarian ideologies — Dogmatics and Polemics. Muhammad had started with Dogmatics which we find in the earlier *sūrahs* of

---

[15]Cited in Ibid., p. 127.

the Quran. It was not long before he evolved his poisonous Polemics to be hurled recklessly at what he described as *kufr* and *shirk* the religion prevailing among the Pagans of Mecca. He suffered a setback when the Pagans hit back, asking inconvenient questions about his pedigree, his person, his prophethood, his mentors, his promises, and his threats. He was thrown on the defensive, and displayed the first Apologetics in the history of Islam.[16] But he returned rather fast to Dogmatics and Polemics when his own followers showed signs of rebellion against him after he "revealed" the famous verses from Satan in a bid to reach a compromise with the Pagans. Since that time, Islam was never in need of Apologetics as its military machine designed by Muhammad himself continued to march triumphantly in West Asia, North Africa, and parts of Europe. The heresies that arose in subsequent centuries, particularly the Shia sects and the sufi *silsilas*, were more fanatic and fundamentalist than the four Sunni *mazhabs* — Hanafi, Hanbali, Māliki, and Shāfii.

The development that really shook Islam for the first time was the breakdown of the Safavi empire in Iran, the Mughal empire in India, and the Ottoman empire spread over West Asia, North Africa and southeastern Europe. European empires had risen everywhere on the debris. The reaction among a section of Muslim "intellectuals" has been what H. Lammens labels as "modernism" and K.S. Lal describes as "hiding the true face of Islam", particularly in Turkey, Egypt, and India. "The most moderate amongst them," observes Lammens, "have undertaken the mission of showing the complete agreement between Islām sanely interpreted, and the progress and aspirations of modern times. They protest that misunderstanding has given rise to a belief in their antinomy and they are resolved to dissipate it."[17] Again, "All vie zealously with one another in the apologia of Islām. They often

---

[16]See Sita Ram Goel, *Hindu Temples: What Happened to Them*, Second Enlarged Edition, New Delhi, 1993, Volume II, Section IV, Chapter 15, 'Muhammad and the Meccans', pp. 327-40.

[17]H. Lammens, *Islam: Beliefs and Institutions*, London, 1929, New impression, 1968, p. 206.

enhance the credit of Quranic institutions by pointing to the temperance campaign and the recrudescence of divorce among Christian peoples. Above all, the progressivists boast they can prove that as far as liberty of conscience, the *rights of man* and other 'conquests' of modern civilization are concerned, Islām is several centuries ahead of Europe... All are agreed in affirming that, judiciously interpreted, the Qorān not only proclaims the complete equality of sexes, but that in its efforts to raise the status of woman, it has outstripped all other religions."[18]

Coming to India, Lammens traces the rise of "modernism" to Sir Syed Ahmad Khan and his Aligarh movement. "Very eclectic in the matter of traditions, they do not trouble about the *hadīth*, when the latter fail to accord with modern progress; they then refute them unhesitatingly by recourse to inner criticism. Here again their line of argument which is entirely subjective, is lacking in logic and does not shrink from distorting history, for instance, to suit their ends. They describe the life of Medina in the first century A.H. and the reign of the four first Caliphs as inspired by tendencies of the most advanced liberalism. A Persian newspaper *Al-Ḥabl al-matīn* (27th of May, 1915) [published in India], shows us Fātima and 'Ayesha in the intimate circle of the Prophet engaged in philosophical arguments."[19] Again, "According to them, Muhammad was the declared adversary of slavery. If any mistake has been made on the subject, it is through misinterpretation of the Qorānic texts which appear to make this institution lawful... The *jehād* troubles them considerably... Their theory is that the Qorān contemplated only defining [defensive?] warfare and that its recommendations, were valid only in the Prophet's own time."[20]

Much water has gone down the Ganges after Lammens wrote in 1929. Islamic Apologetics in India since then has progressed by leaps and bounds. The Quran has been roped in to prove that Islam

---

[18]Ibid., pp. 214-15. Italics in the original.
[19]Ibid., p. 209.
[20]Ibid., pp. 214-15.

stands for equality of all religions and religious tolerance. "There are some," writes Dr. Harsh Narain (1990), "who find in the Qu'rān glimpses of equal respect for all religions, indeed for polytheism and idolatry as well. One of its verses relied upon by them runs thus: 'Unto you your religion, and unto me my religion.' But this verse teaches nothing like respectability of all religions." After quoting the full verse (109.6), he cites renowned Islamic theologians — Jalāluddin Siyūti, Hussain Waiz Kāshfi, Ibn Kathir, Abul Alā Maududi, Ashraf Ali Thanawī and Abdul Majid Daryābādi — who either say that this verse has been abrogated by the verse on *jihād* (*āyat* as-sayf, 9.5) or that it means the opposite of what it is being made to mean by modern apologists. "In other words, Islam is Islam and Kufr is Kufr, and never the twain can meet."[21]

"Another oft-quoted verse," he continues, "is, 'There is no compulsion in religion.' From it, too, the unwary or the unscrupulous are wont to hear a declaration of religious tolerance and peaceful coexistence of Islam with other religions." Again, after quoting the full verse (2.256), he cites Islamic theologians to the effect that this verse, too, has been abrogated by the aforesaid verse on *jihād*. "Shah Walī Allāh interprets it in such a way, however, that it ceases to rule out the use of force in propagation of Islam and, instead, provides a basis for just the use of such force. He writes: 'There is no compulsion for the sake of religion, that is, the doctrine of Islam has been demonstrated. Hence it is not tantamount to compulsion, as it were, though compulsion it is, on the whole.'"[22]

Even if we accept that these verses mean what the apologists say they mean, it has to be pointed out that the exercise only proves the poverty of the Quran in matters of tolerance and peaceful coexistence. One wonders why it does not occur to them that they are able to quote only one line each from two long verses

[21]Harsh Narain, *Myths of Composite Culture and Equality of Religions*, Voice of India, New Delhi, 1990 (reprinted 1997), pp. 57-59.

[22]Ibid., pp. 59-60.

out of the more than 6,200 verses which comprise the Quran. Why do they fail to take into account the rest of the Quran which is brimful of transparent intolerance and vociferous war-mongering? Are they fools or knaves to go on parroting ad nauseam these 15 words out of the more than 3,23,600 words which Allah is supposed to have addressed to their prophet?

Dr. Harsh Narain has not mentioned many other acrobatics of modern Islamic Apologetics in India because he was dealing only with the myth of equality of all religions. That has been taken care of by Prof. K.S. Lal in his latest (1999) book. "These days," he writes, "a group of Muslim writers is busy making an all out effort to present Islam with a benign face. A long series of defeats at the hands of Christian Europe and persistent resistance of Hindus in India, has resulted in inculcating in the Muslim masses a hatred of the West and the Hindus. At the same time it has prompted some Muslim scholars to present Islam as religion of peace, to put it on par with, say, Hinduism, Jainism or Buddhism..."[23] He quotes at some length the "prolific writer" Asghar Ali Engineer who says in so many words that "*jihād* is essentially a war for justice, not for aggression or lust for power", that sufis practised "absolute non-violence", and that "Islam is as non-violent a religion as any religion can be".[24] And Maulana Wahiduddin of the Islamic Centre in New Delhi who writes that "Islam is as tolerant a religion as any other", that "so far as forced conversion is concerned it is totally unlawful in Islam", and that although the Prophet "was persecuted by others, he strictly avoided confrontation, and followed the path of forbearance".[25] And Zafar Jung, President of the Muslim Mainstream Movement, New Delhi, who proclaims that "the word Islam means peace", and that "the Quran and Hadīth foster communal harmony".[26]

These writers, observes Prof. Lal, may be sympathised with as they are not historians and belong to institutions which receive

---

[23]K.S. Lal, *Theory and Practice of Muslim State in India*, op. cit., pp. 285-86.
[24]Ibid., p. 286.
[25]Ibid., p. 288.
[26]Ibid., p.289.

liberal funds from Gulf states for giving a face-lift to Islam. What he finds inexcusable is that renowned historians have joined the game. "Many writers on medieval Indian history find in conversion of many low caste Hindus to Islam a hand of the oppression of Hindu upper castes, or the Hindu caste system itself, and the attraction of the 'democratic spirit of Islamic brotherhood and equality'."[27] He cites Muhammad Mujeeb in this context who "misinterprets well-known facts in cleverly carved language", and tries to prove that "Islam was adopted by families or groups of families who were regarded as outcasts in Hindu society".[28] And Mohammad Habib who proclaims that the Muslim state in medieval India "was not a theocratic state in any sense of the term" and that "its foundation was non-religious and secular".[29]

Prof. Lal wonders why these Muslim apologists ignore "what has been said by contemporary chroniclers of the medieval period". His explanation is that "Probably they are shocked at the barbarous conduct of their medieval brethren and want to salvage the reputation of Islam, although whatever was done was done in accordance with the canons of their creed". He goes on to show how the two versions of medieval Muslim history — medieval chroniclers' and the modern apologists' — contradict one another. "Muslim historians of the medieval period honestly state that non-Muslims were converted to Islam through force; modern Muslim apologists claim that conversions were effected through peaceful means. Medieval chroniclers take pride in the iconoclastic zeal and achievements of their heroes; modern apologists plead otherwise. Medieval historians credit Muslim invaders with fighting Jihad for spreading Islam; modern Muslim writers say that their motive was economic — that the invaders were interested in loot and plunder and had little to do with religion. It needs to be emphasized that the truth here does not lie midway. It lies on the side of the medieval chroniclers. Still the apologists

---

[27]Ibid., p. 120.
[28]Ibid., p. 289.
[29]Ibid., p. 25.

complicate matters by contradicting the versions of their own co-religionists who were closer and more intimately associated with events about which they wrote than our modern apologists. The idea of a secular Muslim state is an innovation of a few 'progressive' writers who wish to bracket Muslim civilization with tolerant civilizations."[30]

He continues, "This phenomenon baffles Indian Muslims to this day — why could India not be made a Muslim country despite the exertion of more than a thousand years? The apologists try to explain it by 'discovering' that Muslim state was a secular state. They do not attribute it to persistent Hindu resistance, nor to the continuance of the great Hindu civilization to which should go the real credit."[31] Again: "There is no need to feel apologetic if most conversions were forcible. Force and violence have special place in Islamic history throughout the world. The heroes of Islam in India are men like Muhammad bin Qasim, Mahmud of Ghazni, Timur and Aurangzeb. They, their poets and chroniclers, all become lyrical when they describe their achievements in the service of Allah which included conversions by force. There is no justification for M. Mujeeb to unseat these old Muslim heroes from their ferocious pedestals and turn them into pacifists like Hindus and Buddhists."[32]

We are afraid, Justice Basak's comments on the Quran appear to be more in line with modern Islamic Apologetics than with Islamic Dogmatics and Polemics which still dominate the overwhelming majority of Muslims in this country as well as elsewhere. Modern apologists of Islam have been increasingly marginalised by the resurgence of Islamic fanaticism since the seventies of this century. Oil wealth of the Arab countries has encouraged and equipped Islam to go on the offensive everywhere, particularly against the West and Hindu India which it perceives as stumbling blocks in the way of its triumphant march

---

[30]Ibid., pp.22-23.
[31]Ibid., p. 41.
[32]Ibid., p. 293.

towards world domination. Muslim seminaries everywhere are training terrorists for doing service to Allah, and Muslim publishing houses are flooding the markets with primary source materials on Islamic theology and history. The Quran is now available in authentic translations undertaken by orthodox Muslim scholars. The picture of Islam that emerges from this material is being presented in the pages that follow.

Comprehensive concept of *Jihād*

Modern writers by and large including modern apologists of Islam state that *āyāts* on *jihād* were "revealed" to the Prophet after his migration to Medina. They explain that *jihād* was the last course to which the Prophet was forced to resort because his "peaceful preaching in Mecca" was not only rebuffed but also met with "persecution by the Meccan pagans". They locate and give a count of the *āyats* on *jihād* in the Medinan *surāhs*. Brigadier S.K. Malik has collected these *āyats* in the context of military strategy; they add up to 267 spread over 17 *sūrahs* out of around 1457 *āyats* spread over 23 *sūrahs* which were received by the Prophet at Medina.[33] The rest of the *āyats* in the Quran — around 4754 in 91 Meccan *sūrahs* and around 1190 in 23 Medinan *sūrahs* —, the apologists insist, pertain to other subjects such as beliefs, prayers, rituals, ethics, social rules and regulations etc.

Brigadier Malik, however, does not agree with this concept of *jihād* which, according to him, is far more comprehensive. Let us listen to what he has to say on the subjects. He writes:

The first step to this study is to understand the difference between total strategy, that is Jehad, and military strategy. *The term, Jehad, so often confused with military strategy, is, in fact, the near-equivalent of total or grand strategy or policy in execution.* Jehad entails the comprehensive direction and application of 'power' while military strategy deals only with the preparation for and application of force. *Jehad is a*

[33] *The Quranic Concept of War*, op. cit., pp. 149-50.

continuous and never-ending struggle waged on all fronts including political, economic, social, psychological, domestic, moral and spiritual to attain the object of policy. It aims at attaining the overall mission assigned to the Islamic State, and military strategy is *one of the means* available to it to do so. It is waged at the individual as well as collective level; and at internal as well as external front.

Waged in its true spirit, and *with multiple means* available to it, the Islamic concept of total strategy has the capacity to produce direct results. Alternately, however, *it creates conditions conducive to the military strategy to attain its objectives speedily and economically.* Military strategy thus draws heavily on the total strategy (Jehad) for its successful application. Any weakness or strength in the formulation, direction or application of the total strategy would affect military strategy in like manner. In the absence of Jehad, the preparation for and application of 'force' to its best advantage would be a matter of exception, not rule. Conversely, optimum preparation and application of military instrument forms an integral part of Jehad.[34]

The Hadis collections, commentaries on the Quran (*tafsīr*), and treatises on this specific Islamic lore also proclaim that the so-called *āyats* on *jihād* "revealed" at Medina pertain to only one form of *jihād*, namely, *jihād bil saif* — striving by the sword. At the same time they mention three other forms of *jihād* as follows:

1. *jihād bil nafs*: striving by the heart or conscience, that is, cursing the Kāfirs silently or in private if conditions do not permit cursing them publicly by means of speech and writing etc.

2. *jihād bil lasān*: striving by the tongue or word of mouth, that is, preaching against the Kāfirs publicly, pasting pejorative labels on them, and threatening them with the defeat and disgrace which await them in this world, and the doom hereafter.

---

[34]Ibid., pp. 54-55, emphasis added.

3. *jihād bil qalam*: striving by the pen, that is, writing down on paper and other materials what one has harboured in one's heart or harangued in one's speeches or plans to say at the appropriate opportunity. The written material is used for preservation of the Polemics as well as for its wider circulation.

Looked at from this comprehensive perspective, the whole of the Quran comes out unmistakably as a compendium on *jihād*. It contains *āyats* which were "revealed" to the Prophet vis-à-vis *kufr* (unbelief) and *shirk* (idolatry) while Islam was preached by him in private, and the small number of converts were organized in a secret society. These *āyats* were recited by the faithful individually and silently, or in private gatherings of a few people. They constitute *jihād bil nafs*. Next, came the *jihād bil lasān* either joined to *jihād bil qalam* or undertaken separately or simultaneously. That was when Allah commanded the Prophet to preach Islam publicly after Muslims had functioned underground for three years and grown in numbers as well as in terms of self-confidence. During the next ten years — from 613 CE to 622 CE — the Quran grew considerably in size as well as subject-matter as it included not only those *āyāts* which had been "revealed" before 613 but also those which "came down" subsequently.

As regards *āyāts* which do not directly denounce or warn the unbelievers, they are obviously of an auxiliary or supplementary character; they are meant for marshalling the Muslims into a militant fraternity (*ummah*) on the basis of a common belief system, a common set of rituals, and a common code of conduct. *Jihād* in any form can be practised only when there is an organized and disciplined community, small or large, to practise it. And *jihād* in the service of the *only god*, the *only prophet*, the *only book*, the *only dīn*, needs above all an *only ummah*.

So each of the five pillars of Islam — the only themes elaborated in the Quran — is a component of *jihād*. Among them the first and topmost place goes to *shahādah* or *Kalimah* (confession of faith, *īmān*); it is a loud and clear declaration of *jihād* or war on the unbelievers, made repeatedly and endlessly in every tenet and ritual of Islam. The other four pillars — *salāt* or *namāz* (prayers), *zakāt* (poor-tax), *saum* or *rozah* (fasting during Ramzan), and *hajj* (pilgrimage to Mecca) — are aimed at fortifying the first pillar in the hearts and minds of the believers so that it becomes a passion and a war-cry. In short, we can conclude as follows:

Firstly, the Quran is an exposition of the *Kalimah* or proclamation of *jihād* in all its aspects, implications, dimensions and dynamics.

Secondly, it is an exhortation towards marshalling a gang of desperados for imposing the *Kalimah* on the rest of mankind by every means including the sword.

And *jihād bil saif* prescribed in the *āyats* "revealed" at Medina and practised by the Prophet during the last ten years of his life — from 622 CE to 632 CE — is only the crowning piece in the Quran. Let the crowning piece stand where it does in all its glamour and glory, but the edifice which sustains it should not be viewed as something different or alien or antagonistic to it. The Quran as a whole is a unique piece of unity which runs throughout its seemingly diverse themes.

Jihād bil Saif

The book by Brigadier S.K. Malik to which we have referred above is a study of "striving by the sword" as elaborated in the Quran. It carries a Foreword by the late General Zia-ul-Haq who had seized power in Pakistan in 1977 after being appointed the Chief of the Army by Z.A. Bhutto, who was dictator of that country for more than a decade, and who promoted the concept of "proxy" or "low intensity" war against India — a war which continues in various forms and on several fronts till today. The General says:

Jehad fi sabilallah is not the exclusive domain of the professional soldier, nor is it restricted to the application of military force alone.

This book brings out with simplicity, clarity and precision the Quranic philosophy on the application of military force

within the context of the totality that is *Jehad*. The professional soldier in a Muslim army, pursuing the goals of a
Muslim state, *cannot* become 'professional' if in all his
activities he does not take the 'colour of Allah'. The non-
military citizen of a Muslin state must, likewise, be aware of
the kind of soldier that his country must produce and the *only*
pattern of war that his country's armed forces must wage.[35]

Allah Bukhsh K. Brohi who served for some years as the
Advocate-General of Pakistan, and who was that country's
ambassador in India at one time, has written a Preface for Malik's
book. He makes the following points:

1. The book is "a valuable contribution to Islamic
   jurisprudence".[36]
2. "The most glorious word in the vocabulary of Islam is
   Jehad, a word which is untranslatable in English but,
   broadly speaking, means 'striving', 'struggling', 'trying' to
   advance the Divine causes or purposes."[37]
3. "Islam views the world as though it were bipolarised in two
   opposite camps — *Darul-Salam* facing *Darul-Harb* —; the
   first one is submissive to Allah's purpose ... but the second
   one is engaged in perpetuating defiance of Allah."[38]
4. "The idea of Ummah of Mohammad, the Prophet of Islam,
   is incapable of being realized within the framework of
   territorial states."[39] He being the Last Prophet, his "Ummah
   participates in this (i.e. prophetic) heritage by a set pattern
   of thought, belief and practice ... and supplies the spiritual
   principle of integration of mankind — a principle which is
   supra-national, supra-racial, supra-linguistic and *supra-
   territorial*".[40]
5. The role of Muslims on the earth "is to communicate the

---

[35]Ibid., p. i, italics in the original.
[36]Ibid., p. iii.
[37]Ibid., pp. iii-iv, italics in the original.
[38]Ibid., p. viii, italics in the original.
[39]Ibid., p. x.
[40]Ibid., p. xi-xii, emphasis in the original.

same message of Allah and his practice (*Sunnah*) which they have inherited from their Prophet and if there be any one who stifles their efforts ... he will be viewed as *constituting membership of Darul-Harb and liable to be dealt with as such*".[41]

6. "The law of war and peace in Islam is as old as the Quran itself... In Islamic international law this conduct [of one state in relation to another] is, strictly speaking, regulated between Muslims and non-Muslims, there being viewed from Islamic perspective, no other nation... *In Islam, of course, no nation is sovereign since Allah alone is the only sovereign in Whom all authority vests.*"[42]

Malik himself starts his exercise with an Author's Note in which he says:

1. "The Holy Quran is a source of eternal guidance for mankind."[43]

2. "As a complete Code of Life, the Holy Quran gives us a philosophy of war as well. *This divine philosophy is an integral part of the Quranic ideology.* It is a philosophy which is controlled and conditioned by the word of Allah from its conception till conclusion."[44]

3. "The Quranic military thought can be studied from several angles. It has its historical, political, legalistic and moralistic ramifications. This study is essentially a technical and professional research into the subject... Such a research is essential to put our subsequent study of the Muslim military history in its correct perspective."[45]

The book has ten chapters and seven appendices attached to chapter nine which deals with 'The Application of the Quranic Military Thought' with particular reference to major battles fought

---

[41]*Ibid.*, p. xii, emphasis in the original.
[42]Ibid., pp. xii-xiii, emphasis added.
[43]Ibid., p. xvii.
[44]Ibid., pp. xvii-xviii, emphasis added.
[45]Ibid., p. xviii.

by the Prophet — Badr, Uhud, Khandaq, Hodaibiyyah, Tabuk. In Appendix I, however, the author provides a complete list of 'The Holy Prophet's Military Campaigns' from 622 CE to 632 CE. It comprises 26 *ghazwahs* (expeditions led by the Prophet himself) and 55 *saryas* (expeditions sent by the Prophet under other commanders) — a total of 81 campaigns. He divides them into six periods as follows:[46]

1. Campaigns after migration to Medina (622 CE) and upto the Battle of Badr (624 CE) — 4 *ghazwahs* and 4 *saryas,* a total of 8.

2. Campaigns from the Battle of Badr (624 CE) to the Battle of Uhud (625 CE) — 6 *ghazwahs* and 5 *saryas,* a total of 11.

3. Campaigns from the Battle of Uhud (625 CE) to the Battle of Khandaq (627 CE) — 6 *ghazwahs* and 5 *saryas,* a total of 11.

4. Campaigns from the Battle of Khandaq (627 CE) to the Conquest of Khyber (628 CE) — 5 *ghazwahs* and 14 *saryas,* a total of 19.

5. Campaigns from the Conquest of Khyber (628 CE) to the Conquest of Mecca (630 CE) — 3 *ghazwahs* and 17 *saryas,* a total of 20.

6. Campaigns from the conquest of Mecca (630 CE) to the time of the Prophet's death (632 CE) — 2 *ghazwahs* and 10 *saryas,* a total of 12.

The most significant revelations from the viewpoint of *jihād bil saif* are provided by the author in Appendices II, IV, V and VI. They relate to the battles of Badr, Uhud, Khandaq, Hodaibiyyah and Tabuk — *sūrahs* 8, 3, 33, 48 and 9 respectively. In Appendix III, he provides in great detail 'A Case Study of the Battle of Uhud' — from 11 March 625 CE when the Muslim army marched out of Medina, to 24 March when the Quraish retreated after inflicting a defeat on the faithful. He lists 6 psychological shocks suffered by the Muslims during this battle. These shocks are supposed to carry lessons for Muslims when they are faced with adversity.[47]

---

[46]Ibid., pp. 99-103.
[47]Ibid., pp. 109-26.

Now we can take up Malik's thesis, chapter by chapter.

1. *Introduction*

"Divine in conception, the Quranic philosophy of war ... can particularly absorb a great deal of the modern military science at the operational level, without sacrificing its own distinctive and fundamental features and principles."[48] The Quran "lays down its own *mystic doctrine as to the three categories of human beings and how they receive Allah's message*".[49] First, there are the Faithful who believe in Allah's revelations and his prophet (2.2-5; 5.17-18). Second, there are the Unbelievers who "reject the Faith" (2.7). Third, there are the Hypocrites who "outwardly profess Faith but harbour treacherous designs inwardly" (2.16). The Quranic philosophy of war has, therefore, to be studied with a view to how the Prophet conducted his military campaigns with the help of the first category of people, and against the other two categories. For the Quran itself says that the Prophet provides a beautiful pattern for Muslims to copy, everywhere and at all times (33.21).[50]

2. *Historical Perspective*

When the Prophet of Islam "voiced his Divinely-ordained mission in Arabia" in 610 CE, there were four major global powers — Eastern Roman empire, the Persian empire, India, and China. The Romans who were Christian and the Persians who were Zoroastrian, had been engaged in mutual warfare from 480 CE onwards. When the Romans suffered a defeat at the hands of the Persians in 621 CE, the Arab Pagans and the Jews were delighted. But the Prophet predicted a victory for the Romans (30.1-5), which the latter achieved in 628 CE. At that time, the Prophet had not yet turned against the Christians. But after he started operating as a warlord from Medina in 622 CE and succeeded in putting down the Jews and the Pagan tribes of Arabia, he denounced the

---

[48]Ibid., p. 3.
[49]Ibid., p. 4, emphasis added.
[50]Ibid., p. 5.

Christians also. In 629 CE, his army started measuring swords with the Romans. After the Prophet died in 632CE, the Muslim armies started battling simultaneously against both the Romans and the Persians. "Under the rising sun of Islam," brags Malik, "the Persian empire disappeared from the map of the world by 680 AD. By about that time, the Muslims had conquered Syria, Egypt, Anatolia, Cyranica, Tripolatania and Armenia from the Romans as well."[51] He does not say in so many words that this triumphant sweep of the Islamic sword should be credited to the "beautiful pattern" followed by the Muslim invaders. But that is what he means, following in the footsteps of earlier Muslim historians.

3. *The Causes of War*

"The central theme behind the causes of war as spelt out by the Holy Quran, was the cause of Allah (2.190, 244; 4.84)."[52] It was essentially a war fought by the Faithful against the Unbelievers (4.76). Malik goes on to summarise what another Muslim scholar, Dr. Hamid Ullah, has stated on the subject. "In his opinion war could be entered upon if the enemy physically invaded the Muslim territory or behaved in an unbearable and provocative manner short of actual invasion. War could also be waged for punitive, retaliatory and preventive purposes. Permissible also would it be to resume a war stopped temporarily. A Muslim state could also enter into armed hostilities in sympathy with their brethren living in another [no-Muslim] state..."[53] So the "cause of Allah" gives a very wide latitude to the Faithful to unleash a war against the Unbelievers on any pretext, whenever the former find or feel that they are in a position of strategic or tactical advantage over the latter.

4. *The Object of War*

The Quran commands the Faithful to keep on fighting "until there is no more tumult or oppression, and there prevails justice

[51]Ibid., p. 15.
[52]Ibid., p. 20.
[53]Ibid., pp. 23-24.

and faith in Allah" (2.193; 8.40). Here the language is deceptive as in all cases of double-speak. The words "tumult and oppression" stand for opposition to Islam, for whatever reason. So the Muslims are to continue waging wars so long as there are non-Muslims anywhere in the world. Of course, Muslims are free to sign treaties of peace with non-Muslims whenever such treaties serve their purpose. But they are also free to violate the treaties of peace whenever they find war more profitable than peace; they can always accuse the Unbelievers of planning treachery (8.56-58). "The Book, however, kept the doors of compassion and forgiveness open for those who offered genuine repentance", that is, embraced Islam under duress (9.3, 5, 11).[54] Another concession is reserved for those who, though defeated, refuse to become Muslim. They can pay *jizyah* and live as *zimmis* (non-citizens) in an Islamic state.[55] But no quarter is to be given to those who are suspected of being either "hypocrites" or "hidden enemies". They are to be slaughtered straight-away (4.89, 91).[56] And these guidelines laid down by Allah in the Quran and practised by the Prophet in his own life-time, are valid for all times and places in a permanent war which is still being waged by the Faithful on many fronts.

5. *The Nature and Dimensions of War*

"The dimensions given to war by the Holy Quran," observes Malik, "take into account the divine purpose behind the creation of Man and guide him to his ultimate destiny... the Book commands the Muslims to wage their war with the spirit of a religious duty and obligation (2.216) ... it also looks upon war as something virtuous for the Faithful and beneficial for the rest of humanity."[57] To those who fight for the "cause of Allah", the Quran promises "generous heavenly assistance" (47.7; 3.160; 4.22-23).[58] In fact,

---

[54]Ibid., pp. 30 and 32.
[55]Ibid., p. 33.
[56]Ibid., pp. 34-35.
[57]Ibid., pp. 37-38.
[58]Ibid., pp. 38-39.

this "divine war" is a profitable bargain also because Allah guarantees an eternal paradise to those who engage in it (66.10-13; 9.111).[59] At the same time, Allah is committed to punish with the torments of an everlasting hell those Believers who refuse to participate in this "holy war" (9.24, 38-39, 81-82). There are, however, certain tests which Believers who aspire to obtain heavenly help, have to pass. Allah expects his flock to remain firm in their Faith even if they suffer defeat or face adversity (2.214; 3.141-42).[60] Staying at home when a "holy war" is on or running away from the battlefield serves no purpose because death is inevitable, and it is better to die for "Allah's cause" than without hope for his grace (2.28, 218; 3.156-57; 4.74, 77; 22.58).[61] The "divine reward" varies according to the "performance of the Believers". Those who participate in the "divine war" stand higher in the eyes of Allah than those who stay at home even if the latter are pious otherwise and practise other tenets of Islam. (4.95-96). And the highest favour from Allah goes to those who are slain in Allah's cause; for they are not dead but very much alive in Allah's presence, that is, in paradise (2.154; 3.157, 169-70).[62]

Strangely enough, Malik does not mention in this context the worldly rewards like plunder including prisoners of war who can be sold as slaves, and living on the fat of the lands conquered and labour of the subjugated people. He has a lot to hide because Islam has to be presented as a "noble and humanitarian" religion and it is no more *correct* to glorify what was glorified till only the other day.

6. *The Ethics of War*

This is the briefest chapter in Malik's vociferous book on the "divine war". He cites only four verses from the Quran, three of which exhort Muslims "not to commit aggression" (2.190-91, 194) and the fourth one (47.4) recommends "generosity or

---

[59]Ibid., pp. 39-40.
[60]Ibid., pp. 40-41.
[61]Ibid., pp. 41-43.
[62]Ibid., pp. 42-43.

ransom" after the Faithful have had their fill of slaughter and taken prisoners. It is obvious that he has not found any verses about the "ethics of war" in the Quran, because he is palpably dishonest in interpreting the verses he has cited. Yet he concludes, "A Muslim's cause of war is just, noble, righteous and humanitarian. A victory in Islam is a victory of Islam. So noble and humanitarian a cause cannot be allowed to be attained through inhuman and undignified ways."[63] Instead of delivering a sermon, he should have cited some verses of the Quran which sound "just, noble, righteous and humanitarian". Or has he made a mistake by talking about ethic of war vis-à-vis the Quran? In any case, we see in the next chapter the *ethics* which the Quran stands for.

7. *The Strategy of War*

"Instructions pertaining to the divine theory of military strategy are found in the revelations pertaining to the battles of Badr, Ohad, Khandaq, Tabuk and Hodaibiyya" (3.124-26; 8.9-10, 11, 59-60). All these "revelations" urge the Faithful "*to prepare for war to the utmost in order to strike terror into the hearts of the enemies...*"[64]

Malik elaborates as follows:

> *Terror struck into the hearts of the enemies is not only a means, it is the end in itself...* It is the point where the means and the end meet and merge. Terror is not a means of imposing decision upon the enemy. It is the decision we wish to impose upon him...
>
> *Terror ... can be instilled only if the opponent's Faith is destroyed.* Psychological dislocation is temporary; spiritual dislocation is permanent. Psychological dislocation can be produced by a physical act but this does not hold good of the spiritual dislocation. To instil terror into the hearts of the enemy, it is essential, in the ultimate analysis, to dislocate his Faith...[65]

---

[63]Ibid., p. 50.
[64]Ibid., p. 58, emphasis in the original.
[65]Ibid., p. 60, emphasis added.

Does it sound diabolical? Not to Muslim ears, for sure. Terrorism in all its forms has been the most effective weapon in the armoury of Islam ever since its advent. Great terrorists have been the heroes whom Muslims cherish the most. And it is terror which has seen to it that the victims do not remember what they were subjected to before they were forced into the fold of the Faithful. The victims are expected and exhorted to become — and do become in most cases — terrorists in their own turn!

8. The Conduct of War

"The Holy Quran wishes to see the Muslim armies always in an uppermost, dominating and commanding position over those of the adversaries (9.5)... The Book wants the Muslims to retain the initiative to themselves through bold, aggressive but calculated and deliberate planning and conduct of war."[66] The Muslims are to be harangued constantly and roused to commit aggression again and again (8.65). A determined minority always succeeds if the victims of aggression do not understand the game, even if the latter are larger in number and more prosperous. That is how the Christians succeeded in the Roman empire, the Muslims in Arabia, the Communists in Russia and China, and the Nazis in Germany. It is as simple as that. And Malik does not have more than that to say in this chapter except for invoking the Quran to call upon the Believers "to display the highest standards of mutual love, affection, respect and concern" (3.200) and warn them "to guard against disunity among their ranks" (8.46).[67]

But history of Islam is a witness that the call as well as the warning failed whenever Muslims could not target or were incapable of fighting Unbelievers. Prof. K.S. Lal observes, "Such is the important place given to violence in Islam that when there are no non-Muslims to fight, the Muslims call one another Kafir and fight Jihad."[68] Malik does not deal with this boomerang as is

---

[66]Ibid., p. 66.
[67]Ibid., p. 69.
[68]*Theory and Practice of Muslim State in India*, op. cit., p. xii.

the case with other Muslim savants who use it in order to explain away the defeats and decline of Islam.

9. *The Application of Quranic Military Thought*

This chapter with seven appendices deals with the career of the Prophet as a warlord from 622 CE to 632 CE. Malik and Muslim scholars of his ilk want us to believe that the Muslim armies succeeded in these campaigns because they practised the strategies of war reposited in the Quran. This is a Big Lie. They succeeded because the Pagan Arabs lived in a series of tribal settlements and did not understand Muhammad's game, while Muslims at Medina built up a formidable war machine with the help of plunder obtained in raids, and by recruiting desperadoes from all over Arabia through lure of loot and bloodlust. Later on, the militarized Arabs succeeded in overrunning the Persian and Roman empires because the two empires had exhausted themselves through mutual warfare for a thousand years.

First of all, it has to be pointed our that the Prophet did not evolve the so-called strategies on the eve of battles he fought. The strategies were "revealed" to him after the battles were over. Which means that in every case, the strategy was an after-thought on the part of Muhammad. The only credit he can take is as a perceptive person who learnt from his experience, while the Arab Pagans failed to do so. Secondly, Malik and his tribe have to explain why the same strategies failed when it came to Christianized Europe, China and India. In Europe, Muslim armies were driven out of Spain and, iter on, from the Balkans. In China, those armies failed even to make a dent. In India, the Muslim sword took 500 years to reach Delhi, and another 500 to sweep over the South. But it failed to convert the country to Islam even after invoking the Quran and practising its strategies for more than a thousand years. Lastly, what happened to those strategies when Muslims were faced with the Mongols of Chingiz Khan and Halaku who massacred millions of Muslims, sacked many a metropolis of Islamdom and finished the Abbasid Caliphate by beating the last Caliph to pulp? And why did those strategies fail to work when a resurgent Christian imperialism swept over the Mediterranean and the Indian Ocean, and crushed Turkish and Arabian navies from the fifteen the century of the Christian era onwards? Why did the mighty Muslim empires crumble and disappear from the map when faced with superior art of warfare developed by modern Europe?

10. *Summary and Major Conclusions*

This chapter in Malik's book has nothing new to say. He repeats what he has already said in the earlier chapters. He, however, continues in this chapter the message that the Quran is a Manual on War. That is what we also say, except that it is not the only Manual of its kind nor the best known to the history of mankind. There are many other Manuals in comparison to which the Quran stands reduced to no more than childish prattle, and which do not need an Almighty Allah or his Last Prophet for elucidating what has always been and remains a mundane theme. Looking at the advances made by the modern art of warfare, the Quran as a Manual on War can serve only one purpose — it can spread an epidemic of madness among the Muslim masses so that creed-drunk mullahs and cynical adventurers can use them as cannon-fodder in private bids for power and pelf. There can be nothing more foolish than presenting madrasas and masjids as training camps for warriors who will conquer the world for Islam. These institutions can train only terrorists and assassins who waste their own lives and inflict wanton suffering on their innocent victims, here and there. They can never match the military academies of the modern world or the arsenals produced by armament industries in the advanced countries.

The Ideology of Islam

Taking into account the character of the basic text of Islam — the Quran — as a Manual on War, Islam cannot pass as a spiritual doctrine in any sense of the term. On the contrary, it stands exposed as a political ideology of predatory imperialism like

Christianity, Communism and Nazism with all of which its shares its source, namely, the Bible, as well as many psychopathological traits. Professor K.S. Lal has studied and taught the history of Islam in India for the last more than fifty years. He has written a dozen books, starting with his famous *History of the Khaljis* (1950). In his latest book (1999), he has reviewed the history of Islam in India in the light of Islamic scriptures — the Quran, the Hadis, the Sunnah, and the Shariat. His characterization of Islam as an ideology is being presented below:

1. "Islam is understood more correctly when it is called Muhammadanism. Muhammad is the central figure in Islam. He controls the hearts and minds of all Muslims everywhere..."[69]

2. "Fundamentalism is not accidental but essential to Islam... It sees unchangeability as strength. That is why the word reform is so abhorrent to Muslim thinkers and religious leaders..."[70]

3. "In Islam truth is established by the sword... dissent is hated as heresy and stamped out as infidelity..."[71] early medieval Indian Muslim chronicles mention the sword as the greatest harvester of converts. Islam was made to spread, as the old saying goes, with Quran in one hand and sword in the other. Sword was freely used in forcing people to become Musalmans..."[72]

4. "There is a uniqueness about Islam. Non-Muslims are to be converted to Islam freely. But once a Kafir becomes a Musalman, he has to remain one for ever thereafter. He is not permitted to renounce Islam or revert to his original faith. Punishment for such apostasy is death..."[73]

5. "Islam lacks any doctrine of coexistence... Muslim madrasas cannot shed their Kafir complex... The present adjustment of coexistence is a temporary expediency in India...74 It is the teaching of Islam to shun contact with non-Muslims except with a

---

[69]Ibid., p. 337.
[70]Ibid., p. 10.
[71]Ibid., p. 34.
[72]Ibid., p. 285-89.

view to converting them... Muslim separatism expresses itself in many ways..."[75]

6. "In Islam all human beings are not treated as equals. It makes a distinction between Muslims and non-Muslims. A non-Muslim is a Kafir, an inferior being. Non-Muslims do not enjoy any human right in this world; they cannot enter Paradise after death..."[76] Islam has two sets of principles of morality, ethics and justice: one is for Muslims and the other for non-Muslims. Sincerity, well-wishing and brotherhood are for the believers and faithful..."[77] Islamic scriptures recommend setting Muslims against non-Muslims, believers against infidels to defend Islam and destroy unbelief. Individual and group killings of Kafirs is encouraged..."[78]

7. "Islam recommends Jihad or permanent war on adherents of other religions... This makes Islam a totalitarian and terrorist cult which it has remained ever since its birth.[79]... There have been wars but wars fought by Muslims are in the service of Allah. This gives Islamic belligerency divine sanction and terrorism becomes a divine command..."[80]

8. "Like proselytization, desecrating and demolishing the temples of non-Muslims is also central to Islam. Iconoclasm derives its justification from the Quranic revelations and the Prophet's Sunnah or practice...[81] non-Muslims cannot reclaim their desecrated temples. This is the law of Islam..."[82]

9. "Islam has all the ingredients of imperialism found anywhere in the world in any age...[83] By destroying the national spirit of non-Arab Muslims, Islam has demolished the Asian centres of civilization such as Egypt, Iran and India..."[84]

---

[75]Ibid., p. 256.
[76]Ibid., p. 251-52.
[77]Ibid., p. 15.
[78]Ibid., p. 78.
[79]Ibid., p. 5.
[80]Ibid., p. 55-56.
[81]Ibid., p. 305.
[82]Ibid., p. 307.
[83]Ibid., p. 68.
[84]Ibid., p. 276.

10. "The Islamic principles of denigrating the non-Muslims, of aggression and violence against them — principles that perpetually incite to riot and rapine — have boomeranged. However brave face the fundamentalists may try to put up, the victims of Islam today are by and large Muslims themselves. The Prophet must have known that violence begets violence and repeatedly exhorted Muslims not to kill one another after his death. He also had a premonition that violence of Islam against non-Muslims will be met with a backlash. There is a *hadis* in *Sahih Muslim* which says that once the Rasul opined that Islam which began in poverty in Medina would one day return to Medina in poverty. 'Just as a snake crawls back and coils itself into a small hole, so will Islam be hunted out from everywhere and return to be confined to Mecca and Medina.' The increasing power of the non-Muslim West and the disenchantment of Muslim dissidents point towards that possibility, howsoever remote."[85]

Prof Lal has presented many other facets of Islam such as that Islam has no word for democracy; that secularism and Islam are mutually exclusive; that Islam can set up only a theocratic state; that Islam has institutionalised slavery and degraded women; and that Islam has laid waste many countries. But here we have been discussing Islam as "a religion of peace".

---

[85]Ibid., p. 296-97.

Chapter 4

The Prophet sets the Pattern

Prophecy about the Prophet

[A Jew from Syria had migrated to Medina some years before Muhammad proclaimed his prophethood in 610 CE.]
Later when he knew that he was about to die he said, "O Jews, what do you think made me leave a land of bread and wine to come to a land of hardship and hunger?" When we [the Jews] said that we could not think why, he said that he had come to this country expecting to see the emergence of a prophet whose time was at hand. This was the town where he would migrate and he was hoping that he would be sent so that he could follow him. "His time has come," he said, "and don't let anyone get to him before you, O Jews; *for he will be sent to shed blood and to take captive the women and children of those who oppose him.* Let not that keep you back from him."[1]

First Blood shed in Islam (Between 610 and 613 CE)

[To start with Muhammad had organised a secret society in Mecca. His followers used to congregate for prayers in unfrequented spots outside the city.]
When the apostle's companions prayed they went to the glens

---

[1]*Sīrat Rasūl Allāh* of Ibn Isḥāq translated by A. Guillaume, OUP, Karachi, Eighth Impression, 1987, p. 94. Emphasis added.

so that their people could not see them praying, and while Sa'd b. Abū Waqqāṣ was with a number of the prophet's companions in one of the glens of Mecca, a band of polytheists came upon them while they were praying and rudely interrupted them. They blamed them for what they were doing until they came to blows, and it was on that occasion that Sa'd smote a polytheist with the jawbone of a camel and wounded him. *This was the first blood to be shed in Islam.*[2]

The Prophet promises Slaughter (Between 613 and 614 CE)

[Muhammad proclaimed his prophethood publicly only when he had acquired a following large enough to make him feel confident that his voice would carry weight.]

People began to accept Islam, both men and women, in large numbers until the fame of it was spread throughout Mecca, and it began to be talked about. Then Allah commanded His apostle to declare the truth of what he had received and to make known His commands to men and to call them to Him. Three years elapsed from the time that the apostle concealed his state until Allah commanded him to publish his religion, according to information which has reached me. Then Allah said, 'Proclaim what you have been ordered and turn aside from the polytheists.'[3]

Yaḥyā b.'Urwa b. al-Zubayr on the authority of his father from 'Abdullah b.'Amr b. al-'Āṣ told me that the latter was asked what was the worst way in which Quraysh showed their enmity to the apostle. He replied: 'I was with them one day when the notables had gathered in the Ḥijr and the apostle was mentioned. They said that they had never known anything like the trouble they had endured from this fellow; *he had declared their mode of life foolish, insulted their forefathers, reviled their religion, divided*

---

[2]Ibid., p. 118. Emphasis added.

[3]Ibid., p. 117. Quran, 15.94. Read 'Allah' wherever the translator has written 'God'. Allah of the Quran is not God but the old gangster, Yahweh, of the Bible. Allah is an ancient Arab name for God, and means God only when some Pagan Arab utters this name.

the community, and cursed their gods. What they had borne was past all bearing, or words to that effect.'[4]

While they were thus discussing him the apostle came towards them and kissed the black stone, then he passed them as he walked round the temple. As he passed they said some injurious things about him. This I could see from his expression. He went on and as he passed them the second time they attacked him similarly. This I could see from his expression. Then he passed the third time, and they did the same. He stopped and said, 'Will you listen to me O Quraysh? *By him who holds my life in His hand I bring you slaughter.*' This word so struck the people that not one of them but stood silent and still; even one who had hitherto been most violent spoke to him in the kindest way possible, saying, 'Depart, O Abū'l-Qāsim, for by God you are not violent.' So the apostle went away, and on the morrow they assembled in the Ḥijr, I being there too, and they asked one another if they remembered what had taken place between them and the apostle so that when he openly said something unpleasant they let him alone. While they were talking thus the apostle appeared, and they leaped upon him as one man and encircled him, saying, 'Are you the one who said so-and-so against our gods and our religion?' The apostle said, 'Yes, I am the one who said that.' And I saw one of them seize his robe. Then Abū Bakr interposed himself weeping and saying. 'Would you kill a man for saying Allah is my Lord?' Then they left him. *That is the worst that anyone ever saw Quraysh do to him.*"[5]

Muhammad's Faction acquires Strength (Between 614 and 616 CE)

[Hamza, one of Muhammad's uncles, was a well-known warrior of Mecca. He heard that Abū Jahl, a leading citizen, had spoken harshly to his nephew.]

Ḥamza was filled with rage, for Allah purposed to honour him, so he went out at a run and did not stop to greet anyone, meaning to

[4]Ibid., pp. 130-31. Emphasis added.
[5]Ibid., p. 131. Emphasis added. Stories that Muhammad was molested by the Meccans in all sorts of ways are latter-day inventions for justifying his violence.

punish Abū Jahl when he met him. When he got to the mosque he saw him sitting among the people, and went up to him until he stood over him, when *he lifted up his bow and struck him a violent blow with it*, saying, 'Will you insult him when I follow his religion, and say what he says? Hit me back if you can!' Some of B. Makhzūm got up to go to Abū Jahl's help, but he said, 'Let Abū Umāra alone for, by God, I insulted his nephew deeply.' *Hamza's Islam was complete, and he followed the apostle's commands.* When he became a Muslim the Quraysh recognized that the apostle had become strong, and had found a protector in Hamza, and so they abandoned some of their ways of harassing him.[6]

When 'Umar became a Muslim, he being a strong, stubborn man whose protégés none dare attack, the prophet's companions were so fortified by him and Hamza that they got the upper hand of Quraysh. 'Abdullah b. Mas'ūd used to say, 'We could not pray at the Ka'ba until 'Umar became a Muslim, and then he fought the Quraysh until he could pray there and we prayed with him.' 'Umar became a Muslim after the prophet's companions had migrated to Abyssinia.[7]

Abyssinian invasion invited (615 CE)

[Meanwhile, Muhammad had sent some of his followers to Abyssinia where Negus, the Christian emperor, was informed that what Muhammad was preaching in Mecca was the same as Christianity. The Negus was also reminded of earlier Abyssinian invasions of Arabia, and invited to intervene again in favour of Muhammad and his Muslims.]

When the apostle saw the affliction of his companions and that though he escaped it because of his standing with Allah and his uncle Abū Ṭālib, he could not protect them, he said to them: 'If you were to go to Abyssinia (it would be better for you), for the

---

[6]Ibid., p. 132. Emphasis added. Abū Jahl (father of foolishness) was the name which Muhammad had bestowed on Abū Hakīm (father of wisdom), his foremost opponent in Mecca.

[7]Ibid., p. 155.

king will not tolerate injustice and it is a friendly country, until such time as Allah shall relieve you from your distress.' Thereupon his companions went to Abyssinia, being afraid of apostasy and fleeing to Allah with their religion. This was the first hijra in Islam.[8]
[But Abyssinian intervention failed to materialize because the Negus got involved in domestic trouble].

The Satanic Verses (615 CE)

When Quraysh perceived that the apostle's companions had settled in a land in peace and safety, and that the Negus has protected those who sought refuge with him, and that 'Umar had become a Muslim and that both he and Ḥamza were on the side of the apostle and his companions, and that Islam had begun to spread among the tribes, they came together and decided among themselves to write a document in which they should put a boycott on B. Hāshim and B. Muṭṭalib that they should not marry their women nor give women to them to marry; and that they should neither buy from them nor sell to them, and when they agreed on that they wrote it in a deed. Then they solemnly agreed on the points and hung the deed up in the middle of the Ka'ba to remind them of their obligations.[9]

When the apostle saw that his people turned their backs on him and he was pained by their estrangement from what he brought them from Allah he longed that there should come to him from Allah a message that would reconcile his people to him. Because of his love for his people and his anxiety over them it would delight him if the obstacle that made his task so difficult could be removed; so that he meditated on the project and longed for it and it was dear to him. Then Allah sent down 'By the star when it sets your comrade errs not and is not deceived, he speaks not from his own desire,' and when he reached His words 'Have you thought of

---

[8]Ibid., p. 146.
[9]Ibid., p. 159.

al-Lāt and al-'Uzzā and Manāt the third, the others', Satan, when he was meditating upon it, and desiring to bring it (*sc.* reconciliation) to his people, put upon his tongue 'these are the exalted Gharānīq whose intercession is approved.' When Quraysh heard that, they were delighted and greatly pleased at the way in which he spoke of their gods and they listened to him.[10]

[Muhammad's followers were annoyed with him for alienating them from their own people and then seeking reconciliation to save himself and his own clan from trouble. So Muhammad had to beat a hasty retreat and repudiate the latest revelation from Allah. Salman Rushdie has dramatised in his novel, *The Satanic Verses*, the tension which arose between Muhammad and his Muslims.]

Then Gabriel came to the apostle and said, 'What have you done, Muhammad? You have read to these people something I did not bring you from Allah and you have said what He did not say to you. The apostle was bitterly grieved and was greatly in fear of Allah. So Allah sent down (a revelation), for He was merciful to him, comforting him and making light of the affair and telling him that every prophet and apostle before him desired as he desired and wanted what he wanted and Satan interjected something into his desires as he had on his tongue. *So Allah annulled what Satan had suggested and Allah established His verses* i.e. you are just like the prophets and apostles. Then Allah sent down: 'We have not sent a prophet or apostle before you but when he longed Satan cast suggestions into his longing. But Allah will annul what Satan has suggested. Then Allah will establish his verses, Allah being knowing and wise.' Thus Allah relieved his prophet's grief, and made him feel safe from his fears and annulled what Satan had suggested in the words used above about their gods by his revelation.[11]

---

[10]Ibid., pp. 165-66.
[11]Ibid., p. 166. Emphasis added. See Quran, 53.1-27. The words 'these are exalted Gharānīq whose intervention is approved' were substituted by others in verses 21-23 when the Quran was finally compiled, and the incident was suppressed by latter-day Muslim historians and orthodox commentators on the Quran. For Allah's volte face in this episode, see Quran, 22.52.

[This episode revealed the quality of Allah's revelations. Muhammad received one kind of revelations when he felt weak and wanted to compromise with the Meccans, and another kind of revelations when his followers raised a storm against the concession he had made in favour of the Meccan Goddesses.]

Uncompromising Aggression (620 CE)

[The Meccans had made many attempts to persuade Muhammad against insulting their religion and their forefathers. They made another attempt at compromise when Abū Ṭālib, Muhammad's uncle and protector, fell ill and was reported as dying.]

Abū Sufyān with sundry other notables went to Abū Ṭālib and said: 'You know your rank with us and now that you are at the point of death we are deeply concerned on your account. You know the trouble that exists between us and your nephew, so call him and let us make an agreement that he will leave us alone and we will leave him alone; let him have his religion and we will have ours.' When he came Abū Ṭālib said, 'Nephew, these notables have come to you that they may give you something and to take something from you.' 'Yes,' he answered, 'you may grant me one word by which you can rule the Arabs and subject the Persians to you.' 'Yea,' said Abū Jahl, 'and ten words.' He said: 'You must say There is no God but Allah and you must repudiate what you worship beside him.' They clapped their hands and said, 'Do you want to make all the gods into one God, Muhammad? That would be an extraordinary thing.' Then they said one to another, 'This fellow is not going to give you anything you want, so go and continue with the religion of your fathers until God judge between us.' So saying they departed... Then Abū Ṭālib died.[12]

---

[12]Ibid., p. 191-92. Muhammad's obstinacy was confirmed by Allah in a revelation that followed soon after the Meccan chiefs went away. Allah also threatened punishment to the unbelievers (Quran, 38.4-15).

Attempt to raise Tā'if against Mecca (620 CE)

In consequence of the growing hostility of Quraysh after Abū Ṭālib's death the apostle went to Ṭā'if to seek help from Thaqīf and their defence against his tribe. Also he hoped that they would receive the message which Allah had given him. He went alone.[13]

When the apostle arrived at al-Ṭā'if he made for a number of Thaqīf who were at that time leaders and chiefs, namely three brothers... One of them had a Quraysh wife of the B. Jumaḥ. *The apostle sat with them and invited them to accept Islam and asked them to help him against his opponents at home.* One of them swore that he would tear up the covering of the Ka'ba if God had sent him. The other said, "Could not God have found someone better than you to send?" The third said, "By God, don't let me ever speak to you. If you are an apostle from God as you say you are, you are far too important for me to reply to, and if you are lying against God it is not right that I should speak to you!" So the apostle got up and went, despairing of getting any good out of Thaqīf. *He said to them, "Seeing that you have acted as you have, keep the matter secret," for he was loath that his people should hear about it, so that they would be still further emboldened against him.*[14]

Muhammad conspires with Medina (620 to 622 CE)

The apostle offered himself to the tribes of Arabs at the fairs whenever opportunity came, summoning them to Allah and telling them that he was a prophet who had been sent. He used to ask them to believe in him and protect him until Allah should make clear to them the message with which he had charged his prophet.[15]

When Allah wished to display His religion openly and to glorify His prophet and to fulfil His promise to him, the time came when he met a number of the Helpers at one of the fairs; and while he

---

[13]Ibid., p. 192.
[14]Ibid., pp. 192-93. Emphasis added.
[15]Ibid., p. 194.

was offering himself to the Arab tribes as was his wont he met at al-'Aqaba a number of the Khazraj whom Allah intended to benefit.[16]

When the apostle met them he learned by inquiry that they were of the Khazraj and allies of the Jews. He invited them to sit with him and expounded to them Islam and recited the Qurān to them. Now Allah had prepared the way for Islam in that they lived side by side with the Jews who were people of the scriptures and knowledge, while they themselves were polytheists and idolaters. They had often raided them in their district and whenever bad feeling arose the Jews used to say to them, '*A Prophet will be sent soon. His day is at hand. We shall follow him and kill you by his aid.*' So when they heard the apostle's message they said one to another: 'This is the very prophet of whom the Jews warned us. Don't let them get to him before us!' Thereupon they accepted his teaching and became Muslims, saying, 'We have left our people, for no tribe is so divided by hatred and rancour as they. Perhaps Allah will unite them through you. So let us go to them and invite them to this religion of yours; and if Allah unites them in it, then no man will be mightier than you.' Thus saying they returned to Medina as believers.[17]

In the following year twelve Helpers attended the fair and met at al-'Aqaba — this was the first 'Aqaba — where they gave the apostle the 'pledge of women'. This was before the duty of making war was laid upon them.[18]

When Allah gave permission to his apostle to fight, the second 'Aqaba contained conditions involving war which were not in the first act of fealty. Now they bound themselves to war against all

---

[16]Ibid., p. 197. The term 'Helpers' (Anṣār) has been used here in anticipation. It became current only after Muhammad migrated to Medina and was used for his Medinan followers as distinguished from the Meccans who became known as Emigrants (Muhājirūn).

[17]Ibid., pp. 197-98. Emphasis added.

[18]Ibid., p. 198. For 'pledge of women' see Quran, 60.12. It means that the Medinans who came to the first 'Aqaba were not yet prepared to wage war for Islam.

and sundry for Allah and his apostle, while he promised them for faithful service thus the reward of paradise. 'Ubāda b. al-Walīd b. 'Ubāda b. al-Ṣāmit from his father from his grandfather 'Ubāda b. al-Ṣāmit who was one of the Leaders told me, 'We pledged ourselves to war in complete obedience to the apostle in weal and woe, in ease and hardship and evil circumstances; that we would not wrong anyone; that we would speak the truth at all times; and that in Allah's service we would fear the censure of none.' 'Ubāda was one of the twelve who gave his word at the first 'Aqaba.[19]

Formation of the *Ummah* (623 CE)

[Following the second 'Aqaba, Muhammad migrated to Medina and laid foundation of his blood-thirsty brotherhood.]

The apostle wrote a document concerning the emigrants and the helpers in which he made a friendly agreement with the Jews and established them in their religion and their property, and stated the reciprocal obligations, as follows: In the name of Allah the Compassionate, the Merciful. This is a document from Muhammad the prophet [governing the relations] between the believers and Muslims of Quraysh and Yathrib, and those who followed them and joined them and laboured with them. They are one community (*umma*) to the exclusion of all men. The Quraysh emigrants according to their present custom shall pay the bloodwit within their number and shall redeem their prisoners with the kindness and justice common among believers.[20]

A believer shall not take as an ally the freedman of another Muslim against him. The Allah-fearing believers shall be against the rebellious or him who seeks to spread injustice, or sin or enmity, or corruption between believers; the hand of every man shall be against him even if he be a son of one of them. A believer

---

[19]Ibid., 208. Emphasis added.
[20]Ibid., pp. 231-32. Yathrib was the real name of the city which came to be known as Medina after Muhammad started living (*madīnat*) there.

shall not slay a believer for the sake of an unbeliever, nor shall he aid an unbeliever against a believer. Allah's protection is one, the least of them may give protection to a stranger on their behalf. Believers are friends one to the other to the exclusion of outsiders. To the Jew who follows us belong help and equality. He shall not be wronged nor shall his enemies be aided. The peace of the believers is indivisible. No separate peace shall be made when believers are fighting in the way of Allah.

It shall not be lawful to a believer who holds by what is in this document and believes in Allah and the last day to help an evil-doer or to shelter him. The curse of Allah and His anger on the day of resurrection will be upon him if he does, and neither repentance nor ransom will be received from him. Whenever you differ about a matter it must be referred to Allah and to Muhammad.[21]

Muhammad turns against the Jews (623 CE)

About this time the Jewish rabbis showed hostility to the apostle in envy, hatred, and malice, because Allah had chosen His apostle from the Arabs. They were joined by men from al-Aus and al-Khazraj who had obstinately clung to their heathen religion. *They were hypocrites, clinging to the polytheism of their fathers denying the resurrection; yet when Islam appeared and their people flocked to it they were compelled to pretend to accept it to save their lives.* But in secret they were hypocrites whose inclination was towards the Jews because they considered the apostle a liar and strove against Islam.

It was the Jewish rabbis who used to annoy the apostle with questions and introduce confusion, so as to confound the truth with falsity. The Quran used to come down in reference to these questions of theirs.[22]

The first hundred verses of the *sūra* of the Cow came down in reference to these Jewish rabbis and the hypocrites of Aus and

[21]Ibid., p. 232.
[22]Ibid., p. 239. Emphasis added.

Khazraj, according to what I have been told, and Allah knows best.[23]

There were two parties: The B. Qaynuqā' and their adherents, allies of Khazraj; and al-Naḍīr and Qurayza and their adherents allies of Aus. When there was war between Aus and Khazraj the B. Qaynuqā' went out with Khazraj, and al-Naḍīr and Qurayza with Aus, each side helping his allies against his own brethren so that they shed each other's blood, while the Torah was in their hands by which they knew what was allowed and what was forbidden them. Aus and Khazraj were polytheists worshipping idols knowing nothing about paradise and hell, the waking and the resurrection, the scriptures, the permitted and the forbidden.[24]

The apostle summoned the Jewish scripture folk to Islam and made it attractive to them and warned them of Allah's punishment and vengeance. Rāfi' b. Khārija and Mālik b. 'Auf said to him that they would follow the religion of their fathers, for they were more learned and better men than they. So Allah sent down concerning their words: 'And when it is said to them, Follow what Allah has sent down, they say: Nay, but we will follow what we found our fathers doing. What! even if their fathers understood nothing and were not rightly guided?'[25]

Some Muslims remained friends with the Jews because of the tie of mutual protection and alliance which had subsisted between them, so Allah sent down concerning them and forbidding them to take them as intimate friends: 'O you who believe, do not choose those outside your community as intimate friends. They will spare no pains to corrupt you longing for your ruin. From their mouths hatred has already shown itself and what their breasts conceal is greater. We have made the signs plain to you if you will understand.'[26]

Abū Bakr went into a Jewish school and found a good many

---

[23]Ibid., p. 247. See Quran, 2.1-100. The Prophet was always ready to produce revelations in his own and his followers' favour.

[24]Ibid., p. 253.

[25]Ibid., p.259.

[26]Ibid., pp. 262-63. Quran, 3.118.

men gathered round a certain Finḥāṣ, one of their learned rabbis, and another rabbi called Ashyaʿ. Abū Bakr called on the former to fear Allah and become a Muslim because he knew that Muhammad was the apostle of Allah who had brought the truth from Him and that they would find it written in the Torah and the Gospel. Finḥāṣ replied: 'We are not poor compared to Allah but He is poor compared to us. We do not humble ourselves to Him as He humbles Himself to us; we are independent of Him while He needs us.'

Abū Bakr was enraged and hit Finḥāṣ hard in the face, saying, 'Were it not for the treaty between us I would cut off your head, you enemy of Allah!' Finḥāṣ immediately went to the apostle and said, 'Look, Muhammad, at what your companion has done.' The apostle asked Abū Bakr what had impelled him to do such a thing and he answered: 'The enemy of Allah spoke blasphemy. He alleged that Allah was poor and that they were rich and I was so angry that I hit his face.' Finḥāṣ contradicted this and denied that he had said it, so Allah sent down refuting him and confirming what Abū Bakr had said: 'Allah has heard the speech of those who say: "Allah is poor and we are rich." We shall write what they say and their killing the prophets wrongfully and we shall say, Taste the punishment of burning."[27]

A Cruel Custom revived by Muhammad (622 CE)

Jewish rabbis had gathered in their school when the apostle came to Medina. A married man had committed adultery with a married woman and they said: 'Send them to Muhammad and ask him what the law about them is and leave the penalty to him. If he prescribes *tajbīh* (which is scourging with a rope of palm fibre smeared with pitch, the blackening of their faces, mounting on two donkeys with their faces to the animal's tail) then follow him, for he is a king and believe in him. If he prescribes stoning for them, he is a prophet so beware lest he deprive you of what you hold.'

---

[27]Ibid., p. 263. Emphasis added. Quran, 3.181.

They brought the pair to Muhammad and explained the position.[28]

When the apostle gave judgement about them he asked for a Torah. A rabbi sat there reading it having put his hand over the verse of stoning. 'Abullah b. Salām struck the rabbi's hand, saying, 'This, O prophet of Allah, is the verse of stoning which he refuses to read to you.' The apostle said, 'Woe to you Jews! What has induced you to abandon the judgement of Allah which you hold in your hands?' They answered: 'The sentence used to be carried out until a man of royal birth and noble origin committed adultery and the king refused to allow him to be stoned. Later another man committed adultery and the king wanted him to be stoned but they said No, not until you stone so-and-so. And when they said that to him they agreed to arrange the matter by *tajbīh* and they did away with all mention of stoning.' The apostle said: 'I am the first to revive the order of Allah and His book and to practise it.' They were duly stoned and 'Abdullah b. 'Umar said, 'I was among those that stoned them.'

The apostle ordered them to be stoned, and they were stoned at the door of his mosque. And when the Jew felt the first stone he crouched over the woman to protect her from the stones until both of them were killed. This is what Allah did for the apostle in exacting the penalty for adultery from the pair.[29]

According to a tradition from 'Umar, the second caliph, Muhammad not only participated in stoning the Jewish couple but also received a revelation which is not found in the Quran as we have it at present. According to a *hadis* from 'Ā'isha, the page on which the revelation was written was lying on her bed when it was eaten by a goat.

'Umar sat in the pulpit, and when the muezzins were silent he praised Allah as was fitting and said: 'I am about to say to you today something which Allah has willed that I should say and I do not know whether perhaps it is my last utterance. He who understands and heeds it let him take it with him whithersoever he

---

[28]Ibid., p. 266.
[29]Ibid., p. 267.

goes; and as for him who fears that he will not heed it, he may not deny that I said it. Allah sent Muhammad and sent down the scripture to him. Part of what he sent down was the passage on stoning; we read it, we were taught it, and we heeded it. *The apostle stoned (adulterers) and we stoned them after him.* I fear that in time to come men will say that they find no mention of stoning in Allah's book and thereby go astray by neglecting an ordinance which Allah has sent down. Verily stoning in the book of Allah is a penalty laid on married men and women who commit adultery, if proof stands or pregnancy is clear or confession is made. Then we read in what we read from Allah's book: "Do not desire to have ancestors other than your own for it is infidelity so to do."'[30]

Allah sanctions War against Unbelievers (622 CE)

When Quraysh became insolent towards Allah and rejected His gracious purpose, accused His prophet of lying, and ill treated and exiled those who served Him and proclaimed His unity, believed in His prophet, and held fast to His religion, He gave permission to His apostle to fight and to protect himself against those who wronged them and treated them badly.[31]

The first verse which was sent down on this subject from what I have heard from 'Urwa b. al-Zubayr and other learned persons was: 'Permission is given to those who fight because they have been wronged. Allah is well able to help them, — those who have been driven out of their houses without right only because they said Allah is our Lord. Had not Allah used some men to keep back others, cloisters and churches and oratories and mosques wherein the name of Allah is constantly mentioned would have been destroyed. Assuredly Allah will help those who help Him. Allah is Almighty. Those who if we make them strong in the land will establish prayer, pay the poor-tax, enjoin kindness, and forbid

---

[30]Ibid., p. 684. Emphasis added.
[31]Ibid., p. 212.

iniquity. To Allah belongs the end of matters.' Then Allah sent down to him: 'Fight them so that there be no more seduction,' i.e. until no believer is seduced from his religion. 'And the religion is Allah's', i.e. Until Allah alone is worshipped.[32]

When Allah had given permission to fight and this clan of the Anṣār had pledged their support to him in Islam and to help him and his followers, and the Muslims who had taken refuge with them, the apostle commanded his companions, the emigrants of his people and those Muslims who were with him in Mecca, to emigrate to Medina and to link up with their brethren the Anṣār. 'Allah will make for you brethren and houses in which you may be safe.' So they went out in companies, and the apostle stayed in Mecca waiting for Allah's permission to leave Mecca and migrate to Medina.[33]

Wars led by Muhammad in Person (623 to 631 CE)

Then the apostle prepared for war in pursuance of Allah's command to fight his enemies and to fight those polytheists who were near at hand whom Allah commanded him to fight. This was thirteen years after his call.[34]

The apostle took part personally in twenty-seven (Ṭ. six) raids:
Waddān which was the raid of al-Abwā'.
Buwāṭ in the direction of Raḍwā.
'Ushayra in the valley of Yanbu'.
The first fight at Badr in pursuit of Kurz b. Jābir.
The great battle of Badr in which Allah slew the chiefs of Quraysh (Ṭ. and their nobles and captured many).
Banū Sulaym until he reached al-Kudr.
Al-Sawīq in pursuit of Abū Sufyān b. Ḥarb (Ṭ. until he reached Qarqara al-Kudr).
Ghaṭafān (Ṭ. towards Najd), which is the raid of Dhū Amarr.

---

[32]Ibid., pp. 212-13. Quran, 22.39-41 and 2.193. See also 2.216-18, 4.76-77, 8.38-41 and 9.5-6, 29.
[33]Ibid., p. 213.
[34]Ibid., p.280.

Baḥrān, a mine in the Ḥijāz (Ṭ. above al-Furu')
Uḥud
Ḥamrā'u'l-Asad.
Banū Naḍīr.
Dhātu'l-Riqā' of Nakhl.
The last battle of Badr.
Dūmatu'l-Jandal.
Al-Khandaq.
Banū Qurayza.
Banū Liḥyān of Hudhayl.
Dhū Qarad.
Banū'l-Muṣṭaliq of Khuzā'a.
Al-Ḥudaybiya not intending to fight where the polytheists opposed his passage.
Khaybar.
Then he went on the accomplished pilgrimage.
The occupation of Mecca.
Ḥunayn,
Al-Ṭā'if
Tabūk.
He actually fought in nine engagements: Badr; Uḥud; al-Khandaq; Qurayza; al-Muṣṭaliq; Khaybar; the occupation; Ḥunayn; and al-Ṭā'if.[35]

Expeditions and Raiding Parties sent by Muhammad (622 to 632 CE)

These were thirty-eight (Ṭ. thirty-five) in number (Ṭ. between the time of his coming to Medina and his death).
'Ubayda b. al-Ḥārith was sent to the lower part (Ṭ. to the tribes) of Thaniyatu'l-Mara (Ṭ. which is in the Hijaz); Ḥamza b. 'Abdu'l-Muṭṭalib to the coast in the direction of al-'Iṣ. (Some people date Ḥamza's raid before that of Ubayda); Sa'd b. Abū Waqqāṣ to al-

---

[35]Ibid., pp. 659-60. Ṭ stands for the famous historian Jarīr al-Ṭabarī, 839-922 CE. His biography of the Prophet, *Sīrat an-Nabī*, is considered orthodox. Ṭabari does not count al-Hudaybia as war; according to him it was pilgrimage.

Kharrār (Ṭ. in the Hijaz); 'Abdullah b. Jahsh to Nakhla; Zayd b. Ḥāritha to al-Qarda (Ṭ. a well in Najd); Muhammad b. Maslama's attack on Ka'b b. al-Ashraf; Marthad b. Abū Marthad al-Ghanawī to al-Rajī'; al-Mundhir b. 'Amr to Bi'r Ma'ūna: Abū 'Ubayda b. al-Jarrāḥ to Dhū'l-Qaṣṣa on the Iraq road; 'Umar b. al-Khaṭṭāb to Turba in the B. 'Āmir country ; 'Alī b. Abū Ṭālib to the Yaman; Ghālib b. 'Abdullah al-Kalbī, the Kalb of Layth, to al-Kadīd where he smote B. al-Mulawwaḥ.[36] 'Ali to B. 'Abdullah b. Sa'd of Fadak; Abū'l-'Aujā' al-Sulamī to B. Sulaym country where he and all his companions were killed; 'Ukkāsha b. Miḥṣan to al-Ghamra; Abū Salama b. 'Abdu'l-Asad to Qaṭan, a well of B. Asad in the direction of Najd. Mas'ūd b. 'Urwa was killed there; Muhammad b. Maslama, brother of b. Ḥāritha, to al-Quraṭā' of Hawāzin; Bashīr b. Sa'd to B. Murra in Fadak; Bashīr b. Sa'd in the direction of Khaybar; Zayd b. Ḥāritha to al-Jamūm in B. Sulaym country; Zayd also to Judhām in Khushayn country. So says Ibn Hishām, but al-Shāfi'ı from 'Amr b. Ḥabīb from Ibn Isḥāq say 'in Ḥismā country'.[37]

Violation of the Sacred Month (623 CE)

The apostle sent 'Abdullah b. Jahsh b. Ri'āb al-Asadī in Rajab on his return from the first Badr. He sent with him eight emigrants, without any of the Anṣār. He wrote for him a letter, and ordered him not to look at it until he had journeyed for two days, and to do what he was ordered to do, but not to put pressure on any of his companions.[38]

When 'Abdullah had travelled for two days he opened the letter and looked into it and this is what it said: 'When you have read this letter of mine proceed until you reach Nakhla between Mecca and Al-Ṭa'if. Lie in wait for Quraysh and find out for us what they are doing.'... A caravan of Quraysh carrying dry raisins and leather

---

[36]Ibid., p. 660.
[37]Ibid., pp. 661-62.
[38]Ibid., pp. 286-87.

and other merchandise of Quraysh passed by them, 'Amr b. al-Ḥaḍramī, 'Uthmān b. Abdullah b. al-Mughīra and his brother Naufal the Makhzūmites, and al-Ḥakam b. Kaysān, freedman of Hishām b. al-Mughīra being among them. When the caravan saw them they were afraid of them because they had camped near them. 'Ukkāsha, who had shaved his head, looked down on them, and when they saw hiɱ they felt safe and said, 'They are pilgrims, you have nothing to fear from them.' The raiders took council among themselves, for this was the last day of Rajab, and they said, 'If you leave them alone tonight they will get into the sacred area and will be safe from you; and if you kill them, you will kill them in the sacred month,' so they were hesitant and feared to attack them. Then they encouraged each other, and decided to kill as many as they could of them and take what they had. Wāqid shot 'Amr b. al-Ḥaḍramī with an arrow and killed him, and 'Uthmān and al-Ḥakam surrendered. Naufal escaped and eluded them. 'Abdullah and his companions took the caravan and the two prisoners and came to Medina with them.[39]

When they came to the apostle, he said, 'I did not order you to fight in the sacred month,' and he held the caravan and the two prisoners in suspense and refused to take anything from them. When the apostle said that, the men were in despair and thought that they were doomed. Their Muslim brethren reproached them for what they had done, and the Quraysh said 'Muhammad and his companions have violated the sacred month, shed blood therein, taken booty, and captured men.' The Muslims in Mecca who opposed them said that they had done it in Sha'bān. The Jews turned this raid into an omen against the apostle. 'Amr b. al-Ḥaḍramī whom Wāqid had killed they said meant 'amarati'l-ḥarb (war has come to life), al-Ḥaḍramī meant haḍarati'l-ḥarb (war is present), and Wāqid meant waqadati'l-ḥarb (war is kindled); but Allah turned this against them, not for them, and when there was much talk about it, Allah sent down to his apostle: 'They will ask you about the sacred month, and war in it. Say, war therein is a

_____
[39] Ibid., p. 287.

serious matter, but keeping people from the way of Allah and disbelieving in Him and in the sacred mosque and driving out His people therefrom is more serious with Allah.'[40]

When 'Abdullah and his companions were relieved of their anxiety when the Quran came down, they were anxious for reward, and said, 'Can we hope that it will count as a raid for which we shall be given the reward of combatants?' So Allah sent down concerning them: 'Those who believe and have emigrated and fought in the way of Allah, these may hope for Allah's mercy, for Allah is forgiving, merciful.' That is, Allah gave them the greatest hopes therein.[41]

Allah sanctions Booty and Terrorism (624 CE)

When [Battle of] Badr was over, Allah sent down the whole *Sūra Anfāl* (eighth *sūra*) about it. With regard to their quarrelling about the spoils there came down: 'They will ask you about the spoils, say, the spoils belong to Allah and the apostle, so fear Allah and be at peace with one another, and obey Allah and His apostle if you are believers.'[42]

Then He taught them how to divide the spoil and His judgement about it when He made it lawful to them and said: 'And know that what you take as booty a fifth belongs to Allah and the apostle.'[43]

Then Allah reproached him about the prisoners and the taking of booty, no other prophet before him having taken booty from his enemy. Muhammad Abū Ja'far b. 'Alı b. al-Ḥuṣayn told me that the apostle said: 'I was helped by fear; the earth was made a place to pray, and clean; I was given all-embracing words; booty was made lawful to me as to no prophet before me; and I was given the power to intercede; five privileges accorded to no prophet before me.'[44]

---

[40]Ibid., pp. 287-88. Quran, 2.217.
[41]Ibid., p. 288. Quran, 9.20.
[42]Ibid., p. 321. Quran, 8.1.
[43]Ibid., p. 324. Quran, 8.41.
[44]Ibid., p. 326.

Allah said, 'It is not for any prophet; i.e. before thee, 'to take prisoners' from his enemies 'until he has made slaughter in the earth,' i.e. slaughtered his enemies until he drives them from the land. 'You desire the lure of this world,' i.e. its goods, the ransom of the captives. 'But Allah desires the next world,' i.e. their killing them to manifest the religion which He wishes to manifest and by which the next world may be attained. 'Had there not previously been a book from Allah there would have come upon you for what you took,' i.e. prisoners and booty, 'an awful punishment,' i.e. had it not previously gone forth from Me that I would punish only after a prohibition — and He had not prohibited them — I would have punished you for what you did. Then He made it lawful to him and to them as a mercy from Him and a gift from the Compassionate, the Merciful. He said, 'So enjoy what you have captured as lawful and good, and fear Allah. Allah is Forgiving, Merciful.'[45]

Captives killed after the Battle of Badr (624 CE)

Then the apostle began his return journey to Medina with the unbelieving prisoners, among whom were 'Uqba b. Abū Mu'ayṭ and al-Naḍr b. al-Ḥārith. The apostle carried with him the booty that had been taken from the polytheists and put 'Abdullah b. Ka'b in charge of it.

When the apostle was in al-Ṣafrā, al-Naḍr was killed by 'Alī, as a learned Meccan told me. When he was in 'Irqu'l-Ẓabya 'Uqba was killed.

When the apostle ordered him to be killed 'Uqba said, 'But who will look after my children, O Muhammad?' 'Hell', he said, and 'Āṣim b. Thābit b. Abū'l-Aqlaḥ al-Anṣārī killed him.[46]

Assassination of Abū 'Afak (CE 624)

Abū 'Afak was one of B. 'Amr b. 'Auf of the B. 'Ubayda clan.

---

[45]Ibid., pp. 326-27. Quran 8.67-69.
[46]Ibid., p. 308.

He showed his disaffection when the apostle killed al-Ḥārith b. Suwayd b. Ṣāmit. [Suwayd's fault was that he had killed his father's murderer who happened to be a favourite of Muhammad.] The apostle said, 'Who will deal with this rascal for me?' whereupon Sālim b. 'Umayr, brother of B. 'Amr b. 'Auf one of the 'weepers', went forth and killed him.[47]

Assassination of 'Asmā' D. Marwān (624 CE)

She was of B. Umayya b. Zayd. When Abū 'Afak had been killed she displayed disaffection. 'Abdullah b. al-Ḥārith b. al-Fuḍayl from his father said that she was married to a man of B. Khaṭma called Yazīd b. Zayd. Blaming Islam and its followers she said:

I despise B. Mālik and al-Nabīt
And 'Auf and B. al-Khazraj.
You obey a stranger who is none of yours,
One not of Murād or Madhhij.
Do you expect good from him after the killing of your chiefs
Like a hungry man waiting for a cook's broth?[48]

When the apostle heard what she had said he said, 'Who will rid me of Marwān's daughter?' 'Umayr b. 'Adīy al-Khaṭmī who was with him heard him, and that very night he went to her house and killed her. In the morning he came to the apostle and told him what he had done and he said, 'You have helped Allah and His apostle, O 'Umayr!' When 'Umayr asked if he would have to bear any evil consequences the apostle said, 'Two goats won't butt their heads about her.' So 'Umayr went back to his people.

Now there was a great commotion among B. Khaṭma that day about the affair of Bint Marwān. She had five sons, and when 'Umayr went to them from the apostle he said, 'I have killed Bint Marwān, O sons of Khaṭma. Withstand me if you can; don't keep me waiting.' That was the first day that Islam became powerful

---

[47]Ibid., p. 675.
[48]Ibid., pp. 675-76.

among B. Khaṭma; before that those who were Muslims concealed the fact. The first of them to accept Islam was 'Umayr b. 'Adīy who was called 'the Reader', and 'Abdullah b. Aus and Khuzayma b. Thābit. *The day after Bint Marwān was killed the men of B. Khaṭma became Muslims because they saw the power of Islam.*[49]

Banū Qaynuqā' expelled from Medina (624 CE)

Meanwhile there was the affair of the B. Qaynuqā'. The apostle assembled them in their market and addressed them as follows: 'O Jews, beware lest Allah bring upon you the vengeance that He brought upon Quraysh and become Muslims. You know that I am a prophet who has been sent — you will find that in your scriptures and Allah's covenant with you.' They replied, 'O Muhammad, you seem to think that we are your people. Do not deceive yourself because you encountered a people with no knowledge of war and got the better of them; for by Elohim if we fight you, you will find that we are real men!'

A freedman of the family of Zayd b. Thābit from Sa'īd b. Jubayr or from 'Ikrima from Ibn 'Abbās told me that the latter said the following verses came down about them:

'Say to those who disbelieve: you will be vanquished and gathered to Hell, an evil resting place. You have already had a sign in the two forces which met', i.e. the apostle's companions at Badr and the Quraysh. 'One force fought in the way of Allah; the other, disbelievers, thought they saw double their own force with their very eyes. Allah strengthens with His help whom He will. Verily in that is an example for the discerning.'

The apostle besieged them until they surrendered unconditionally. 'Abdullah b. Ubayy b. Salūl went to him when Allah had put them in his power and said, 'O Muhammad, deal kindly with my clients' (now they were allies of Khazraj), but the apostle put him off. He repeated the words, and the apostle turned away from him,

---

"Ibid., p. 676. Emphasis added. Muhammad had demonstrated the effectiveness of terror.

whereupon he thrust his hand into the collar of the apostle's robe; the apostle was so angry that his face became almost black. He said, 'Confound you, let me go.' He answered, 'No, by Allah, I will not let you go until you deal kindly with my clients. Four hundred men without mail and three hundred mailed protected me from all mine enemies; would you cut them down in one morning? By Allah, I am a man who fears that circumstances may change.' The apostle said, 'You can have them.'[50]

[This Jewish tribe was expelled from Medina.]

Assassination of Ka'b B. al-Ashraf (624 CE)

After the Quraysh defeat at Badr the apostle had sent Zayd b. Ḥāritha to the lower quarter and 'Abdullah b. Rawāḥa to the upper quarter to tell the Muslims of Medina of Allah's victory and of the polytheists who had been killed.[51]

Ka'b b. al-Ashraf who was one of the Ṭyyi' of the subsection B. Nabhān whose mother was from the B. al-Naḍīr, when he heard the news said, 'Is this true? Did Muhammad actually kill these whom these two men mention? (i.e. Zayd and 'Abdullah b. Rawāḥa). These are the nobles of the Arabs and kingly men; by Elohim, if Muhammad has slain these people 'twere better to be dead than alive.'

When the enemy of Allah became certain that the news was true he left the town and went to Mecca to stay with al-Muṭṭalib b. Abū Wadā'a b. Ḍubayra al-Sahmi who was married to 'Atika d. Abu'l-'Is b. Umayya b. 'Abdu Shams b. 'Abdu Manāf. She took him in and entertained him hospitably. He began to inveigh against the apostle and to recite verses in which he bewailed the Quraysh who were thrown into the pit after having been slain at Badr.[52]

[Then Ka'b came back to Medina and recited more verses.] The

---

[50]Ibid., p. 363. See Quran, 3.12-13.
[51]Ibid., p. 364.
[52]Ibid., p. 365.

apostle said, 'Who will rid me of Ibnu'l-Ashraf?' Muhammad b. Maslama, brother of the B. 'Abdul'l-Ashhal, said, 'I will deal with him for you, O apostle of Allah, I will kill him.' He said, 'Do so if you can.' So Muhammad b. Maslama returned and waited for three days without food or drink, apart from what was absolutely necessary. When the apostle was told of this he summoned him and asked him why he had given up eating and drinking. He replied that he had given him an undertaking and he did not know whether he could fulfil it. The apostle said, 'All that is incumbent upon you is that you should try.' He said, 'O apostle of Allah, we shall have to tell lies.' He answered, 'Say what you like, for you are free in the matter.' Thereupon he and Silkān b. Salāma b. Waqsh who was Abū Nā'ila one of the B. 'Abdul'l-Ashhal, foster-brother of Ka'b, and 'Abbād b. Bishr b. Waqsh, and al- Hārith b. Aus b. Mu'ādh of the B. 'Abdul'l-Ashhal and Abū 'Abs b. Jabr of the B. Hāritha conspired together and sent Silkān to the enemy of Allah, Ka'b b. Ashraf, before they came to him. He talked to him some time and they recited poetry one to the other, for Silkān was fond of poetry. Then he said, 'O Ibn Ashraf, I have come to you about a matter which I want to tell you of and wish you to keep secret.' 'Very well,' he replied. He went on, 'The coming of this man [Muhammad] is a great trial to us. It has provoked the hostility of the Arabs, and they are all in league against us. The roads have become impassable so that our families are in want and privation, and we and our families are in great distress.' Ka'b answered, 'By Elohim, I kept telling you, O Ibn Salāma, that the things I warned you of would happen.' Silkān said to him, 'I want you to sell us food and we will give you a pledge of security and you deal generously in the matter... I have friends who share my opinion and I want to bring them to you so that you may sell to them and act generously, and we will give you enough weapons for a good pledge.' Silkān's object was that he should not take alarm at the sight of weapons when they brought them. Ka'b answered, 'Weapons are a good pledge.' Thereupon Silkān return-ed to his companions, told them what had happened, and ordered them to take their arms. Then they went away and assembled with him and met the apostle.[53]

The apostle walked with them as far as Baqi'u'l-Gharqad. Then he sent them off, saying, 'Go in Allah's name; O Allah help them.' So saying, he returned to his house. Now it was a moonlight night and they journeyed on until they came to his castle, and Abū Nā'ila called out to him. He had only recently married, and he jumped up in the bedsheet, and his wife took hold of the end of it and said, 'You are at war, and those who are at war do not go out at this hour.' He replied, 'It is Abū Nā'ila. Had he found me sleeping he would not have woken me.' She answered, 'By Elohim, I can feel evil in his voice.' Ka'b answered, 'Even if the call were for a stab a brave man must answer it.' So he went down and talked to them for some time, while they conversed with him. Then Abū Nā'ila said, 'Would you like to walk with us to Shi'b al-'Ajūz, so that we can talk for the rest of the night?' 'If you like,' he answered, so they went off walking together; and after a time Abū Nāi'la ran his hand through his hair. Then he smelt his hand, and said, 'I have never smelt a scent finer than this.' They walked on farther and he did the same so that Ka'b suspected no evil. Then after a space he did it for the third time, and cried, 'Smite the enemy of Allah!' So they smote him, and their swords clashed over him with no effect. Muhammad b. Maslama said, 'I remembered my dagger when I saw that our swords were useless, and I seized it. Meanwhile the enemy of Allah had made such a noise that every fort around us was showing a light. I thrust it into the lower part of his body, then I bore down upon it until I reached his genitals, and the enemy of Allah fell to the ground. Al-Ḥārith had been hurt, being wounded either in his head or in his foot, one of our swords having struck him. ... We carried him and brought him to the apostle at the end of the night. We saluted him as he stood praying, and he came out to us, and we told him that we had killed Allah's enemy. He spat upon our comrade's wounds, and both he and we returned to our families. Our attack upon Allah's

---

[53]Ibid., p. 367.

enemy cast terror among the Jews, and there was no Jew in Medina who did not fear for his life.'[54]

General Order for killing the Jews (624 CE)

The apostle said, 'Kill any Jew that falls into your power.' Thereupon Muḥayyiṣa b. Mas'ūd leapt upon Ibn Sunayna, a Jewish merchant with whom they had social and business relations, and killed him. Ḥuwayyiṣa was not a Muslim at the time though he was the elder brother. When Muḥayyiṣa killed him Ḥuwayyiṣa began to beat him, saying, 'You enemy of God, did you kill him when much of the fat on your belly comes from his wealth?' Muḥayyiṣa answered, 'Had the one who ordered me to kill him ordered me to kill you I would have cut your head off,' The other asked, 'By God, if Muhammad had ordered you to kill me would you have killed me?' He said, 'Yes, by Allah, had he ordered me to cut off your head I would have done so.' He exclaimed, 'By God, a religion which can bring you to this is marvellous!' and he became a Muslim.[55]

A Blind Man killed on the way to Uḥud (625 CE)

Then the apostle asked his companions whether anyone could take them near the Quraysh by a road which would not pass by them. Abū Khaythama, brother of B. Ḥāritha b. al-Ḥārith, undertook to do so, and he took him through the *harra* of B. Ḥāritha and their property until he came out in the territory of Mirbaʿ b. Qayzī who was a blind man, a disaffected person. When he perceived the approach of the apostle and his men he got up and threw dust in their faces saying, 'You may be the apostle of Allah, but I won't let you through my garden!' I was told that he took a handful of dust and said, 'By God, Muhammad, if I could be sure that I should not hit someone else I would throw it in your face.'

---

[54]Ibid., p. 368.
[55]Ibid., p. 369.

The people rushed on him to kill him, and the apostle said, 'Do not kill him, for this blind man is blind of heart, blind of sight.' Sa'd b. Zayd, brother of B. 'Abdu'l-Ashhal, rushed at him before the apostle had forbidden this and hit him on the head with his bow so that he split it open.[56]

Assassination of Khālid B. Sufyān (625 CE)

'Abdullah b. Unays said: The apostle called me and said that he had heard that Ibn Sufyān b. Nubayḥ al-Hudhalī was collecting a force to attack him, and that he was in Nakhla or 'Urana and that I was to go and kill him. I asked him to describe him so that I might know him, and he said, 'If you see him he will remind you of Satan. A sure sign is that when you see him you will feel a shudder.' I went out girding on my sword until I came on him with a number of women in a howdah seeking a halting-place for them. It was the time for afternoon prayer, and when I saw him I felt a shuddering as the apostle had said. I advanced towards him fearing that something would prevent my praying, so I prayed as I walked towards him bowing my head. When I came to him he asked who I was and I answered, 'An Arab who has heard of you and your gathering a force against this fellow [Muhammad] and has come to you.' He said, 'Yes, I am doing so.' I walked a short distance with him and when my chance came I struck him with my sword and killed him, and went off leaving his women bending over him. When I came to the apostle he saw me and said, 'The aim is accomplished.' I said. 'I have killed him, O Apostle,' and he said, 'You are right.'[57]

Banū Al-Naḍīr Jews expelled from Medina (625 CE)

According to what Yazīd b. Rūmān told me the apostle went to B. al-Naḍīr to ask for their help in paying the bloodwit for the two

---

[56]Ibid., pp. 372-73.
[57]Ibid., p. 666.

men of B. 'Āmir whom 'Amr b. Umayya al-Ḍamrī had killed after he had given them a promise of security. There was a mutual alliance between B. al-Naḍīr and B. 'Āmir. When the apostle came to them about the bloodwit they said that of course they would contribute in the way he wished; but they took counsel with one another apart, saying, 'You will never get such a chance again. Who will go to the top of the house and drop a rock on him (Ṭ. so as to kill him) and rid us of him?' The apostle was sitting by the wall of one of their houses at the time. 'Amr b. Jiḥāsh b. Ka'b volunteered to do this and went up to throw down a rock. As the apostle was with a number of his companions among whom were Abū Bakr, 'Umar, and 'Alī, news came to him from heaven about what these people intended, so he got up (Ṭ and said to his companions, 'Don't go away until I come to you') and he went back to Medina. When his companions had waited long for the prophet, they got up to search for him and met a man coming from Medina and asked him about him. He said that he had seen him entering Medina, and they went off, and when they found him he told them of the treachery which the Jews meditated against him. The apostle ordered them to prepare for war and to march against them. Then he went off with the men until he came upon them.

The Jews took refuge in their forts and the apostle ordered that the palm-trees should be cut down and burnt, and they called out to him, 'Muhammad, you have prohibited wanton destruction and blamed those guilty of it. Why then are you cutting down and burning our palm-trees?'

Now there was a number of B. 'Auf b. al-Khazraj among whom were 'Abdullah b. Ubayy b. Salūl and Wadī'a and Mālik b. Abū Qauqal and Suwayd and Dā'is who had sent to B. al-Naḍīr saying, 'Stand firm and protect yourselves, for we will not betray you. If you are attacked we will fight with you and if you are turned out, we will go with you.' Accordingly they waited for the help they had promised, but they did nothing and Allah cast terror into their hearts. They asked the apostle to deport them and to spare their lives on condition that they could retain all their property which they could carry on camels, except their armour, and he agreed. So they loaded their camels with what they could carry. Men were destroying their houses down to the lintel of the door which they put upon the back of their camels and went off with it. Some went to Khaybar and others went to Syria.[58]

They left their property to the apostle and it became his personal property which he could dispose of as he wished. He divided it among the first emigrants to the exclusion of the Anṣār, except that Sahl b. Ḥunayf and Abū Dujāna Simāk B. Kharasha complained of poverty and so he gave them some. Only two of B. al-Nḍīr became Muslims: Yāmīn B. 'Umayr Abū Ka'b b. 'Amr b. Jihāsh and Abū Sa'd b. Wahb who became Muslims in order to retain their property.

Concerning B. al-Naḍīr the *Sūra* of Exile came down in which is recorded how Allah wreaked His vengeance on them and gave His apostle power over them and how He dealt with them. Allah said: 'He it is who turned out those who disbelieved of the scripture people from their homes to the first exile. You did not think that they would go out and they thought that their forts would protect them from Allah. But Allah came upon them from a direction they had not reckoned and He cast terror into their hearts so that they destroyed their houses with their own hands and the hands of the believers.' That refers to their destroying their houses to extract the lintels of the doors when they carried them away. 'So consider this, you who have understanding. Had not Allah prescribed deportation against them,' which was vengeance from Allah, 'He would have punished them in this world,' i.e. with the sword, 'and in the next world there would be the punishment of hell' as well. 'The palm-trees which you cut down or left standing upon their roots.' *Līna* means other than the best kind of dates. 'It was by Allah's permission,' i.e. they were cut down by Allah's order; it was not destruction but was vengeance from Allah, 'and to humble evildoers'. 'The spoil which Allah gave the apostle from them,' i.e. from B. al-Naḍīr. 'You did not urge on your

---

[58]Ibid., p. 437. The story that the Jews had conspired to murder Muhammad is obviously an afterthought. Muhammad was bent upon destroying the Jews since long before this event and the Jews were too terrorized a lot to conspire against him.

cavalry or riding camels for the sake of it, but Allah gives His apostle power over whom He wills and Allah is Almighty,' i.e. it was peculiar to him, 'The spoil which Allah gave the apostle from the people of the towns belongs to Allah and his apostle.'[59]

Raid on Banū al-Muṣṭaliq (626 CE)

The apostle received news that B. al-Muṣṭaliq were gathering together against him, their leader being al-Ḥārith b. Abū Dirār, the father of Juwayriya d. al-Ḥārith (afterwards) wife of the apostle. When the apostle heard about them he went out and met them at a watering place of theirs called al-Muraysī' in the direction of Qudayd towards the shore. *There was a fight and Allah put the B. al-Muṣṭaliq to flight and killed some of them and gave the apostle their wives, children, and property as booty.*[60]

'Ā'isha [who had accompanied the apostle on this expedition] said: When the apostle distributed the captives of B. al-Muṣṭaliq, Juwayriya fell to the lot of Thābit b. Qays b. al-Shammās, or to a cousin of his, and she gave him a deed for her redemption. She was a most beautiful woman. She captivated every man who saw her. She came to the apostle to ask his help in the matter. As soon as I saw her at the door of my room I took a dislike to her, for I knew that he would see as I saw her. She went in and told him who she was — d. of-Ḥārith b. Abū Dirār, the chief of his people. 'You can see the state to which I have been brought. I have fallen to the lot of Thābit or his cousin and have given him a deed for my ransom and have come to ask your help in the matter.' He said, 'Would you like something better than that? I will discharge your debt and marry you,' and she accepted him.[61]

Islam inspires Patricide (626 CE)

While the apostle was by this water [after the raid on Banū

---

[59]Ibid., p. 438. Quran, 59.2-7.
[60]Ibid., p.490. Emphasis added.
[61]Ibid., p. 493.

Muṣṭaliq] a party came down to it. 'Umar had a hired servant from B. Ghifār called Jahjāh b. Mas'ūd who was leading his horse. This Jahjāh and Sinān b. Wabar al-Juhanī, an ally of B. 'Auf b. al-Khazraj, thrust one another away from the water and fell to fighting. The Juhanī called out 'Men of al-Anṣār!' and Jahjāh called out 'Men of the Muhājirūn!'. 'Abdullah b. Ubayy b. Salūl was enraged. With him was a number of his people including Zayd b. Arqam, a young boy. He said, 'Have they actually done this? They dispute our priority, they outnumber us in our own country, and nothing so fits us and the vagabonds of Quraysh as the ancient saying "Feed a dog and it will devour you". By Allah when we return to Medina the stronger will drive out the weaker.' Then he went to his people who were there and said: 'This is what you have done to yourselves. You have let them occupy your country, and you have divided your property among them. Had you but kept your property from them they would have gone elsewhere.' Zayd b. Arqam heard this and went and told the apostle when he had disposed of his enemies. 'Umar, who was with him, said, 'Tell 'Abbād b. Bishr to go and kill him.' The apostle answered, 'But what if men should say Muhammad kills his own companions? No, but give orders to set off.'[62]

[The son of 'Abdullah b. Ubayy] came to the apostle, saying, 'I have heard that you want to kill 'Abdullah b. Ubayy for what you have heard about him. If you must do it, then order me to do it and I will bring you his head, for al-Khazraj know that they have no man more dutiful to his father than I, and I am afraid that if you order someone else to kill him my soul will not permit me to see his slayer walking among men and I shall kill him, thus killing a believer for an unbeliever, and so I should go to hell.'[63]

Signals for waging Wars of Conquest (627 CE)

Salmān al-Fārisī said: I was working with a pick in the trench

---

[62]Ibid., p. 490-91.
[63]Ibid., p. 492.

[during the Battle of the Trench] where a rock gave me much trouble. The apostle who was near at hand saw me hacking and saw how difficult the place was. He dropped down into the trench and took the pick from my hand and gave such a blow that lightning showed beneath the pick. This happened a second and a third time. I said: 'O you, dearer than father or mother, what is the meaning of this light beneath your pick as you strike?' He said: 'Did you really see that, Salmān? The first means that Allah has opened up to me the Yaman; the second Syria and the west; and the third the east.' One whom I do not suspect told me that Abū Hurayra used to say when these countries were conquered in the time of 'Umar and 'Uthmān and after, *'Conquer where you will, by Allah, you have not conquered and to the resurrection day you will not conquer a city whose keys Allah had not given beforehand to Muhammad.'*[64]

Massacre of Banū Qurayza Jews (627 CE)

[After the Battle of the Trench] at the time of the noon prayers Gabriel came to the apostle wearing an embroidered turban and riding on a mule with a saddle covered with a piece of brocade. He asked the apostle if he had abandoned fighting, and when he said that he had he said that the angels had not yet laid aside their arms and that he had just come from pursuing the enemy. 'Allah commands you, Muhammad, to go to B. Qurayza. I am about to go to them to shake their stronghold.'

The apostle ordered it to be announced that none should perform the afternoon prayer until after he reached B. Qurayza. The apostle sent 'Alī forward with his banner and the men hastened to it. 'Alī advanced until when he came near the forts he heard insulting language used of the apostle. He returned to meet the apostle on the road and told him that it was not necessary for

---

[64]Ibid., p. 452. Emphasis added. This, of course, is wisdom by hindsight. But the believers regard it as the Sunnah of the Prophet, and wage wars against mankind.

him to come near those rascals. The apostle said, 'Why? I think you must have heard them speaking ill of me,' and when 'Ali said that was so he added, 'If they saw me they would not talk in that fashion.' When the apostle approached their forts he said, 'You brothers of monkeys, has Allah disgraced you and brought His vengeance upon you?' They replied, 'O Abū'l-Qāsim, you are not a barbarous person.'

The apostle besieged them for twenty-five nights until they were sore pressed and Allah cast terror into their hearts.[65]

Then they sent to the apostle saying, 'Send us Abū Lubāba b. 'Abdu'l-Mundhir, brother of B. 'Amr b. 'Auf (for they were allies of al-Aus), that we may consult him.' So the apostle sent him to them, and when they saw him they got up to meet him. The women and children went up to him weeping in his face, and he felt sorry for them. They said, 'Oh Abū Lubāba, do you think that we should submit to Muhammad's judgement?' He said, 'Yes,' and pointed with his hand to his throat, signifying slaughter. [But they did not get the message].[66]

In the morning they submitted to the apostle's judgement and al-Aus leapt up and said, 'O Apostle, they are our allies, not allies of Khazraj, and you know how you recently treated the allies of our brethren.' Now the apostle had besieged B. Qaynuqā' who were allies of al-Khazraj and when they submitted to his judgement 'Abdullah b. Ubayy b. Salūl had asked him for them and he gave them to him; so when al-Aus spoke thus the apostle said: 'Will you be satisfied, O Aus, if one of your own number pronounces judgement on them?' When they agreed he said that Sa'd b. Mu'ādh was the man.[67]

When Sa'd reached the apostle and the Muslims the apostle told them to get up to greet their leader. The muhājirs of Quraysh thought that the apostle meant the Anṣār, while the latter thought that he meant everyone, so they got up and said 'O Abū 'Amr, the

[65]Ibid., p. 461.
[66]Ibid., p. 462.
[67]Ibid., p. 463.

apostle has entrusted to you the affair of your allies that you may give judgement concerning them.' Sa'd asked, 'Do you covenant by Allah that you accept the judgement I pronounce on them?' They said Yes, and he said, 'And is it incumbent on the one who is here?' (looking) in the direction of the apostle not mentioning him out of respect, and the apostle answered Yes. Sa'd said, *'Then I give judgement that the men should be killed, the property divided, and the women and children taken as captives.'*[68]

Then they surrendered, and the apostle confined them in Medina in the quarter of d. al-Ḥārith, a woman of B. al-Najjār. Then the apostle went out to the market of Medina (which is still its market today) and dug trenches in it. *Then he sent for them and struck off their heads in those trenches as they were brought out to him in batches.* Among them was the enemy of Allah Ḥuyayy b. Akhṭab and Ka'b b. Asad their chief. *There were 600 or 700 in all, though some put the figure as high as 800 or 900.* As they were being taken out in batches to the apostle they asked Ka'b what he thought would be done with them. He replied, 'Will you never understand? Don't you see that the summoner never stops and those who are taken away do not return? By Elohim it is death!' This went on until the apostle made an end of them.[69]

'Ā'isha [who was watching the gory scene] said: 'Only one of their women was killed. She was actually with me and was talking with me and laughing immoderately as the apostle was killing her men in the market when suddenly an unseen voice called her name. 'Good heavens,' I cried, 'what is the matter?' 'I am to be killed,' she replied. 'What for?' I asked. 'Because of something I did,' she answered. *She was taken away and beheaded.*[70]

The apostle had ordered that every adult of theirs should be killed.[71]

Then the apostle divided the property, wives, and children of B. Qurayza among the Muslims, and he made known on that day

---

[68]Ibid., pp. 463-64. Emphasis added.
[69]Ibid., p. 464. Emphasis added.
[70]Ibid., p.464-65. Emphasis added
[71]Ibid., p. 465. Emphasis added.

the shares of horse and men, and took out the fifth. A horseman got three shares, two for the horse and one for his rider. A man without a horse got one share. On the day of B. Qurayza there were thirty-six horses. It was the first booty on which lots were cast and the fifth was taken. *According to its precedent and what the apostle did the divisions were made, and it remained the custom for raids. Then the apostle sent Sa'd b. Zayd al-Anṣāri brother of b. 'Abdu'l Ashhal with some of the captive women of B. Qurayza to Najd and he sold them for horses and weapons.*

The apostle had chosen one of their women for himself, Rayḥāna d. 'Amr b. Khunāfa, one of the women of B. 'Amr b. Qurayza, and she remained with him until she died, in his power. The apostle had proposed to marry her and put the veil on her, but she said: 'Nay, leave me in your power, for that will be easier for me and for you.' So he left her. She had shown repugnance towards Islam when she was captured and clung to Judaism. So the apostle put her aside and felt some displeasure. While he was with his companions he heard the sound of sandals behind him and said, 'This is Tha'laba b. Sa'ya coming to give me the good news of Rayḥāna's acceptance of Islam' and he came up to announce the fact. This gave him pleasure.

Allah sent down concerning the trench and B. Qurayza the account which is found in the *Sūra* of the Confederates.[72]

[Regarding Banū Qurayza, Allah said], 'And Allah turned back those who disbelieved in His wrath' i.e. Quraysh and Gaṭafān... 'And He brought down those of the Scripture people who helped them,' i.e. B. Qurayza, 'from their strongholds' the forts and castles in which they were. 'And he cast terror into their hearts; some you slew and some you captured,' i.e. he killed the men and captured the women and children. 'And caused you to inherit their land and their dwellings, and their property, and a land you had not trod,' i.e. Khaybar. 'For Allah can do all things.'[73]

---

[72]Ibid., p. 466. Emphasis added. Quran, *sūra* 33.
[73]Ibid., p. 468. Quran, 33.26-27.

Raid on Banū al-Mulawwaḥ (627 CE)

We went on until we came to (Ṭ the valley of) al-Kadīd at sunset. We were in the wadi and my companions sent me on to scout for them. So I left them and went on until I came to a hill overlooking the enemy's camp. We gave them time until they quietened down and went to sleep (T. until their cattle returned in the evening and they milked them and lay down quietly, and a third of the night passed) and towards dawn we attacked them and killed some and drove off the cattle. They cried out to one another for aid, and a multitude that we could not resist came at us and we went on with the cattle and passed Ibn al-Barṣā' and his companion and carried them along with us. The enemy were hard on our heels and only the Wadi Qudayd was between us, when Allah sent a flood in the wadi from whence He pleased, for there were no clouds that we could see and no rain. It brought such water that none could resist it and none could pass over. And there they stood looking at us as we drove off their cattle. Not one of them could cross to us as we hurried off with them until we got away; they could not pursue us, and we brought them to the apostle.

A man of Aslam on the authority of another of them told me that *the war-cry of the apostle's companions that night was Slay! Slay!*[74]

Raid on Banū Tamīm (627 CE)

The apostle sent him to raid them, and he killed some and captured others. 'Ā'isha said to the apostle that she must free a slave of the sons of Ismā'īl, and he said, 'The captives of B. al-'Anbar are coming now. We will give you one whom you can set free.' When they were brought to the apostle a deputation from B. Tamīm rode with them until they reached the apostle. They

---

[74]Ibid., p. 661. Emphasis added.

spoke to the apostle on their behalf and he liberated some and accepted ransom for others.[75]

Raid on al-Ghāba (627 CE)

We set forth taking our arrows and swords until we arrived near the settlement in the evening as the sun was setting. I hid at one end and ordered my companions to hide at the other end of the camp and told them that when they heard me cry 'Allah akbar' as I ran to the camp they were to do the same and run with me. There we were waiting to take the enemy by surprise or to get something from them until much of the night had passed. Now they had a shepherd who had gone out with the animals and was so late in returning that they became alarmed on his behalf. Their chief this Rifā'a b. Qays got up and took his sword and hung it round his neck, saying that he would go on the track of the shepherd, for some harm must have befallen him; whereupon some of his company begged him not to go alone for they would protect him, but he insisted on going alone. As he went he passed by me, and when he came in range I shot him in the heart with an arrow, and he died without uttering a word. I leapt upon him and cut off his head and ran in the direction of the camp shouting 'Allah akbar' and my two companions did likewise, and by Allah, shouting out to one another they all fled at once with their wives and children and such of their property as they could lay hands on easily. We drove off a large number of camels and sheep and brought them to the apostle and I took Rifā'a's head to the apostle, who gave me thirteen of the camels to help me with the woman's dowry, and I consummated my marriage.[76]

Raid on the Bajīlīs (627 CE)

In the raid of Muḥārib and B. Tha'laba the apostle had captured

---

[75]Ibid., p. 667.
[76]Ibid., pp. 671-72.

a slave called Yasār, and he put him in charge of his milch-camels to shepherd them in the neighbourhood of al-Jammā'. Some men of Qays of Kubba of Bajīla came to the apostle suffering from an epidemic and enlarged spleens, and the apostle told them that if they went to the milch-camels and drank their milk and urine they would recover, so off they went. When they recovered their health and their bellies contracted to their normal size they fell upon the apostle's shepherd Yasār and killed him and stuck thorns in his eyes and drove away his camels. The apostle sent Kurz b. Jābir in pursuit and he overtook them and brought them to the apostle as he returned from the raid of Dhū Qarad. *He cut off their hands and feet and gouged out their eyes.*[77]

Raid on Banū Judhām (627 CE)

The apostle sent Zayd b. Ḥāritha against them and that was what provoked the raid of Zayd on Judhām... Zayd's force came up from the direction of al-Aulāj and attacked... They rounded up the cattle and men they found and killed al-Hunayd and his son and two men of B. al-Aḥnaf and one of B. al-Khaṣīb.[78]

Raid on Dūmtu'l-Jandal (627 CE)

Then he ordered 'Abdu'l-Raḥmān b. 'Auf to make his preparations for the expedition. In the morning he wore a black turban of cotton. The apostle told him to approach and unwound it and then rewound it leaving four fingers or so loose behind him, saying, "Turban yourself thus, Ibn 'Auf, for thus it is better and neater." Then he ordered Bilāl to give him the standard and he did so. Then he gave praise to Allah and prayed for himself. He then said, "Take it, Ibn 'Auf; *fight everyone in the way of Allah and kill those who disbelieve in Allah. Do not be deceitful with the spoil; do not be treacherous, nor mutilate, nor kill*

---

[77]Ibid., pp. 677-78. Emphasis added.
[78]Ibid., p. 662.

*children. This is Allah's ordinance and the practice of his prophet
among you.*"[79]

Raid on Banū Fazāra (627 CE)

Zayd also raided Wādi'l-Qurā, where he met B. Fazāra and
some of his companions were killed; he himself was carried
wounded from the field. Ward b. 'Amr b. Madāsh, one of B. Sa'd
b. Hudhayl, was killed by one of B. Badr. When Zayd came he
swore that he would use no ablution until he raided B. Fazāra; and
when he recovered from his wounds the apostle sent him against
them with a force. He fought (Ṭ. he met) them in Wādi'l-Qurā and
killed some of them... Umm Qirfa Fāṭima d. Rabī'a b. Badr was
taken prisoner *She was a very old woman,* wife of Mālik. Her
daughter and 'Abdullah b. Mas'ada were also taken. *Zayd ordered
Qays b. al-Musaḥḥar to kill Umm Qirfa and he killed her cruelly
(Ṭ. by putting a rope to her two legs and to two camels and driving
them until they rent her in two).* Then they brought Umm Qirfa's
daughter and Mas'ada's son to the apostle. The daughter of Umm
Qirfa belonged to Salama b. 'Amr b. al-Akwa' who had taken her.
She held a position of honour among her people, and the Arabs
used to say, 'Had you been more powerful than Umm Qirfa you
could have done no more.' *Salama asked the apostle to let him
have her and he gave her to him and he presented her to his uncle
Ḥazn b. Abū Wahb and she bare him 'Abdu'l-Raḥmān b. Ḥazn.*[80]

Assassination of Sallām ibn Abu'l-Ḥuqayq (627 CE)

When the fight at the trench and the affair of the B. Qurayza
were over, the matter of Sallām b. Abū'l-Ḥuqayq known as Abū
Rāfi' came up in connexion with those who had collected the
mixed tribes together against the apostle. Now Aus had killed

---

[79]Ibid., p. 672. Emphasis added. Mutilation of captives and killing of children
was disallowed because they were part of the plunder and were to work or be sold
as slaves.

[80]Ibid., pp. 664-65. Emphasis added. Islam was brutalizing the Arabs very fast.

Ka'b b. al-Ashraf before Uḥud because of his enmity towards the apostle and because he instigated men against him, so Khazraj asked and obtained the apostle's permission to kill Sallām who was in Khaybar.

One of the things which Allah did for His apostle was that these two tribes of the Anṣār, Aus and Khazraj, competed the one with the other like two stallions: if Aus did anything to the apostle's advantage Khazraj would say, 'They shall not have this superiority over us in the apostle's eyes and in Islam' and they would not rest until they could do something similar. If Khazraj did anything Aus would say the same.

When Aus had killed Ka'b for his enmity towards the apostle, Khazraj used these words and asked themselves what man was as hostile to the apostle as Ka'b? And then they remembered Sallām who was in Khaybar and asked and obtained the apostle's permission to kill him.[81]

Five men of B. Salima of Khazraj went to him... As they left, the apostle appointed 'Abdullah b. 'Atīk as their leader, and he forbade them to kill women or children. When they got to Khaybar they went to Sallām's house by night, having locked every door in the settlement on the inhabitants. Now he was in an upper chamber of his to which a (T. Roman) ladder led up. They mounted this until they came to the door and asked to be allowed to come in. His wife came out and asked who they were and they told her that they were Arabs in search of supplies. She told them that their man was here and that they could come in. 'When we entered and we bolted the door of the room on her and ourselves fearing lest something should come between us and him. His wife shrieked and warned him of us, so we ran at him with our swords as he was on his bed. The only thing that guided us in the darkness of the night was his whiteness like an Egyptian blanket. When his wife shrieked one of our number would lift his sword against her; then he would remember the apostle's ban on killing women and withdraw his hand; but for that we would have made an end of her that night.

---

[81]Ibid., p. 482.

When we had smitten him with our swords 'Abdullah b. Unays bore down with his sword into his belly until it went right through him, as he was saying *Qaṭni, qaṭnī*, i.e. It's enough.'[82] Then he came to them and told them the news, and they picked up their companion and took him to the apostle and told him that they had killed Allah's enemy. *They disputed before him as to who had killed him, each of them laying claim to the deed.* The apostle demanded to see their swords and when he looked at them he said, 'It is the sword of 'Abdullah b. Unays that killed him; I can see traces of food on it.'[83]

Killing of Jews by Treachery (628 CE)

'Abdullah b. Rawāḥa raided Khaybar twice; on one occasion he killed al-Yusayr b. Rizām. Now al-Yusayr (Ṭ. the Jew) was in Khaybar collecting Ghaṭafān to attack the apostle. The latter sent 'Abdullah b. Rawāḥa with a number of his companions, among whom were 'Abdullah b. Unays, an ally of B. Salima. When they came to him [al-Yusayr] they spoke to him (Ṭ. and made him promises) and treated him well, saying that if he would come to the apostle he would give him an appointment and honour him. They kept on at him until he went with them with a number of Jews. 'Abdullah b. Unays mounted him on his beast (Ṭ. and he rode behind him) until when he was in al-Qarqara, about six miles from Khaybar, al-Yusayr changed his mind about going to the apostle. 'Abdullah perceived his intention as he was preparing to draw his sword, so he rushed at him and struck him with his sword cutting of his leg. Al-Yusayr hit him with a stick of *shauhaṭ* wood which he had in his hand and wounded his head (Ṭ. and Allah killed Yusayr). All the apostle's companions fell upon their Jewish companions and killed them except one man who escaped on his feet (Ṭ. his beast). When 'Abdullah b. Unays came to the

---

[82]Ibid., pp. 482-83. Killing of women was not allowed because they, too, were prized as plunder. But the ban was not observed in the case of old women as we have seen above — the cruel murder of Umm Qirfa.

[83]Ibid., p. 483. Emphasis added. 'Food' here means 'blood'.

apostle he spat on his wound and it did not suppurate or cause him pain.[84]

Neighbouring Rulers invited to Islam (628 CE)

The apostle went out to his companions and said: 'Allah has sent me as a mercy to all men, so take a message from me, Allah have mercy on you...' Then the apostle divided his companions and sent Salīṭ b. 'Amr b. 'Abdu Shams b. 'Abdu Wudd, brother of B. 'Āmir b. Lu'ayy, to Haudha b. 'Alī ruler of al-Yamāma; al-'Alā' b. al-Ḥaḍramī to al-Mundhir b. Sāwā, brother of B. 'Abdu'l-Qays, ruler of al-Baḥrayn; 'Amr b. al-'Āṣ to Jayfar b. Julandā and 'Abbād his brother the Asdīs, rulers of 'Umān; Ḥātib b. Abū Balta'a to the Muqauqis ruler of Alexandria. He handed over to him the apostle's letter and the Muqauqis gave to the apostle four slave girls, one of whom was Mary mother of Ibrāhīm the apostle's son; Diḥya b. Khalīfa al-Kalbī al-Khazrajī he sent to Caesar, who was Heraclius king of Rome.[85]

Conquest of Khaybar (628 CE)

When the apostle marched from Medina to Khaybar he went by way of 'Iṣr, and a mosque was built for him there; then by way of al-Saḥbā'. Then he went forward with the army until he halted in a wadi called al-Rajī', halting between the men of Khaybar and Ghaṭafān so as to prevent the latter reinforcing Khaybar, for they were on their side against the apostle.

When Ghaṭafān heard about the apostle's attack on Khaybar they gathered together and marched out to help the Jews against him; but after a day's journey, hearing a rumour about their property and families, they thought that they had been attacked during their absence, so they went back on their tracks and left the way to Khaybar open to the apostle.

---

[84]Ibid., pp. 665-66
[85]Ibid., p. 653.

The apostle seized the property piece by piece and conquered the forts one by one as he came to them. The first to fall was the fort of Nā'im; there Maḥmūd b. Maslama was killed by a millstone which was thrown on him from it; then al-Qamūṣ the fort of B. Abū'l-Ḥuqayq. *The apostle took captives from them among whom was Ṣafīya d. Ḥuyayy b. Akhṭab who had been the wife of Kināna b. al-Rabī' b. Abū'l-Ḥuqayq, and two cousins of hers. The apostle chose Ṣafīya for himself.*

Diḥya b. Khalīfa al-Kalbī had asked the apostle for Ṣafīya, and when he chose her for himself he gave him her two cousins. *The women of Khaybar were distributed among the Muslims.* The Muslims ate the meat of the domestic donkeys and the apostle got up and forbade the people to do a number of things which he enumerated.[86]

Kināna b. al-Rabī', who had the custody of the treasure of B. al-Naḍīr, was brought to the apostle who asked him about it. He denied that he knew where it was. A Jew came (Ṭ. was brought) to the apostle and said that he had seen Kināna going round a certain ruin every morning early. When the apostle said to Kināna, "Do you know that if we find you have it I shall kill you?" he said Yes. The apostle gave orders that the ruin was to be excavated and some of the treasure was found. When he asked him about the rest he refused to produce it, *so the apostle gave orders to al-Zubayr b. al-'Awwām, 'Torture him until you extract what he has,' so he kindled a fire with flint and steel on his chest until he was nearly dead. Then the apostle delivered him to Muhammad b. Maslama and he struck off his head.*[87]

When the apostle married Ṣafīya in Khaybar or on the way, she having been beautified and combed, and got in a fit state for the apostle by Umm Sulaym d. Milḥān mother of Anas b. Mālik, *the apostle passed the night with her in a tent of his.* Abū Ayyūb, Khālid b. Zayd brother of B. al-Najjār passed the night girt with his sword, guarding the apostle and going round the tent until in

---

the morning the apostle saw him there and asked him what he meant by his action. He replied, 'I was afraid for you with this woman for you have killed her father, her husband, and her people, and till recently she was in unbelief, so I was afraid for you on her account.' They allege that the apostle said 'O Allah, preserve Abū Ayyūb as he spent the night preserving me.'[88]

When the spoil of Khaybar was divided, al-Shaqq and Naṭā fell to the Muslims while al-Katība was divided into five sections: Allah's fifth; the prophet's share (Ṭ. fifth); the share of kindred, orphans, the poor (Ṭ. and wayfarers); maintenance of the prophet's wives; and maintenance of the men who acted as intermediaries in the peace negotiations with the men of Fadak. To Muḥayyiṣa, who was one of these men, the apostle gave thirty loads of barley and thirty loads of dates. Khaybar was apportioned among the men of al-Hudaybiya without regard to whether they were present at Khaybar or not.[89]

When the apostle had finished with Khaybar, Allah struck terror to the hearts of the men of Fadak when they heard what the apostle had done to the men of Khaybar. They sent to him an offer of peace on condition that they should keep half of their produce. Their messengers came to him in Khaybar or on the road or after he came to Medina, and he accepted their terms. Thus Fadak became his private property, because it had not been attacked by horse or camel.[90]

The apostle took Khaybar by force after fighting and Khaybar was part of what Allah gave to him as booty. The apostle divided it into five parts and distributed it among the Muslims, and after the fighting the population surrendered on condition that they should migrate. The apostle called them and said that if they wished he would let them have the property on condition that they worked it and the produce was equally divided between both parties and he would leave them there as long as Allah let them stay. They

---

[88]Ibid., pp. 516-17. Emphasis added.
[89]Ibid., p. 521.
[90]Ibid., p. 523.

accepted the terms and used to work the property on those conditions. The apostle used to send 'Abdullah b. Rawāḥa and he would divide the produce and make a just assessment. When Allah took away His prophet, Abū Bakr continued the arrangement until his death, and so did 'Umar for the beginning of his amīrate. *Then he heard that the apostle had said in his last illness. 'Two religions shall not remain together in the peninsula of the Arabs'* and he made inquiries until he got confirmation. Then he sent to the Jews saying, 'Allah has given permission for you to emigrate', quoting the apostle's words. 'If anyone has an agreement with the apostle let him bring it to me and I will carry it out; he who has no such agreement let him get ready to emigrate.' Thus 'Umar expelled those who had no agreement with the apostle.[91]

Raid on Mu'ta in Syria (629 CE)

The apostle sent his expedition to Mu'ta in Jumāda'l-Ūlā in the year 8 and put Zayd b. Ḥāritha in command; if Zayd were slain then Ja'far b. Abū Ṭālib was to take command, and if he were killed then 'Abdullah b. Rawāḥa. The expedition got ready to the number of 3,000 and prepared to start. When they were about to set off they bade farewell to the apostle's chiefs and saluted them. When 'Abdullah b. Rawāḥa took his leave of the chiefs he wept and when they asked him the reason he said, 'By Allah, it is not that I love the world and am inordinately attached to you, but I heard the apostle read a verse from Allah's book in which he mentioned hell and I do not know how I can return after I have been in it?[92]

The people went forward until when they were on the borders of the Balqā' the Greek and Arab forces of Heraclius met them in a village called Mashārif. When the enemy approached, the Muslims withdrew to a village called Mu'ta. There the forces met and the Muslims made their dispositions, putting over the right

---

[91]Ibid., pp. 524-25. Emphasis added.
[92]Ibid., p. 532. Quran, 19.71. Fear of hell became no less an incentive for Muslim desperados than the lure of paradise.

wing Quṭba b. Qatāda of the B. 'Udhra, and over the left wing an Anṣārī called 'Ubāya b. Mālik. When fighting began Zayd b. Ḥāritha fought holding the apostle's standard, until he died from loss of blood among the spears of the enemy. Then Ja'far took it and fought with it until when the battle hemmed him in he jumped off his roan and hamstrung her and fought till he was killed. *Ja'far was the first man in Islam to hamstring his horse.* When Ja'far was killed 'Abdullah b. Rawāḥa took the standard and advanced with it riding his horse. He had to put pressure on himself as he felt reluctant to go forward.[93]

Then he dismounted and a cousin of his came up with a meat bone, saying, 'Strengthen yourself with this, for you have met in these battles of yours difficult days.' He took it and ate a little. Then he heard the sounds of confusion in the force and threw it away, saying, 'And you are still living?' He seized his sword and died fighting.[94]

[Khālid b. al-Walīd who had converted to Islam some time earlier and joined this expedition, led the Muslim army in retreat to Medium. Hearing the report] the apostle said: 'Zayd took the standard and fought with it until he was killed as a martyr; then Ja'far took it and fought until he was killed as a martyr.' Then he was silent until the faces of the Anṣār fell and they thought that something disastrous had happened to 'Abdullah b, Rawāḥa. Then he said: 'Abdullah took it and fought by it until he was killed as a martyr. *I saw in a vision that they were carried up to me in Paradise upon beds of gold.* I saw 'Abdullah's bed turning away from the beds of the other two, and when I asked why, I was told that they had gone on but he hesitated before he went forward.'[95]

---

[93]Ibid., pp. 534. Emphasis added. In the history of Islam, hamstringing of horses became an established exhibitionist practice for Muslim desperados as the armies of Islam invaded other people's lands.

[94]Ibid., p. 534-35.

[95]Ibid,. p, 535. Emphasis added. In due course, every Muslim desperado killed in aggressive wars was hailed as a martyr. The Prophet saw them with himself in paradise while he was still alive and on earth!

Vindictive Killings after the Conquest of Mecca (630 CE)

The apostle had instructed his commanders when they entered Mecca only to fight those who resisted them, except a small number who were to be killed even if they were found beneath the curtains of the Ka'ba. Among them was 'Abdullah b. Sa'd, brother of the B. 'Āmir b. Lu'ayy. The reason he ordered him to be killed was that he had been a Muslim and used to write down revelation; then he apostatized and returned to Quraysh and fled to 'Uthmān b. 'Affān whose foster-brother he was. The latter hid him until he brought him to the apostle after the situation in Mecca was tranquil, and asked that he might be granted immunity. They allege that the apostle remained silent for a long time till finally he said yes. When 'Uthmān had left he said to his companions who were sitting around him, 'I kept silent so that one of you might get up and strike off his head!' One of the Ansār said, 'Then why didn't you give me a sign, O apostle of Allah?' He answered that a prophet does not kill by pointing.[96]

Another was 'Abdullah b. Khatal of B. Taym b. Ghālib. He had become a Muslim and the apostle sent him to collect the poor tax in company with one of the Ansār. He had with him a freed slave who served him. (He was a Muslim.) When they halted he ordered the latter to kill a goat for him and prepare some food, and went to sleep. When he woke up the man had done nothing, so he attacked and killed him and apostatized. He had two singing-girls Fartanā and her friend who used to sing satirical songs about the apostle, so he ordered that they should be killed with him.[97]

Another was al-Huwayrith b. Nuqaydh b. Wahb b. 'Abd b. Qusayy, one of those who used to insult him in Mecca.

Another was Miqyas b. Hubāba because he had killed an Ansārī

---

[96]Ibid., p. 550. The reason for 'Abdullah's apostasy was that he found the Prophet incorporating in 'revelations' words suggested by him whenever he saw the Prophet fumbling. Sometimes he wrote whole sentences which the Prophet accepted as dictated by Allah. He became convinced that the Prophet's *wahy* was a fake.

[97]Ibid., pp. 550-51.

who had killed his brother accidentally, and returned to Quraysh as a polytheist. And Sāra, freed slave of one of the B. 'Abdu'l-Muttalib; and 'Ikrima b. Abū Jahl. Sāra had insulted him in Mecca. 'Abdullah b. Khaṭal was killed by Sa'īd b. Ḥurayth al-Makhzūmī and Abū Barza al-Aslamī acting together. Miqyas was killed by Numayla b. 'Abdullah, one of his own people. As for Ibn Khaṭal's two singing-girls, one was killed and the other ran away until the apostle, asked for immunity, gave it her. Similarly Sāra, who lived until in the time of 'Umar a mounted soldier trod her down in the valley of Mecca and killed her. Al-Ḥuwayrith was killed by 'Alī.[98]

The Battle of Ḥunayn (630 CE)

When Hawāzin heard how Allah had given the apostle possession of Mecca, Mālik b. 'Auf al-Naṣrī collected them together. There assembled to him also all Thaqīf and all Naṣr and Jusham; and Sa'd b. Bakr, and a few men from B. Hilāl.[99]

When the prophet heard about them he sent 'Abdullah b. Abū Ḥadrad al-Aslamī to them and ordered him to go among them and stay with them until he learned all about them, and then bring him back the news. 'Abdullah went and stayed with them until he learned that they had decided to fight the apostle and the dispositions of Hawāzin, and then came back to tell the apostle.[100]

Then the apostle marched with 2,000 Meccans and 10,000 of his companions who had gone out with him when he conquered Mecca, 12,000 in all.[101]

[Abū Qatāda, who fought in the battle in the valley of Ḥunayn], said: On the day of Ḥunayn I saw two men fighting, a Muslim and

---

[98]Ibid., p. 551. Apostasy and criticism of the Prophet had been pronounced as offences punishable with death as soon Muhammad floated his cult in secret. They have remained the 'law' of Islam ever since.

[99]Ibid., p. 566.

[100]Ibid., p. 567.

[101]Ibid., p. 567-68.

a polytheist. A friend of the latter was making to help him against the Muslim, so I went up to him and struck off his hand, and he throttled me with the other; and by Allah he did not let me go until I smelt the reek of blood. He had all but killed me and had not loss of blood weakened him he would have done so. But he fell and I struck and killed him, and was too occupied with the fighting to pay any more attention to him. One of the Meccans passed by and stripped him, and when the fighting was over and we had finished with the enemy *the apostle said that anyone who had killed a foe could have his spoil.* I told the apostle that I had killed a man who was worth stripping and had been too occupied with fighting at the time and that I did not know who had spoiled him. One of the Meccans admitted that I had spoken the truth and that the spoil was in his possession. 'So pay him to his satisfaction on my behalf from his spoil.' Abū Bakr said, 'No, by Allah, he shall not "give him satisfaction" from it. Are you going to make one of Allah's lions who fought for His religion go shares with you in his prey? Return the spoil of the man he killed to him!' The apostle confirmed Abū Bakr's words, so I took the spoil from him and sold it and bought with the money a small palm-grove. It is the first property I ever held. One I do not suspect told me: Abū Ṭalḥa alone took the spoil of twenty men.[102]

Rabī'a b. Rufay' b. Uhbān b. Tha'laba b. Rabi'a b. Yarbū' b. Sammāl b. 'Auf b. Imru'ul-Qays who was called after his mother Ibn Dughunna more often overtook Durayd b. al-Ṣimma and took hold of his camel's halter, thinking that he was a woman because he was in his howdah. And lo, it was a man; he made the camel kneel and it was a very old man — Durayd b. al-Ṣimma. The young man did not know him and Durayd asked him what he wanted and what was his name. He told him and said that he wanted to kill him, and struck him with his sword to no effect. Durayd said, 'What a poor weapon your mother has given you!

---

[102]Ibid., p. 571. Living on plunder and its proceeds became in due course the most honourable way of life in Islam, particularly for the sufis who always prayed for the victory of Muslim arms.

Take this sword of mine that is behind the saddle in the howdah and strike me with that above the spine and below the head, for that is the way I used to strike men. Then when you come to your mother tell her that you have killed Durayd b. al-Ṣimma, for many's the day I have protected your women.' The B. Sulaym allege that Rabī'a said, 'When I smote him he fell and exposed himself, and lo his crotch and the inside of his thighs were like paper from riding horses bareback. When Rabī'a returned to his mother he told her that he had killed him and she said, 'By Allah, he set free three mothers and grandmothers of yours.'[103]

Devastation at Ṭā'if (630 CE)

[The apostle] went on until he halted near al-Ṭā'if and pitched his camp there. Some of his companions were killed by arrows there because the camp had come too close to the wall of al-Ṭā'if and the arrows were reaching them. The Muslims could not get through their wall for they had fastened the gate. When these men were killed by arrows he (Ṭ. withdrew and) pitched his camp near where his mosque stands today. He besieged them for some twenty days.

The apostle besieged them and fought them bitterly and the two sides exchanged arrows, until when the day of storming came at the wall of al-Ṭā'if a number of his companions went under a testudo and advanced up to the wall to breach it. Thaqīf let loose on them scraps of hot iron so they came out from under it and Thaqīf shot them with arrows and killed some of them. The apostle ordered that the vineyards of Thaqīf should be cut down and the men fell upon them cutting them down.[104]

Then Khuwayla d. Ḥakīm b. Umayya b. Ḥāritha b. al-Auqaṣ al-Sulamīya, wife of 'Uthmān b. Maz'ūn, asked the apostle to give her the jewellery of Bādiya d. Ghaylān b. Salama, or the jewellery

---

[103]Ibid., p. 574. Durayd represents the character inculcated by Arab Paganism, Rabī'a the transformation brought about by Islam.

[104]Ibid., p. 589. Destroying gardens etc. of an enemy was prohibited by Arab Paganism. It was a practice introduced by Muhammad.

of al-Fāri'a d. 'Aqīl if Allah gave him victory over al-Ṭā'if, for they were the best bejewelled women of Thaqīf. I have been told that the apostle said to her, 'And if Thaqīf is not permitted to me, O Khuwayla?' She left him and went and told 'Umar, who came and asked the apostle if he had really said that. On hearing that he had, he asked if he should give the order to break camp, and receiving his permission he did so.

When the army moved off Sa'īd b. 'Ubayd b. Asīd b. Abū 'Amr b. 'Allāj called out, 'The tribe is holding out.' 'Uyayna b. Ḥiṣn said, Yes, nobly and gloriously.' One of the Muslims said to him, 'Allah smite you, 'Uyayna! Do you praise the polytheists for holding out against the apostle when you have come to help him?' 'I did not come to fight Thaqīf with you,' he answered, 'but I wanted Muhammad to get possession of al-Ṭā'if so that I might get a girl from Thaqīf whom I might tread (Ṭ. make pregnant) so that she might bear me a son, for Thaqīf are a people who produce intelligent children.'[105]

Lust for Loot and Bribes (630 CE)

Then a deputation from Hawāzin came to him in al-Ji'rāna where he held 6,000 women and children, and sheep and camels innumerable which had been captured from them in the Battle of Ḥunayn. The deputation from Hawāzin came to the apostle after they had accepted Islam, saying that the disaster which had befallen them was well known and asking him to have pity on them for Allah's sake. One of the Hawāzin of the clan B. Sa'd b. Bakr (Ṭ. it was they who had provided the fostermother for the apostle) called Zuhayr Abū Ṣurad said: 'O Apostle of Allah, in the enclosures are your paternal and maternal aunts and the women who suckled you who used to look after you.'[106]

The apostle said, 'Which are dearest to you? Your sons and your wives or your cattle?' They replied, 'Do you give us the

---

[105]Ibid., p. 590. Khuwayla and 'Uyayna represent the sort of characters attracted by Islam.
[106]Ibid., p. 592.

choice between our cattle and our honour? Nay, give us back our wives and our sons, for that is what we most desire.' He said, 'So far as concerns what I and the B. 'Abdu'l-Muṭṭalib have they are yours. When I have prayed the noon prayer with the men then get up and say, "We ask the apostle's intercession with the Muslims, and the Muslims' intercession with the apostle for our sons and our wives." I will then give them to you and make application on your behalf.' When the apostle had ended the noon prayers they did as he had ordered them, and he said what he had promised to say. Then the Muhājirs said that what was theirs was the apostle's, and the Anṣār said the same.[107]

The apostle gave 'Alī a girl called Rayṭa d. Hilāl b. Ḥayyān b. 'Umayra b. Hilāl b. Nāṣira b. Quṣayya b. Naṣr b. Sa'd b. Bakr; and he gave 'Uthmān a girl called Zaynab d. Ḥayyān; and he gave 'Umar a girl whom 'Umar gave to his son 'Abdullah.

['Abdullah b. 'Umar related]: I sent her to my aunts of B. Jumaḥ to prepare and get her ready for me until I had circumambulated the temple and could come to them, wanting to take her when I returned. When I had finished I came out of the mosque and lo the men were running about, and when I asked why they told me that the apostle had returned their wives and children to them, so I told them that their woman was with B. Jumah and they could go and take her, and they did so.[108]

When the apostle had returned the captives of Ḥunayn to their people he rode away and the *men followed him, saying, 'O apostle, divide our spoil of camels and herds among us' until they forced him back against a tree and his mantle was torn from him and he cried, 'Give me back my mantle,* men, for by Allah if you had (T. I had) as many sheep as the trees of Tihāma I would distribute them among you; you have not found me niggardly or cowardly or false.'

The apostle gave gifts to those whose hearts were to be won

---

[107]Ibid., pp. 592-93.

[108]Ibid., p. 593. Following the precedent set by the Prophet in the case of Ṣafīya, the heroes of Islam were always in a hurry to drag captured women to their beds.

*over, notably the chiefs of the army, to win them and through them
their people.*[109]
When the apostle had distributed these gifts among Quraysh
and the Bedouin tribes, and the Anṣār got nothing, this tribe of
Anṣār took the matter to heart and talked a great deal about it, until
one of them said, 'By Allah, the apostle has met his own people.'
Saʻd b. ʻUbāda went to the apostle and told him what had
happened. He asked, 'Where do you stand in this matter, Saʻd?'
He said, 'I stand with my people.' 'Then gather your people in this
enclosure,' he said. He did so, and when some of the Muhājirs
came, he let them come, while others he sent back. When he had
got them altogether he went and told the apostle, and he came to
them, and after praising and thanking Allah he addressed them
thus: 'O men of Anṣār, what is this I hear of you? Do you think ill
of me in your hearts? Did I not come to you when you were erring
and Allah guided you; poor and Allah made you rich; enemies and
Allah softened your hearts?' They answered; 'Yes indeed, Allah
and His apostle are most kind and generous.' He continued: 'Why
don't you answer me, O Anṣār?' They said, 'How shall we answer
you? Kindness and generosity belong to Allah and His apostle.'
He said, 'Had you so wished you could have said — and you
would have spoken the truth and have been believed — You came
to us discredited and we believed you; deserted and we helped
you; a fugitive and we took you in; poor and we comforted you.
*Are you disturbed in mind because of the good things of this
life by which I win over a people that they may become Muslims
while I entrust you to your Islam?* Are you not satisfied that
men should take away flocks and herds while you take back with
you the apostle of Allah? By Him in whose hand is the soul of
Muhammad, but for the migration I should be one of the Anṣār
myself. If all men went one way and the Anṣār another I should
take the way of the Anṣār. Allah have mercy on the Anṣār, their

---

[109]Ibid., p. 594. Luring people into the fold of Islam by means of bribes has
been a settled practice since the days of the Prophet.

sons and their sons' sons.' The people wept until the tears ran down their beards as they said: 'We are satisfied with the apostle of Allah as our lot and portion'. Then the apostle went off and they dispersed.[110]

Raid on Banū Tayyi' (631 CE)

['Adīy, the son of Hātim Tayyi', a great hero of pre-Islamic Arabia, had migrated to Syria when he saw Muhammad triumphant. He related]: In my absence the apostle's cavalry came and among the captives they took was Hātim's daughter, and she was brought to the apostle among the captives of Tayyi'. The apostle had heard of my flight to Syria. Hātim's daughter was put in the enclosure by the door of the mosque in which the captives were imprisoned and the apostle passed by her. She got up to meet him, for she was a courteous woman, and said, 'O apostle of Allah, my father is dead and the man who should act for me has gone. If you spare me God will spare you.' He asked her who her man was and when she told him it was 'Adīy b. Hātim he exclaimed, 'The man who runs away from Allah and His apostle.'[111]

Raid on Tabūk (631 CE)

The apostle ordered his companions to prepare to raid the Byzantines at a time when men were hard pressed; the heat was oppressive and there was a drought; fruit was ripe (T. and shade was eagerly sought) and the men wanted to stay in the shade with their fruit and disliked travelling at that season. Now the apostle nearly always referred allusively to the destination of a raid and announced that he was making for a place other than that which he actually intended. This was the sole exception, for he said plainly that he was making for the Byzantines because the journey was

[110]Ibid., p. 596-97. Emphasis added.
[111]Ibid., p. 638

long, the season difficult, and the enemy in great strength, so that the men could make suitable preparations. He ordered them to get ready and told them that he was making for the Byzantines.[112]

The apostle heard that the hypocrites were assembling in the house of Suwaylim the Jew (his house was by Jāsūm) keeping men back from the apostle in the raid on Tabūk. So the prophet sent Ṭalḥa b. 'Ubaydullah with a number of his friends to them with orders to burn Suwaylim's house down on them. Ṭalḥa did so, and al-Daḥḥak b. Khalīfa threw himself from the top of the house and · broke his leg, and his friends rushed out and escaped.[113]

When the apostle reached Tabūk Yuḥanna b. Ru'ba governor of Ayla came and made a treaty with him and paid him the poll tax. The people of Jarbā' and Adhruḥ also came and paid the poll tax. The apostle wrote for them a document which they still have.

Then the apostle summoned Khālid b. al-Walīd and sent him to Ukaydir at Dūma. Ukaydir b.'Abdu'l-Malik was a man of Kinda who was ruler of Dūma; he was a Christian. The apostle told Khālid that he would find him hunting wild cows. Khālid went off until he came within sight of his fort. It was a summer night with a bright moon and Ukaydir was on the roof with his wife. The cows were rubbing their horns against the gate of the fort all the night. His wife asked him if he had ever known anything of the kind in the past, and urged him to go after them. He called for his horse, and when it was saddled he rode off with a number of his family, among them a brother called Ḥassān. As they were riding the apostle's cavalry fell in with them and seized him and killed his brother. Ukaydir was wearing a gown of brocade covered with gold. Khālid stripped him of this and sent it to the apostle before be brought him to him.[114]

Then Khālid brought Ukaydir to the apostle who spared his life and made peace with him on condition that he paid the poll tax. Then he released him and he returned to his town.[115]

---

[112]Ibid., p. 602.
[113]Ibid., p. 782.
[114]Ibid., p. 607.
[115]Ibid., p. 608.

Allah sanctions Breach of Pledge (631 CE)

The apostle ... sent Abū Bakr in command of the *hajj* in the year 9 to enable the Muslims to perform their *hajj* while the polytheists were at their pilgrimage stations. Abū Bakr and the Muslims duly departed.[116]

A discharge came down permitting the breaking of the agreement between the apostle and the polytheists that none should be kept back from the temple when he came to it, and that none need fear during the sacred month. That was a general agreement between him and the polytheists; meanwhile there were particular agreements between the apostle and the Arab tribes for specified terms. And there came down about it and about the disaffected who held back from him in the raid on Tabūk, and about what they said (revelations) in which Allah uncovered the secret thoughts of people who were dissembling. We know the names of some of them, of others we do not. Allah said: 'A discharge from Allah and His apostle towards those polytheists with whom you made a treaty', i.e. those polytheists with whom you made a general agreement. 'So travel through the land for four months and know that you cannot escape Allah and that Allah will put the unbelievers to shame. And a proclamation from Allah and His apostle to men on the day of the greater pilgrimage that Allah and His apostle are free from obligation to the polytheists,' i.e. after this pilgrimage. 'So if you repent it will be better for you; and if you turn back know that you cannot escape Allah. Inform those who disbelieve, about a painful punishment except those polytheists with whom you have made a treaty,' i.e. the special treaty for a specified term, 'since they have not come short in anything in regard to you and have not helped anyone against you. So fulfil your treaty with them to their allotted time. Allah loves the pious. And when the sacred months are passed,' Allah means the four which he fixed as their time, 'then kill the polytheists wherever you find them, and seize them and besiege them and lie

[116]Ibid., p. 617.

in wait for them in every ambush. But if they repent and perform prayer and pay the poor-tax, then let them go their way. Allah is forgiving, merciful.'[117]

Then Allah said: "The polytheists are nothing but unclean, so let them not approach the sacred mosque after this year of theirs, and if you fear poverty' that was because the people said 'the markets will be cut off from us, trade will be destroyed, and we shall lose the good things we used to enjoy,' and Allah said, 'If you fear poverty Allah will enrich you from His bounty,' i.e. in some other way, 'if He will. He is knowing, wise. Fight those who do not believe in Allah and the last day and forbid not that which Allah and His apostle have forbidden and follow not the religion of truth from among those who have been given the scripture until they pay the poll tax out of hand being humbled,' i.e. as a compensation for what you fear to lose by the closing of the markets. Allah gave them compensation for what He cut off from them in their former polytheism by what He gave them by way of poll tax from the people of scripture.[118]

Invasion of Palestine Planned (632 CE)

The apostle sent Usāma to Syria and commanded him to take the cavalry into the borders of the Balqā' and al-Dārūm in the land of Palestine. So the men got ready and all the first emigrants went with Usāma.

While matters were thus the apostle began to suffer from the illness by which Allah took him to what honour and compassion He intended for him shortly before the end of Ṣafar or in the beginning of Rabi'u'l-awwal. It began, so I have been told, when he went to Baqi'u'l-Gharqad in the middle of the night and prayed for the dead. Then he returned to his family and in the morning his sufferings began.[119]

The apostle found the people tardy in joining the expedition of

---

[117]Ibid., pp. 617-18. Quran, 9.1-5.
[118]Ibid., p. 620. Quran, 9.28-29.
[119]Ibid., p. 678.

Usāma b. Zayd while he was suffering, so he went out with his head bound up until he sat in the pulpit. Now people had criticized the leadership of Usāma, saying, 'He has put a young man in command of the best of the emigrants and the helpers.' After praising Allah as is His due he said, 'O men, dispatch Usāma's force, for though you criticize his leadership as you criticized the leadership of his father before him, he is just as worthy of the command as his father was.' Then he came down and the people hurried on with their preparations. The apostle's pain became severe and Usāma and his army went out as far as al-Jurf, about a stage from Medina, and encamped there and men gathered to him. When the apostle became seriously ill Usāma and his men stayed there to see what Allah would decide about the apostle.[120]

Last Will (632 CE)

The apostle wore a black cloak when he suffered severe pain. Sometimes he would put it over his face, at others he would take it off, saying the while, 'Allah slay a people who choose the graves of the prophets as mosques,' warning his community against such a practice.

On the same authority I was told that the last injunction the apostle gave was in his words 'Let not two religions be left in the Arabian peninsula.'

'Ā'isha used to say, 'When the apostle died the Arabs apostatized and Christianity and Judaism raised their heads and disaffection appeared. The Muslims became as sheep exposed to rain on a winter's night through the loss of their prophet until Allah united them under Abū Bakr.'[121]

Islam sustained by the Sword (632 CE)

When the apostle was dead most of the Meccans meditated

---

[120]Ibid., pp. 679-80.
[121]Ibid., p. 689. This was the Prophet's saying which 'Umar, the second Caliph, invoked for expelling all Jews and Christians from Arabia.

withdrawing from Islam and made up their minds to do so. 'Attāb b. Asid[122] went in such fear of them that he hid himself. Then Suhayl b. 'Amr arose and after giving thanks to Allah mentioned the death of the apostle and said, 'That will increase Islam in force. If anyone troubles us we will cut off his head.' Thereupon the people abandoned their intention and 'Attāb reappeared once more. This is the stand which the apostle meant when he said to 'Umar: 'It may well be that he will take a stand for which you cannot blame him.'[123]

Conclusion

Machiavelli who had studied the history of prophets has observed in his magnum opus that "all well-armed prophets have conquered and the unarmed failed".[124]

In fact, prophets other than Muhammad had arisen in Arabia itself, before, alongside and after Muhammad. But all of them had failed because they did not raise armies and assemble arsenals. Muhammad succeeded because he equipped his mission with a mailed fist. It may be noted that while he had only 301 ill-equipped warriors with him in the Battle of Badr (622 CE), he had 10,000 well-equipped men when he marched into Mecca eight years later (630 CE) and 30,000 when he planned an invasion of Palestine on the eve of his death (632 CE).

The term 'jihād' may have acquired a mystic meaning for Muslims who believe in Muhammad's "revelations", and the divinity of Allah. But for the historian who studies recorded facts and uses normal human reason to reach conclusions, 'jihād' is no more than physical aggression preceded by ideological aggression.

---

[122]He was governor of Mecca when the Prophet died.
[123]Ibid., pp. 794-95.
[124]*The Prince*, OUP, 1934, Jaico reprint, Bombay, 1957, p. 32.

Chapter 5

The Orthodox Exposition of *Jihād*

Imam Abu Hanifa, the eighth-century systematizer of Muslim law, is held in the highest regard by Muslims all over the world. He is also the most important authority for Muslims in India, a majority of whom subscribe to his school (*mazhab*). And the most outstanding treatise of his school is the *Hidāyah* compiled by Shaykh Burhan-ud-din Ali who flourished in the 12th century (CE). The Shaykh claims to have studied all earlier commentaries on the Quran and the Hadis belonging to the schools of Mālik, Shāfii and Hanbal, besides that of Hanifa.

The *Hidāyah* in its original Arabic is still the standard textbook for students of *fiqh* (jurisprudence) in famous Muslim seminaries such as the Dar-ul-Ulum at Deoband. It was translated into English for the first time by Charles Hamilton of the East India Company and published from London in 1791. A reprint has been brought out recently by a Muslim publishing house in New Delhi.

This voluminous work deals with all the traditional subjects that are common to this class of commentaries. What interests us in the present context, however, is its Book IX: *The Institutes*. The translator observers: "This book contains a chief part of what may be properly termed the political ordinances of Muhammad and is useful both in a historical and a legal view — in the former, as it serves to explain the principles upon which the Arabians proceeded in their first conquests, (and in which they have been imitated by all successive generations of Mussulmans), and in the iatter, as many of the rules here laid down, with respect to subjugated countries, continue to prevail, in all of that description at the present day."

We shall summarise below some of the chapters from Book IX to show the character of *jihād*. It will be noticed that the learned Shaykh quotes the Quran and the precedents set by the Prophet, in order to clinch every point.

Doctrine of Permanent War

Chapter I introduces *jihād* by stating that it "is established as a divine ordinance, by the word of Allah, who has said, in the Koran, 'Slay the infidels,' and also by a saying of the Prophet, 'War is permanently established until the day of judgment'." But it is not "a positive injunction (*farz-ayn*)" for the individual Muslim and is "enjoined only for the purpose of advancing the true faith." If it is made a "positive injunction," every Muslim everywhere will have to engage in war, "in which case the materials for war (such as horses, armour and so forth) could not be procured." Therefore , "the sacred injunction concerning war is sufficiently served when it is carried on by any one party or tribe of Mussalmans." On the other hand, if "no one Mussalman were to make war, the whole of the Mussalmans would incur the criminality of neglecting it."

War becomes a "positive injunction" when "infidels invade a Mussalman territory" and the Imam (leader) of the time "issues a general proclamation requiring all persons to stand forth and fight." All Muslims "whether men or women" have to obey the Imam whether he be "a just or unjust person." In case the Muslims of the territory invaded fail to "repulse the infidels," war becomes a "positive injunction" for Muslims in the neighbouring lands. "All the Mussalmans from east to west" must move into the war by stages, till the "infidels are repulsed."

In conclusion, it is stated that "the destruction of the sword (*qatl*) is incurred by infidels, although they be not the first aggressors, as appears from various passages in the sacred writings which are generally received to this effect."

Manner of Waging War

Chapter II discusses the "manner of waging war." In principle, Muslims should not invade an "infidel" territory without first inviting the "infidels" to embrace Islam or pay *jizyah* (capitation-tax). The "infidels" must be made to know that they are being "attacked for the sake of religion and not for the sake of taking their property, or making slaves of their children." War is automatically terminated if the "infidels" embrace Islam or agree to pay capitation-tax.

In practice, however, the Muslims can mount surprise attacks "on the infidels, slay them, and take their property." This breach of principle invites no censure because "that which protects (namely, Islam) does not exist in them, nor are they under protection by place," that is, they are not citizens of an Islamic state. It is "laudable" to warn the "infidels" in advance. But it is "not incumbent as it appears in the *Naki Saheeh* that the Prophet plundered and despoiled the tribe of Mooslick by surprise; and he also agreed with Asāma, to make a predatory attack upon Cobna at an early hour, and then set it on fire."

Slaughter of Women and Children

Similarly, "slaying of the women or infant children of infidels" is also prohibited in principle. But if a Muslim slays them, he invites no censure. It may also be noted that slaying of women and children is not prohibited on grounds of mercy but because they constitute a part of the plunder of which Muslim conquerors should not be deprived.

Total War

If the "infidels" refuse to embrace Islam or pay capitation-tax, Muslims should attack them "with all manner of warlike engines (as the Prophet did by the people of Tayeef), and also set fire to their habitations (in the same manner as the Prophet fired Baweera), and must inundate them with water, and tear up their plantations, and tread down their grains." All these methods are "sanctified by the law" because they weaken the "infidels", break their will to resistance and reduce their resources.

Treatment of the Handicapped

Disfiguring of people is also prohibited. Although the Prophet had "disfigured the Oorneans," a subsequent "revelation" abrogated the practice. Muslims should not slay women or children or men who are aged or blind or bed-ridden or paralytic or dismembered of the right hand. Imam Shāfii disagrees. He sanctions slaying of all these categories of "infidels" because, according to him, "infidelity is an occasion of slaughter being allowable." In any case, if "infidels" of these categories get killed in the course of war, it is of no consequence. They can also be slain if they "attempt to fight." A woman who is "a queen or chief" should be slain for sure because she may cause trouble if she remains alive.

A Son can Slay his Father

It is forbidden to a Muslim to slay his father. But if the father happens to be an "infidel" and comes out to fight, the son "should hold him in view" till someone else comes and kills him. In case the father attacks the son, the father can be slain by the son without any hesitation.

Strategies of Peace

Chapter III is on "making peace." If the Imam [leader of the *jihād*] finds that peace with the "infidels" is in the interest of Muslims, he should agree to it, as the Prophet had done with the "infidels" of Mecca. Peace "is war in effect, where the interest of the Mussalmans requires it." But when peace is not in the interest of Muslims, it is not lawful, "as this would be abandoning war, both apparently and in effect."

The Imam can also violate a time-bound truce with the "infidels" and go to war if "it is most advantageous for the Mussalman interest to break it [the truce]." When the circumstances change in favour of the Muslims, observation of an agreed truce is tantamount to "a desertion of war, both in appearance and also in effect, and war is an ordinance of Allah and the forsaking of it is not becoming."

Making peace with the "infidels" in exchange for property is lawful if "the Mussalmans stand in need of the property." But if the property is not needed by the Muslims, it is not lawful to make peace in exchange for it, "since peace is a desertion of war, both in appearance and in effect." Similarly, if the Muslims are harassed by the "infidels" and offered peace in exchange for property, the Imam should not make peace "as this would be a degradation of Mussalman honour." But if the Muslims face extermination, it is lawful to purchase peace with property.

Division of Plunder

Chapter IV deals with "plunder and the division thereof." If an "infidel" country is conquered by force of arms, the Imam can divide it among the Muslims "in the same manner as the Prophet had divided Kheebir among his followers." He can also leave it in the hands of the original inhabitants, "exacting from them a capitation-tax, and imposing a tribute on their lands." He should decide what is best in the circumstances. His decision regarding land should also dictate his disposal of the moveable property of the "infidels". If the "infidels" are to lose their lands, their entire moveable property should also be taken away from them. In case they are to continue with the cultivation of lands, they should be allowed to retain "such a portion of their moveable property as may enable them to perform their business."

War-Prisoners are Part of Plunder

The Imam has three courses open to him regarding "infidels"

captured in war. He can put them to death "because the Prophet put captives to death, and also because slaying them terminates wickedness." Or, he can sell them into slavery so that "the evil of them is remedied, at the same time as the Mussalmans reap an advantage." Or, he can make them *zimmis* " according to what is recorded of Omar." But it is not lawful "to release the idolaters of Arabia or apostates." They are to be slaughtered straight-away.

If the prisoners of war embrace Islam, they should not be put to death. But it is lawful to sell them into slavery even after their conversion "because the reason for making them slaves had existence previous to their embracing the faith."

It is not lawful to exchange "infidel" prisoners in Muslim hands with Muslim prisoners in "infidel" hands. Such an exchange helps the "infidels" because the "infidel" prisoners who are released "will again return to fight the Mussalmans." On the other hand, if Muslim prisoners are left in "infidel" hands, the "injury" is confined only to those Muslims and "does not extend to the other Mussalmans." Release of "infidel" prisoners in exchange for property is also unlawful. But it can also be considered if the Mussalmans need the property "because the Prophet released the captives taken at Biddir for a ransom." An "infidel" prisoner who embraces Islam can also be exchanged for a Muslim prisoner in "infidel" hands, provided "there be no apprehension of his apostatizing."

Imam Shāfii says that "infidel" prisoners can be released gratuitously also in order to confer favour upon them. He cites the example of the Prophet who had released some captives as a matter of favour after the Battle of Badr. But this course of action has been abrogated by "the text of the Quran" which says, "Slay the idolaters, wherever ye find them."

Muslims are free "to feed their cattle with plunder whilst in the enemy's country." They can themselves eat such "plunder as fit food." This is in keeping with what the Prophet had said at Khybar, "Eat the food found in plunder, and feed your cattle with the forage."

Sharing the Property of the Converts and the Killed

If an "infidel" in a hostile land embraces Islam, "his person is his own... because a Mussalman cannot be subjected to bondage." His infant children should also be left with him together with whatever moveable property he may possess. The Prophet had said, "whoever becomes a Mussalman, and is possessed of property in his own hands, such property belongs to him." But his immoveable properties "become the property of the public treasury", that is, should be treated as plunder. So also his wife and "her foetus", if she happens to be pregnant.

The Imam should keep one-fifth of the plunder for himself and divide the rest among the soldiers, "as it was thus the Prophet divided it." There are many minor details regarding the share of a horseman as compared to that of a foot-soldier, rewards to be given to women, children and slaves who helped the army, and "an extraordinary gratuity" to be paid to *zimmis* who worked as guides.

Gratuity should also be paid to particular persons over and above their share of plunder, in case they showed special zeal in killing the "infidels". The Imam can make them zealous in fighting by declaring, "whoever kills an infidel will have his garments." Allah had commended that course to the Prophet in the Quran by saying, "Excite the believers."

Imam Shāfii maintains that "the personal effects of the person slain belong to the slayer." He quotes the Prophet who had said, "whoever slays an infidel is entitled to his personal property." But the Prophet had also said that "No more appertains to you of the property of the person you have slain, than your Imam may think proper to allow." In any case, it should be remembered that personal property means "whatever may be found upon the person of the slain, such as clothes, weapons, and armour, and also the animal upon which he rode, together with the equipage such as the saddle and so forth, or whatever may be found upon him in his girdle or pocket, such as purse or gold and so forth." Anything carried for him "on another animal by his servant", is not to be treated as his personal property.

The Status of *Zimmis*

Chapter VIII concerns *jizyah* or capitation-tax. When Muslims conquer an "infidel" country by force of arms, "the inhabitants, together with their wives and children are all plunder and property of the state, as it is lawful to reduce to slavery all infidels." Imam Shāfii says that "destruction is incurred by all infidels", that is, they should be put to death immediately after they surrender. But the Quran provides for capitation-tax by paying which the *kitābis* (People of the Book) can buy their lives. The Prophet had also said, "Take from every male and female and adult one Deenar or cloth to that value." All others, particularly the idolaters (*mushriks*), are "subject to the original penalty, which is destruction."

Kitābis can become *zimmis* on agreeing to pay capitation-tax. They have to live under certain disabilities. They cannot build new churches or synagogues. The rule, however, applies only to cities because "the tokens of Islam (such as public prayer, festivals, and so forth) appear in cities." New places of worship can be built by the *zimmis* in the villages. They can also repair old places of worship which fall into decay.

The *zimmis* should also look distinct from Muslims "in point both of garments and equipage." They should not be "allowed to ride upon horses, or to use armour, or to use the same saddles and wear the same garments or headgear as the Mussalmans." The reason for this distinction in dress and equipage is that "Mussalmans may be held in honour." If the *zimmis* look no different, Mussalmans may salute them first, which is dishonourable. The *zimmis* should, therefore, be made to wear "a woollen cord or belt round their waists or outside of their garments." In no case should this cord or belt be made of silk.

The wives of *zimmis* should be "kept separate from the wives of Muslims, both in public roads, and also in the baths." The *zimmis* should put some distinctive sign on their houses so that "beggars who come to their door may not pray for them." Some theologians recommend that *zimmis* should not be "permitted to ride at all, except in cases of absolute necessity." In any case, a *zimmi* should alight "wherever he sees any Mussalmans assembled." Rich *zimmis* should be "prohibited from wearing rich garments."

The Hadis on *Jihād*

The doctrine of *jihād* is expounded in numerous books on the Shariat, as also in collections of *fatwas* such as *Fatāwa-ī-'Alamgīri* compiled in the reign of Aurangzeb. In India, the "infidels" referred to were always Hindus. The only exception was a call for *jihād* against the Christian invaders of an Islamic kingdom in India. The book was written by Shykh Zeenu'd-Din, a Muslim theologian who lived in the reign of Ali I Adil Shah (1557-1580 CE) of Bijapur. His aim was "the arousing of the faithful to engage in holy warfare against the worshippers of crucifixes [Portuguese Christians]" who were engaged in "infamous machinations against the religion of Islamism" in Malabar. We have chosen him also because he cites in full many sayings of the Prophet recorded in various collections of Hadis. We quote him verbatim.

He introduces the doctrine in the following words written in his preface to the book:

'Further, the Imam-Ahmud (on whom be peace!) has related on the authority of Al-Mikdad that he heard the Prophet (for ever blessed) to exclaim: "There shall not remain a dwelling in the city, or on the plain, on which Allah shall not cause to descend the word of Islamism, which shall dignify him [who is] already righteous, and condemn him who lives in sin, to the salvation of the one, and the everlasting ruin of the other." For those whom "Allah would exalt, will he make of the number of true believers, whilst, those whose destruction has been predetermined, shall seal it by rejecting this holy faith, which indeed," said I, "has Allah for its author and its end." Now be it known, that Allah most high hath willed, that the faith of Islamism should flourish throughout the chief of the inhabited regions of the earth; *in some countries making the sword and compulsion the means of its dissemination, in others preaching and exhortation...*'[1]

Coming to the doctrine itself, he continues in the main text:

'Know then, that infidels shall be regarded in two distinct points of view. And first: those who are dwelling peaceably in their own countries, and against whom if one person only from any party of Moslems shall go forth to war, the divine command on this subject will have been sufficiently observed, and the remainder of his brethren are not called upon to proceed against them. But should no one be found thus to offer himself as the holy champion of his party, then it becomes the duty of all to arm. Secondly: The case of infidels who shall invade the territories of the Moslems, as is now the case in the contest in which we are engaged. Now to attack these, becomes an act of paramount duty for every pious Mahomedan, and for all who would support their religion, whether bond or free, male for female, of the city or of the plain, without being dependent on or guided by the consent or refusal of master, husband, father or creditor, or of any other person to whom he or she might in other matters owe obedience; since to engage in this warfare is imperative on every person whether within three days' journey of the position of the infidels or beyond that distance; should the forces of the faithful not be sufficiently strong to admit of their services being dispensed with. It is the duty of him who is the leader in this holy war to take counsel, and concert measures with his companions, regarding the manner in which hostilities should be carried on, setting in order their ranks: and, should any plunder fall into their hands, first causing it to be collected into one place, and afterwards distributing it, giving the effects of the slain to those by whose swords they fell. And regarding this subject of the division of booty, whatever shall have been the personal property of the infidel (for instance, his clothes, boots, waistbelt, purse of money, or any cash or portion of his pay, or rings of silver

---

[1] *Tuhfat-ul-Mujahideen* translated from Arabic by M.J. Rowlandson, London, 1933, pp. 3-5. Emphasis added.

or gold that shall be found on his person, with his weapons and horse, and saddle and bridle), of all these the chief shall make an equal division into five shares. Of these shares, one being again divided by him into five portions. And of these portions, one shall be set aside for the general good of the Moslems, to be appropriated in the repairing of breaches, the building of fortifications and bridges, the raising of mosques, and for defraying the salaries of Cazees and Imams. Another shall be given to the descendants of the Prophet (upon whom be the blessing and peace of Allah!), to the descendants of Hashum and the descendants of Motalleb. One portion shall be distributed amongst those who are orphans, and one amongst the poor and destitute, in whose number the fakeers shall be included. The fifth portion shall go to travellers. And the four shares out of five that remain shall be the property of the captors and those who were present at the time of the battle, and who actually were engaged in it. Further, he who combats against infidels, should offer up prayers and supplication to Allah for victory; occupying himself in the performance of acts of piety, reposing especially his whole trust in Allah (most high), before engaging in this holy warfare: for Allah it is who makes to prosper...[2]

'Verily, Almighty and all Hallowed, hath said, "It has been written; that war against infidels is incumbent on you; nevertheless ye are averse to engage in it. Take care, however, that herein ye do not refuse that which is profitable for you, and perchance desire that which shall injure you, for the Lord is omniscient, whilst your understandings are blinded."[3] Further he said, "Surely Allah has purchased of the faithful their lives and possessions, in that he has vouchsafed unto them the blessings of paradise if they will fight for the cause of Allah; and whether they kill others or be themselves slain, of this the promises are made sure to them, both by the Tourat, the Injeel, and the Koran. And who shall be more faithful to his covenant than Allah! Rejoice ye,

---

[2] Ibid., pp. 15 21.
[3] Quran, 2.216.

then, in the covenant which ye have made, for by it shall ye obtain great happiness."⁴ And he said, "Those who expend their wealth in the cause of Allah and to advance his religion, may be compared to a grain of corn, which produces seven ears, and in each of which are a hundred grains; for Allah giveth increase where he will, and is all-bounteous and all-wise."⁵ And he said, "Consider not those who have been slain in the cause of Allah as dead, but rather as yet alive in the presence of their Allah, being filled with joy for that of which, by the grace of Allah, they have been thought worthy, rejoicing for the sake of those who following, have not hitherto arrived where they themselves are, seeing that both fear and grief are far from them."⁶ And it is related in the Soheih of Bookharee and Moossellim, upon the authority of Abu-Horeirah (of whom may Allah approve!), that it was once asked of the Prophet (upon whom may the blessing and peace of Allah for ever rest!) what act was of all the most meritorious: he answered, "faith in Allah, and in his prophet; after this," added he, "fighting in the cause of religion;" and then, "pilgrimage to Mecca." Moreover the same authors, upon the same authority, have written, that the Prophet (upon whom be the blessing and peace of Allah!) declared, "Allah has made it incumbent upon him who goes forth in his cause, that he should do so with firm trust in him, and with faith in his prophet. *If he shall return in safety he shall be rewarded by the plunder which he shall have acquired; but if he shall be slain, then paradise awaits him.*" Abu-Horeirah also has said, the Prophet declared (on him be peace!), "I swear by him from whom I have derived my being, that there exists not amongst the faithful one who can reject me, and who shall be found to deny that merit which I have ascribed to fighting for the sake of Allah; and I swear by him in whose hands is my life, that I not only desire to die in so holy a cause, but that if I possessed three lives, I would cheerfully resign them all in the same manner!" Abu Horeirah

---

⁴Quran, 9.111.
⁵Quran, 2.261.
⁶Quran, 3.169-70.

further says, the Prophet (on whom be peace!) declared, "He who goes forth to contend for Allah, shall be considered equal in merit to those who practise upon themselves all the austerities and bodily mortifications which have been commanded by Allah; nor shall the holy warrior be considered to have omitted either prayer or self-discipline whilst he shall be absent in this warfare." Further, on the authority of the same associate, the Prophet (on him be peace!) is declared to have said, "There has no one been wounded in fighting for Allah but that it is known to Allah, and who shall not appear on the last day; from whose wound also the blood that flows shall be of a golden hue, and its odour that of musk." Anas moreover has related that the Prophet (on him be peace!) declared, "Although to fight in the cause of Allah is a service of mortal danger, yet of all things in the world it is the best which a man can perform, and shall afford the most satisfaction." Further, said he, the Prophet (on him be peace!) declared, "There is no one who has found admission into paradise, who would desire to return again into the world, except it were that he might find the glorious death of a martyr; for nothing could be an inducement to him to leave the happiness of paradise for this world, unless he could for ten times make surrender of his life for Allah." Also Jaber (Allah rest satisfied with him!), relates, that a man said to the Prophet (on him he peace!) on the fatal day of Ohod, "O thou Prophet! I discern that my death draws nigh, where shall my spirit be?" He answered, "in paradise." On hearing this, the warrior cast from him the dates that were in his hands, and rushing into the conflict, fought desperately until he was slain. And Sahal Ben-Saad relates, that the Prophet (on him be peace and blessing!) declared, "To sit astride your horse, for one day in contending for Allah, is a higher satisfaction than all else that the world can afford." Abu Moosa also relates, that one came to the Prophet (on whom be the blessing and peace of Allah!) and asked, "the man who slays to obtain plunder, or he who fights to perpetuate his fame, or he who enters the combat in order that he may obtain martyrdom and behold the place prepared for him, which of these three fights most for Allah, and serves him in the truest way?" He answered, "He who fights in observance of the word of Allah, he it is who is before all, and he who renders to Allah the most faithful service." And Abu Saud-ul-Hazree relates, that the Prophet (on him be peace!) declared, "He of all mankind is the most righteous whose faith is sincere, and who freely expends his life and substance in fighting for Allah." Bookharee also, upon the authority of Abu Horeirah, that the Prophet (on him be peace!) declared, "Verily, in paradise there are a hundred degrees of elevation, and each distinct; and Allah has promised to those who fight for his sake, the intermediate space between one degree and the other, as the space which exists between the heavens and the earth. When Allah shall enquire of you, which degree ye desire, then answer ye, 'Firdoos, since it is in the centre of paradise, and situated in the most delightful and exalted part of it; above being the throne of the All-merciful, and out of it the rivers of paradise flowing." Further, Abu-Abas has related, that the Prophet (on him be peace!) declared, "He who shall not arouse himself from slumber, and exert himself in the service of Allah, him shall the fire of hell receive." And Abu-Kais also says, "I heard Saad relate, that he, with certain Arabs (of whom he was chief) had gone out to fight for Allah against unbelievers, the Prophet (on whom be peace!) being also of their company; and no food being procurable, except the leaves of trees, one of their party devoured a quantity of these, equal to what a camel or sheep would eat, nevertheless he suffered no harm!" Moreover Abu Horeirah (Allah rest satisfied with him!) related, that the Prophet (on him be peace!) declared, "He who shall bestow a horse upon one who would enlist himself under the banner of the Most High, and be one who has faith in Allah and in his promises, surely both the food of that horse and the sustenance of his rider, with the ordure of the former, shall be placed in the scales for his advantage on the day of judgment." Moossellim further relates from that commentator (Abu Horeirah), that the Prophet (on him be peace!) declared, "He who shall die without having fought for Allah, or who never proposed that duty to himself, verily consigns himself to destruction by his hypocrisy." Again, "The infidel, and he who slays him, shall not be gathered in the fire together!" Again, "Of mankind he is the most meritorious, who shall urge on his horse when fighting for Allah; flying forward, as it were, upon his back; disregardless of whatever shall reach his hearing, although horrible; neither being averted by any sounds of lamentation that shall assault him, although so terrible, indeed, as to frighten away from him all sense of death and destruction: for neither the man who shall seize upon the plunder of infidels (and whose head shall be almost turned with his good fortune), or he who in the solitude of the desert shall mortify his body by rigid privations and prayer, and so shall have obtained full knowledge of Allah, shall be compared with him first spoken of, although they shall not be without their reward." And Jabir Ben Surmah relates, that the Prophet (on him be peace!) declared, "Verily the true faith shall stand first, and the wearers of the turbans shall fight in defence of it until the last day." Soliman the Persian also relates, that he heard the Prophet (on him be peace!) declare, "To urge forward a horse in this holy warfare for one night and one day, is better than fasting for a whole month, or than the practice of rigid watchfulness during all that time. Now if when so engaged he shall be slain, he has accomplished that for which he lived, and has obtained a provision for himself, being placed beyond the reach of all further perfidy and trouble." And Akbat Ben Aamir relates: "I heard the Prophet (on him be peace!) when mounted in the pulpit, exclaim, O Moslems, promise that only which ye are able to perform, for instance, the exertion of your strength and skill in shooting arrows. Your archery it is that I require; your archery only will serve me." Further he said: "I heard the Prophet (on him be peace!) declare, He who learnt the art of archery and afterwards neglected it, is not of our number." Again Abu Masood-ul Ansaree relates, that a man approaching the Prophet with a bridled camel in his hand said to him, "This I devote to the service of Allah;" whereupon the Prophet exclaimed (on him be peace!), "Unto thee on the day of the resurrection shall seven hundred camels be given, all of them bridled." Musrooh relates, also: "We asked of Abdullah Ben Masood regarding the following saying: 'Ye shall not consider those who have been slain in the cause of Allah as dead, but rather as yet alive in the presence of their Allah, enjoying that which has been provided for them."[7] He answered, 'We indeed inquired of the Prophet regarding this saying, when he declared to us, — Their spirits are in the belly of the green bird, to enlighten which candles are suspended from the throne of Allah (by which is implied paradise), where all desires are fulfilled. Then they (these spirits) shall desire the sights of these candles, when Allah shall make visible to them his etherical presence, to the extent of their capability of discernment. For when Allah said, 'what desire ye?' they answered, 'what can we desire, we who are placed in paradise, where all our wishes are anticipated.' Then Allah spoke to them after the same manner three times; and when they perceived that he had ceased to address them, they prayed to him, saying: 'O Lord, we desire that our souls may return again to their bodies, in order that we may again surrender up our lives for thy sake.' But He, the Almighty, knowing that this was not necessary for them, ceased to converse with them." And upon the authority of Abdullah Ben Omar Ben Aas, it is related, that the Prophet (on him be peace!) declared, "In the conflict for the cause of Allah all earthly things shall perish, save only the true faith." Anas also relates. "I had gone forth with the Prophet and with his companions, when he was attacked by the infidels, who furiously assaulted him. Then the Prophet (blessing and peace be upon him!) exclaimed: 'Prepare ye to enter paradise, which exceeds in expanse both heaven and earth.' The Amir Ben-al-Himam upon this cried out, 'Huzzah, Huzzah!' The Prophet demanded (on him be peace!) 'What meanest thou in thus shouting, Huzzah! Huzzah?' He answered: 'O Prophet, I take Allah to witness that I so exclaimed, only from the hope that is before me of becoming one of the inhabitants of paradise.' The Prophet replied, 'Behold! thou art already one.' He added, 'Cast from thee the dates that thou holdest in thy hand, in order that thou mayest partake of those

---

[7]Quran, 3.169.

that thou shalt find in paradise.' Further, the Prophet said, 'I also would desire of those dates prepared for me, and which shall give life without end.' Al-Himam exclaimed, 'Thou hast said truly:' and thereupon throwing from him the dates that he had in his hand, he rushed forward to the combat, slaying all around him, till he himself fell." Further Tirmuzee and Abu Daood have related, upon the authority of Fuzalut-Ben-Abeed, that the Prophet (on him be peace!) exclaimed, "Whenever one shall resign his breath, at that hour his work is finished; except him only who dies when charging the enemies of Allah, and whose account shall not be closed until the last day, who shall be delivered also from the purgatory of the grave." Again Abu Daood, from Abu-Humamah, relates that the Prophet (on him be peace!) declared, "He who has not fought for Allah, and has not given of his substance to those who have, or who has dissuaded any one of his people from that meritorious work, Allah verily has cast that person into hell-fire already, not reserving him for the last day." Imam-Ben-Hussain has related also, that the Prophet (on him be peace!) declared, "There shall always remain for me a tribe of my people, who shall fight and slay in the cause of truth, and whose exterior shall give evidence of their inward feelings, until that time when they shall last of all destroy the Antichrist." And Tirmuzee relates, upon the authority of Ibn-Abbas, that the Prophet (on him be peace!) declared, "There are two descriptions of eyes, which the fire of hell shall not destroy; the eyes that weep in contemplating the indignation of Allah, and the eyes which are closed when in the act of combat for the cause of Allah." Again Abu-Horeirah; that one of the associates of the Prophet (on him be peace!) when proceeding to battle, having turned aside into a cave in which were grapes and a limpid stream, exclaimed, "If those who are my companions will excuse me from proceeding with them further, I will take up my dwelling in this cave." On his saying this before the Prophet (on him be peace!), he answered, "Thou shalt not do this, for *the merit of all of you who go out to fight for Allah, is greater than what ye could acquire, if ye were to spend seventy years in offering up prayers in the house of Allah:*[8] for if, indeed, ye desire to be forgiven of Allah, and to be hereafter admitted into paradise, then must ye go forth to fight for Allah, since he who in this holy warfare shall wound but a she-camel, he is truly deserving of paradise." Further, Abu-Tirmuzee and Al-Nusaeee, upon the authority of Abu-Horeirah, relate that the Prophet (on whom be peace!) declared, "He who falls a martyr experiences none of the pangs of death; except, indeed, it be such sensations as men experience when surprised by joy." And Haram-Ben-Ateek relates, that the Prophet (on him be peace!) declared, "He who shall bestow any of his substance in the cause of Allah, or for the support of his religion, there shall be written down for him seven hundred-fold." And Ibn-Inajih has related it upon the authority of Alee, and Abu Adruda, and Abu Horeirah, and Abu-Amamah, and Abdullah-Ben-Omar, and Ben-Abdullah, and Imran Ben-Hoossain (with all of whom may Allah rest satisfied! and who all agree in this account), that the Prophet (on him be peace!) declared, "He who has contributed of his wealth to those who fight for Allah, and remained at home, for every dirhem that he has so expended, he shall receive seven hundred-fold." And after declaring this, he recited the following saying: "For Allah shall give increase where he will, He who is all beneficent and all wise." And Abu-Daood has related upon the authority of Ibn-Abbas (Allah rest satisfied with him!) that the Prophet (on him be peace!) declared to his associates, "When your brethren were slain on the day of Ohod, Allah transported their souls into the belly of the green bird, from whence the rivers of paradise flow forth, and where they partake of its fruits, and behold the candles of Allah suspended in the shadow of his throne. Now when they perceived the purity and sweetness of their food and drink, and the pleasantness of their places of rest, they exclaimed, 'Oh! where shall we find one who shall carry intelligence to our brethren on earth that we are in paradise, where the practice of mortifications

---

[8]The temple or sacred mosque of Mecca is probably here meant.

is not required, or the severities of war experienced.' And Allah, most High, whose name be praised, made answer, 'I will disclose this for your sakes.' Therefore, Allah most High revealed that, saying, 'Consider not those as dead who have fallen in the cause of Allah, but as yet living:'" — besides many other passages of the same import. Further, Hakim relates, from Abu-Moosa Al-Asharee, that the Prophet (on him be peace!) declared — "*in the shades of the scymitars is paradise prefigured.*" And Ibn-Majah has narrated it from Anas, that the Prophet (on him be the blessing and the peace of Allah!) declared, "He who shall resign his life in the cause of Allah, whatever pollutions he shall have collected about him shall be changed into musk on the last day." Al-Tibranee also has related it, (in the Kubeer), on the authority of Ibn-Omar, that the Prophet (on him be peace!) declared, "*He who shall afflict his head with pain in the cause of Allah, whatever crime was before this lying at his charge, shall now be pardoned.*" And Waellah relates, that the Prophet (on him be peace!) declared, "Whoever has lost his life in my cause may hereafter contend in the deep."[9] Ad-Dillumee also, in his work called the Musnud-al-Firdous, relates, that Abu-Horeirah said, that the Prophet (on him be peace!) declared, "*that to fight for one hour in supporting the religion of Allah, was better than to make fifty pilgrimages to Mecca.*" By which he meant to say, that the future reward that shall await the first act shall exceed that awarded to pilgrimages, however many in number. And the cause of this pre-eminence being given to the holy warrior is this, that he truly risks his life and all that he possesses for the sake of Allah, whilst others also reap the advantage of this self-devotion, which cannot be said of pilgrimages to Mecca, where the benefit extends no further than to the pilgrim himself.'[10]

---

[9]The allusion in this passage is obscure. The Prophet's meaning probably is, that having thus established his devotion and courage, he is prepared to meet any danger. The sea, from the monsters that inhabit it, is generally quoted by eastern writers as the climax of all that is horrible.

[10]*Tuhfat-ul-Mujahideen*, pp. 25-46. Emphases added.

Conclusion

This is the authentic exposition of *jihād* to which many passages of the Writ Petition refer. It is a far cry from the "defensive war" it has been made into by S.D. Collet in her *Life and Letters of Raja Rammohan Roy,* quoted by the Attorney-General of India in his submissions and commended by Justice Basak in his judgment. There should be no doubt that *jihād* is an out and out aggressive war to be waged by Muslims, ceaselessly and in an uncompromising manner, for the total destruction of non-Muslims. Of course, there is provision in it for change of strategy and tactics to suit the size of Muslim strength in a given situation. But that does not affect its essential character.

True Character of the Quran

The fact is that the Quran can pass as a religious scripture only so long as its verses are not related to their concrete context in the life of the Prophet. Once we learn to do that from the theologians of Islam, the Quran comes out in its true colour as a comprehensive compendium on continued and total war against the "infidels". Allah also drops his mask and shows up in his real role as a *deux ex machina* prompted to pronounce pieces which suit the stage-manager's convenience. Swami Dayananda saw through the whole game when he nailed down Allah as "Muhammad's domestic servant".

The swordsmen of Islam have always felt self-righteous and believed fervently that they are carrying out the commandments of Allah when they practise *jihād* as per prescriptions of the Prophet. The Quran gives them a clean conscience for committing the most heinous crimes and heaping unbelievable cruelties on helpless human beings.

Chapter 6

Jihād in India's History

The principles of *jihād* elaborated in countless compendia composed by Islamic scholars, have been generalized from concrete practices of the Prophet, and confirmed by Allah through "revelations" in the Quran. In turn, these principles have guided all swordsmen of Islam throughout these fourteen countries and in many lands.

India has had a prolonged experience of *jihād* from the day when the first Muslim army stepped into Sindh in 712 CE and won its first victories after suffering a number of defeats for 78 years. Lands in Seistan, Khurasan, Transoxiana and Afghanistan where Hindu religion and culture had flourished for long, had been subjected to *jihād* in earlier years. We are citing some of the prominent *jihāds* waged in India by the most famous *mujāhids*.

The citations that follow are from the well-known Muslim chronicles composed in medieval times. The only change we have made is to replace the word "God" by the word "Allah" in order to make the translation more faithful. God of the Pagan pantheon has nothing to do with Allah of the Quran, who is only a projection of the evil in man and his baser drives for self-aggrandisement, as is obvious from the deeds that Allah sanctions.

MUHAMMAD BIN QASIM (712-15 CE)

After Muhammad bin Qasim had reduced some forts in Sindh, he wrote to Hajjaj, his uncle and governor of Iraq: "The forts of

Siwistan and Sisam have been already taken. The nephew of Dahir, his warriors, and principal officers have been despatched, and the infidels converted to Islam or destroyed. Instead of idol temples, mosques and other places of worship have been built, pulpits have been erected, the Khutba is read, the call to prayers is raised, so that devotions are performed at the stated hours. The *takbīr*[1] and praise to the Almighty Allah are offered every morning and evening."[2]

Bounties bestowed by Allah

The narrative proceeds: "Muhammad took the fort [of Rawar] and stayed there for two or three days. He put six thousand fighting men, who were in the fort, to the sword, and shot some with arrows. The other dependents and servants were taken prisoners, with their wives and children... When the number of the prisoners was calculated, it was found to amount to thirty thousand persons, amongst whom thirty were the daughters of chiefs, and one of them was Rai Dahir's sister's daughter, whose name was Jaisiya. They were sent to Hajjaj. The head of Dahir and the fifth part of the prisoners were forwarded in charge of Ka'ab, son of Mharak. When the head of Dahir, the women, and the property all reached Hajjaj, he prostrated himself before Allah, offered thanks-givings and praises... Hajjaj then forwarded the head, the umbrellas, and wealth, and the prisoners to Walid the Khalifa. When the Khalifa of the time had read the letter, he praised Almighty Allah. He sold some of those daughters of the chiefs, and some he granted as rewards... It is said that after the conquest was effected and the affairs of the country were settled and the report of the conquest had reached Hajjaj, he sent a reply to the following effect. 'O my cousin! I received your life-inspiring letter. I was much pleased and over-joyed when it reached me. The events were recounted in an excellent and beautiful style, and

---

[1]The Muslim war-cry of *Allāhu-akbar*.
[2]Elliot and Dowson, *History of India as told by its own Historians*, Volume I, p. 164. Translation is that of the *Chachnama* by an unknown Muslim author.

I learnt that the ways and rules you follow are conformable to the Law. Except that you give protection to all, great and small alike, and make no difference between enemy and friend. Allah says, — Give no quarter to Infidels, but cut their throats. Then know that this is the command of the great Allah...[3]

Slaughter and Plunder at Brahmanabad

"Muhammad Kasim marched from Dhalila, and encamped on the banks of the stream of the Jalwali to the east of Brahmanabad. He sent some confidential messengers to Brahmanabad to invite its people to submission and to the Muhammadan faith, to preach to them Islam, to demand the Jizya, or poll-tax, and also to inform them that if they would not submit, they must prepare to fight...[4]

"They sent their messengers, and craved for themselves and their families exemption from death and captivity. Muhammad Kasim granted them protection on their faithful promises, but put the soldiers to death, and took all their followers and dependents prisoners. All the captives, up to about thirty years of age, who were able to work, he made slaves, and put a price upon them...[5]

"When the plunder and the prisoners of war were brought before Kasim, and enquiries were made about every captive, it was found that Ladi, the wife of Dahir, was in the fort with two daughters of his by his other wives. Veils were put on their faces, and they were delivered to a servant to keep them apart. One-fifth of all the prisoners were chosen and set aside; they were counted as amounting to twenty thousand in number, and the rest were given to the soldiers. Protection was given to the artificers, the merchants, and the common people, and those who had been seized from those classes were all liberated.[6] But he (Kasim) sat on the seat of cruelty, and put all those who had fought to the sword.

---

[3]Ibid., pp. 172-73.

[4]Ibid., p. 176.

[5]Ibid., p. 179.

[6]Muslim conquerors spared the common people from death or enslavement only to turn them into hewers of wood and drawers of water for the new master class and keep the economy going.

It is said that about six thousand fighting men were slain, but, according to some, sixteen thousand were killed, and the rest were pardoned.[7]

Rates of *Jizyah*

"Muhammad Kasim fixed a tax upon all the subjects, according to the laws of the Prophet. Those who embraced the Muhammadan faith were exempted from slavery, the tribute, and the poll-tax, and from those who did not change their creed a tax was exacted according to three grades. The first grade was of great men, and each of these was to pay silver, equal to forty-eight dirams in weight, the second grade twenty-four dirams, and the lowest grade twelve dirams. It was ordered that all who should become Musulmans at once should be exempted from the payment, but those who were desirous of their old persuasion must pay the tribute and poll-tax. Some showed an inclination to abide by their creed, and some having resolved upon paying tribute, held by the faith of their forefathers, but their lands and property were not taken from them...[8]

Hajjaj recommends Harsh Measures

"The agriculturists in this part of the country were Jats, and they made their submission and were granted protection. When all these circumstances were communicated to Hajjaj, he sent an emphatic answer, ordering that those who showed fight should be destroyed, or that their sons and daughters should be taken as hostages and kept. Those who choose to submit, and in whose throats the water of sincerity flowed,[9] were to be treated with mercy, and their property secured to them...[10]

---

[7]Ibid., p. 181.
[8]Ibid., p. 182.
[9]Those who became Muslims.
[10]Ibid., p. 190.

Massacre at Multan

"A mine was dug, and in two or three days the walls fell down, and the fort of Multan was taken. Six thousand warriors were put to death, and all their relations and dependents were taken as slaves. Protection was given to the merchants, artisans and the agriculturists. Muhammad Kasim said the booty ought to be sent to the treasury of the Khalifa; but as the soldiers have taken so much pains, have suffered so many hardships, have hazarded their lives, and have been so long a time employed in digging the mine and carrying on the war, and as the fort is now taken, it is proper that the booty should be divided, and their dues given to the soldiers. Then all the great and principal inhabitants of the city assembled together, and silver to the weight of sixty thousand dirams was distributed, and every horseman got a share of four hundred dirams weight."[11]

SUBUKTIGIN (977-997 CE)

"The Sultan therefore sharpened the sword of intention in order to make an incursion upon his [Jayapal's] kingdom, and cleanse it from impurity and from his rejection of Islam... The Amir marched out towards Lamghan, which is a city celebrated for its great strength and abounding in wealth. He conquered it and set f   i   r   e to the places in its vicinity which were inhabited by infidels, and demolishing the idol-temples, he established Islam in them. He marched and captured other cities and killed the polluted wretches, destroying the idolatrous and gratifying the Musulmans. After wounding and killing beyond all measure, his hands and those of his friends became cold in counting the value of the plundered property. On the completion of his conquest he returned and promulgated accounts of the victories obtained for Islam, and

---

[11]Ibid , p 205.

every one, great and small, concurred in rejoicing over this result and thanking Allah."[12]

MAHMUD GHAZNAVI (997-1030 CE)

"Sultan Mahmud at first designed in his heart to go to Sijistan, but subsequently preferred engaging previously in a holy war against Hind, and he distributed arms prior to convening a council on the subject, in order to secure a blessing on his designs, of exalting the standard of religion, of widening the plain of right, of illuminating the words of truth, and of strengthening the power of justice. He departed towards the country of Hind, in full reliance on the aid of Allah, who guiding by his light and by his power, bestowed dignity upon him, and gave him victory in all expeditions. On his reaching Purshaur (Peshawar), he pitched his tent outside the city...[13]

Dealing with a Defeated Enemy

"Noon had not arrived when the Musulmans had wreaked their vengeance on the infidel enemies of Allah, killing 15,000 of them, spreading them like a carpet over the ground, and making them food for beasts and birds of prey... The necklace was taken off the neck of Jaipal, — composed of large pearls and shining gems and rubies set in gold, of which the value was two hundred thousand dinars; and twice that value was obtained from necks of those of his relatives who were taken prisoners, or slain, and had become the food of the mouths of hyenas and vultures. Allah also bestowed upon his friends such an amount of booty as was beyond all bounds and all calculation, including five hundred thousand slaves, beautiful men and women. The Sultan returned with his followers to his camp, having plundered immensely, by Allah's aid, having obtained the victory, and thankful to Allah... This

---

[12]Ibid., Volume II, p. 22. Translation is that of *Tārīkh-i-Yamīni* of al-Utbi.
[13]Ibid., pp. 24-25.

splendid and celebrated action took place on Thursday, the 8th of Muharram, 392 H., 27th November, 1001 AD...[14]

Jihād preferred over Personal Comfort

"The Sultan, contrary to the disposition of man, which induces him to prefer a soft to a hard couch, and the splendour of the cheeks of pomegranate-bosomed girls to well-tempered sword blades, was so offended at the standard which Satan had raised in Hind, that he determined on another holy expedition to that land...[15]

Plunder Paraded

"After this he returned to Ghazna in triumph; and, on his arrival there, he ordered the court-yard of his palace to be covered with a carpet, on which he displayed jewels and unbored pearls and rubies shining like sparks, or like wine congealed with ice, and emeralds like fresh springs of myrtle, and diamonds in size and weight like pomegranates. Then ambassadors from foreign countries, including the envoy from Taghan Khan, king of Turkistan, assembled to see the wealth which they had never yet even read of in books of the ancients....[16]

Sack of Narain (or Nardin)[17]

"The Sultan again resolved on an expedition to Hind, and marched towards Narain, urging his horses and moving over ground, hard and soft, until he came to the middle of Hind, where he reduced chiefs, who, up to that time obeyed no master, overturned their idols, put to the sword the vagabonds of that

---

[14]Ibid., p. 27.
[15]Ibid., p. 33.
[16]Ibid., p. 35.
[17]Narayanpur in Alwar district of Rajasthan.

country, and with delay and circumspection, proceeded to accomplish his design. He fought a battle with the chiefs of the infidels, in which Allah bestowed upon him much booty in property, horses, and elephants, and the friends of Allah committed slaughter in every hill and valley. The Sultan returned to Ghazna with all the plunder he had obtained....[18]

Plunder of Nandana[19]

"After the Sultan had purified Hind from idolatry, and raised mosques therein, he determined to invade the capital of Hind, to punish those who kept idols and would not acknowledge the unity of Allah. He collected his warriors and distributed money amongst them. He marched with a large army in the year 404 H., 1013 AD during a dark night...[20]

"The Sultan returned, marching in the rear of this immense booty, and slaves were so plentiful that they became very cheap; and men of respectability in their native land, were degraded by becoming slaves of common shopkeepers. But this is the goodness of Allah, who bestows honours on his religion and degrades infidelity...[21]

Massacre at Thanesar

"The chief of Tanesar was on this account obstinate in his infidelity and denial of Allah. So the Sultan marched against him with his valiant warriors, for the purpose of planting the standards of Islam and extirpating idolatry... The blood of the infidels flowed so copiously that the stream was discoloured, and people were unable to drink it. Had not night come on and concealed the traces of their flight, many more of the enemy would have been

---

[18]Ibid., p. 36.
[19]Capital of the Hindu Shahis after they lost Udbhandapur near Peshawar.
[20]Ibid., p. 37.
[21]Ibid., p. 39.

slain. The victory was gained by Allah's grace, who has established Islam for ever as the best of religions, notwithstanding that idolators revolt against it. The Sultan returned with plunder which it is impossible to recount — Praise be to Allah, the protector of the world, for the honour he bestows upon Islam and Musulmans!...[22]

Allah at Asni

"When Chandal[23] heard of the advance of the Sultan, he lost his heart from excess of fright, and as he saw death with its mouth open towards him, there was no resource to him but flight. The Sultan ordered therefore that his five forts should be demolished from their foundations, the inhabitants buried in their ruins, and imprisoned. The Sultan, when he heard of the flight of Chandal, was sorely afflicted, and turned his horse's head towards Chand Rai, one of the greatest men in Hind, who reigned in the fort of Sharwa [Siraswa]...[24]

Slaughter at Siraswa[25]

"The Sultan summoned the most religiously disposed of his followers, and ordered them to attack the enemy immediately. Many infidels were consequently slain or taken prisoners in this sudden attack, and the Musulmans paid no regard to the booty till they had satiated themselves with the slaughter of the infidels and worshippers of the sun and fire. The friends of Allah searched the bodies of the slain for three whole days, in order to obtain booty... The booty amounted in gold and silver, rubies and pearls, nearly to three thousand thousand dirhams, and the number of prisoners may be conceived from the fact, that each was sold for from

---

[22]Ibid., pp. 40-41.
[23]Bhur King Chandrapal of Asni near Fatehpur in Uttar Pradesh.
[24]Ibid., p. 47.
[25]Town near Saharanpur in Uttar Pradesh.

two to ten dirhams. These were afterwards taken to Ghazna, and merchants came from distant cities to purchase them, so that the countries of Mawarau-n nahr, Irak and Khurasan were filled with them, and the fair and the dark, the rich and the poor, were commingled in one common slavery."[26]

MUHAMMAD GHURI (1173-1206 CE)

The editor introduces Muhammad Ghuri in the *Taj-ul-Maasir* of Hasan Nizami as follows: "After dwelling on the advantage and necessity of holy wars, without which the fold of Muhammad's flock could never be filled, he says that such a hero as these obligations of religion require has been found, 'during the reign of the lord of the world Mu'izzu-d dunya wau-d din, the Sultan of Sultans, Abu-l Muzaffar Muhammad bin Sam bin Husain... the destroyer of infidels and plural-worshippers etc.,' and that Almighty Allah had selected him from amongst the kings and emperors of the time, 'for he had employed himself in extirpating the enemies of religion and the state, and had deluged the land of Hind with the blood of their hearts, so that to the very day of resurrection travellers would have to pass over pools of gore in boats, — had taken every fort and stronghold which he attacked, and ground its foundations and pillars to powder under the feet of fierce and gigantic elephants, — had sent the whole world of idolatry to the fire of hell, by the well-watered blade of his Hindi sword, — had founded mosques and colleges in the places of images and idols'."[27]

The narrative proceeds: "Having equipped and set in order the army of Islam, and unfurled the *standards of victory and the flags of power*, trusting in the *aid of the Almighty*, he proceeded towards Hindustan...[28]

---

[26]Ibid., pp. 49-50.
[27]Ibid., p. 209.
[28]Ibid., p. 212. Emphases in the original translation.

Islam imposed on Ajmer

"Such was the man[29] who was sent on an *embassy* to Ajmir, in order that the Rai (Pithaura) of that *country* might see the right way without the *intervention* of the sword, and that he might incline from *the track of opposition into the path of propriety,* leaving his *airy* follies for the *institutes* of the knowledge of Allah, and acknowledging the *expediency of uttering the words of martyrdom and repeating the precepts of* the law, and might abstain from *infidelity and darkness,* which entails *the loss of this world and that to come,* and might place in his ear *the ring* of slavery to the *sublime* Court (*may Allah exalt it!*) which is *the centre of justice and mercy, and the pivot of the Sultans of the world and* by these *means and modes might cleanse the fords of good life from the sins of impurity…*[30]

"The army of Islam was completely victorious, and 'an hundred thousand grovelling Hindus swiftly departed to the fire of hell'… After this great victory, the army of Islam marched forward to Ajmir, where it arrived at a fortunate moment and under an auspicious bird, and obtained so much booty and wealth, that you might have said that the secret depositories of the seas and hills had been revealed.

"While the Sultan remained at Ajmir, he destroyed the pillars and foundations of the idol temples, and built in their stead mosques and colleges, and the precepts of Islam, and the customs of the law were divulged and established…[31]

Qutb-ud-din "cleanses" Kohram

"The Government of the fort of Kohram and of Samana was made over by the Sultan to Kutbu-d din… [who] by the aid of

---

[29]Sadr Kiwam-l mulk Ruhu-d din Hamza.
[30]Ibid., p. 213. Emphases in the original translation.
[31]Ibid., p. 215.

his sword of Yemen and dagger of India became established in independent power over the countries of Hind and Sind... He purged by his sword the land of Hind from the filth of infidelity and vice, and freed the whole of that country from the thorn of God-plurality, and the impurity of idol-worship, and by his royal vigour and intrepidity, left not one temple standing...[32]

Destruction and Conversion of Temples at Delhi

"The conqueror entered the city of Delhi, which is the source of wealth and the foundation of blessedness. The city and its vicinity was freed from idols and idol-worship, and in the sanctuaries of the images of the Gods, mosques were raised by the worshippers of one Allah...[33]

"Kutub-d-din built the Jami Masjid at Delhi, and 'adorned it with the stones and gold obtained from the temples which had been demolished by elephants,' and covered it with 'inscriptions in Toghra, containing the divine commands.'...[34]

Iconoclasm at Varanasi

"From that place the royal army proceeded towards Benares 'which is the centre of the country of Hind, and here they destroyed nearly one thousand temples, and raised mosques on their foundations; and the knowledge of the law became promulgated, and the foundations of religion were established.'...[35]

Ghāzis in Gujarat

"In the middle of the month of Safar, 593 H. (Jan. 1197), the world-conquering Khusru departed from Ajmir, and with every description of force turned his face towards the annihilation of the

---

[32]Ibid., pp. 216-17.
[33]Ibid., p. 219.
[34]Ibid., p. 222.
[35]Ibid., p. 223.

Rai of Nahrwala.... A severe action ensued from dawn to mid-day when 'the army of idolatry and damnation turned its back in flight from the line of battle. Most of their leaders were taken prisoners, and nearly fifty thousand infidels were despatched to hell by the sword, and from the heaps of the slain, the hills and the plains became of one level... More than twenty thousand slaves, and twenty elephants, and cattle and arms beyond all calculation, fell into the hands of victors.' You would have thought that the treasures of the kings of all the inhabited world had come into their possession...[36]

Kalima comes to Kalinjar

"The fort of Kalinjar which was celebrated throughout the world for being as strong as the wall of Alexander was taken. 'The temples were converted into mosques and abodes of goodness and the calculations of the bead-counters and the voices of the summoners to prayer ascended to the highest heaven, and the very name of idolatry was annihilated... Fifty thousand men came under the collar of slavery, and the plain became black as pitch with Hindus.' Elephants and cattle, and countless arms also, became the spoil of the victors...[37]

"Purification" of Delhi

"The Sultan then returned[38] to Delhi, 'which is the capital of prosperity and the place of glory,' and after his arrival, 'not a vestige or name remained of the idol temples which had reared their heads on high; and the light of faith shone out from the darkness of infidelity, like the sun from a curtain of sorrow, or after its emerging from an eclipse, and threw its shade over the

---

[36]Ibid., p. 230. What Hasan Nizami does not tell at this point is that the army of Islam had to beat a hasty retreat from Gujarat in the face of a fierce Hindu counter-offensive.

[37]Ibid., p. 231.

[38]Hindus had reconquered Delhi after their first defeat.

provinces of Hind and Sind, the far and near countries of idolatry; and the moon of religion and the State became resplendent from the heaven of prosperity and glory'."[39]

ALAUDDIN KHILJI (1296-1316 CE)

"When Sultan Alau-d din, the Sultan of Delhi, was well established in the centre of his dominion and had cut off the heads of his enemies and slain them, the vein of the zeal of religion beat high for the subjection of infidelity and destruction of idols, and in the month of Zi'l-hijja 698 H. (1298 AD) his brother Malik Mu'izzu-d din and Nusrat Khan, the chief pillar of the state and the leader of his armies, a generous and intelligent warrior, were sent to Kambayat,[40] the most celebrated of the cities of Hind in population and wealth... With a view of holy war, and not for the lust of conquest, he enlisted under their banners about 14,000 cavalry and 20,000 infantry, which in their language, are called *dakk*.[41]

Ghāzis visit Gujarat Again

"They went by daily marches through the hills, from stage to stage, and when they arrived at their destination at early dawn they surrounded Kambayat and the idolaters were awakened from their sleepy state of carelessness and were taken by surprise, not knowing where to go, and mothers forgot their children and dropped them from their embrace. The Muhammadan forces began to 'kill and slaughter on the right and on the left unmercifully, throughout the impure land, for the sake of Islam,' and blood flowed in torrents. They plundered gold and silver to an extent greater than can be conceived, and an immense number of brilliant precious stones, such as pearls, diamonds, rubies, and

---

[39]Ibid., pp. 238-39.
[40]Khambat or Cambay in Gujarat.
[41]Ibid., Volume III, pp. 42-43. Translation of *Tārīkh-i-Wassāf* of Abdullah Wassaf.

emeralds, etc. as well as a great variety of cloths, both silk and cotton, stamped, embroidered, and coloured.[42]

Plunder and Iconoclasm

"They took captive a great number of handsome and elegant maidens, amounting to 20,000, and children of both sexes, 'more than the pen can enumerate'... In short, the Muhammadan army brought the country to utter ruin, and destroyed the lives of the inhabitants, and plundered the cities, and captured their off-spring, so that many temples were deserted and the idols were broken and trodden under foot, the largest of which was one called Somnat... The fragments were conveyed to Delhi, and the entrance of the Jami Masjid was paved with them, that people might remember and talk of this brilliant victory."[43]

Allah appears in South India

"The tongue of the sword of the Khalifa of the time, which is the tongue of the flame of Islam, has imparted light to the entire darkness of Hindustan by the illumination of its guidance... On the other side, so much dust arose from the battered temple of Somnat that even the sea was not able to lay it, and on the right hand and on the left hand the army has conquered from sea to sea, and several capitals of the gods of the Hindus, in which Satanism has prevailed since the time of the Jinns, have been demolished. All these impurities of infidelity have been cleansed by the Sultan's destruction of idol-temples, beginning with his first holy expedition against Deogir,[44] so that the flames of the light of the law illumine all these unholy countries, and places for the criers to prayer are exalted on high, and prayers are read in mosques. Allah be praised!...[45]

---

[42]Ibid., p. 43.
[43]Ibid., p. 44.
[44]Devagiri in Maharashtra, renamed Daulatabad by Muhammad bin Tughlaq.
[45]Ibid., p. 85. Translation of *Tārīkh-i-'Alāi* of Amir Khusru, poet and sufi disciple of Nizamuddin Awliya, the far-famed Chishtiyya sufi of Delhi.

"On Sunday, the 23rd, after holding a council of chief officers, he [Malik Kafur, converted Hindu and commander of the Muslim army] took a select body of cavalry with him and pressed on against Billal Deo, and on the 5th of Shawwal reached the fort of Dhur Sammund[46] after a difficult march of twelve days over the hills and valleys, and through thorny forests. 'The fire-worshipping' Rai, when he learnt that 'his idol-temple was likely to be converted into a mosque,' despatched Kisu Mal... The commander replied that he was sent with the object of converting him to Muhammadanism, or of making him a *zimmi*, and subject to pay tax, or of slaying him if neither of these terms were assented to. When the Rai received this reply, he said he was ready to give up all he possessed, except his sacred thread."[47]

TIMUR (1398-99 CE)

"About this time there arose in my heart the desire to lead an expedition against the infidels, and to become a *ghāzi;* for it had reached my ears that the slayer of infidels is a *ghāzi,* and if he is slain he becomes a martyr. It was on this account that I formed this resolution, but I was undetermined in my mind whether I should direct my expedition against the infidels of China or against the infidels and polytheists of India. In this matter I sought an omen from the Kuran, and the verse I opened upon was this, 'O Prophet, make war upon infidels and unbelievers, and treat them with severity.'[48] My great officers told me that the inhabitants of Hindustan were infidels and unbelievers. In obedience to the order of Almighty Allah I ordered an expedition against them...[49]

"Then the Prince Muhammad Sultan said: 'The whole country of India is full of gold and jewels, and in it there are seventeen mines of gold and silver, diamond and ruby and emerald and tin and steel and copper and quicksilver, etc., and of the plants which

---

[46]Dwarasamudra in Karnataka, Capital of the Hoysala Kingdom at that time.
[47]Ibid., pp. 88-89.
[48]Quran, 66.9.
[49]Ibid., 394-95. Translation of *Malfūzāt-i-Timūri* of Timur.

grow there are those fit for making wearing apparel, and aromatic plants, and the sugar-cane, and it is a country which is always green and verdant, and the whole aspect of the country is pleasant and delightful. Now, since the inhabitants are chiefly polytheists and infidels and idolators and worshippers of the sun, by the order of Allah and his prophet, it is right for us to conquer them.'[50]

Ulema and Sufis advocate *Jihād* against Hindus

"Some of the nobles said, 'By the favour of Almighty Allah we may conquer India, but if we establish ourselves permanently therein, our race will degenerate and our children will become like the natives of those regions, and in a few generations their strength and valour will diminish.' The *amirs* of regiments (*kushunat*) were disturbed at these words, but I said to them, 'My object in the invasion of Hindustan is to lead an expedition against the infidels that, according to the law of Muhammad (upon whom and his family be the blessing and peace of Allah), we may convert to the true faith the people of that country, purify the land itself from the filth of infidelity and polytheism; and that we may overthrow their temples and idols and become *ghāzis* and *mujāhids* before Allah.' They gave an unwilling consent, but I placed no reliance upon them. At this time the wise men of Islam came before me, and a conversation began about the propriety of a war against infidels and polytheists; they gave it as their opinion that it is the duty of the Sultan of Islam, and all the people who profess that 'there is no god but Allah, and Muhammad is the prophet of Allah,' for the sake of preserving their religion and strengthening their law, to exert their utmost endeavour for the suppression of the enemies of their faith. And it is the duty of every Muslim and true believer to use his utmost exertions in obedience to his ruler. When the edifying words of the wise men reached the ears of the nobles, all their hearts were set upon a holy war in Hindustan, and throwing themselves on their knees, they repeated the Chapter of Victory.[51]

---

[50]Ibid., pp. 396-97.
[51]Ibid., p. 397. *Sūrat-ul-Fātihat*, the opening chapter of the Quran.

"When I girded up my loins for the expedition, I wrote to Hazrat Shaikh Zainu-d-din[52] to the effect that I had determined on a religious expedition to Hindustan. He wrote in the margin of my letter: 'Be it known to Abu-l-Ghazi Timur (whom may Allah assist) that great prosperity in this world and the next will result to you from this undertaking, and you will go and return in safety.' He also sent me a large sword which I made my sceptre...[53]

Kalima comes to Kator

"The ruler of Kator[54] had a fort, on one side of which was a river, and beyond the river a lofty mountain reaching down to the water... When I advanced into the neighbourhood of the fort I did not perceive a trace of the infidels, and when I came to the place itself I saw that they had abandoned it and fled. I obtained a booty of many sheep and some other things here, and ordered that they should set fire to the houses and buildings of the city, in the midst of which the fort was built, and that they should level it with the ground. Then crossing the river in haste and pursuing the track of the enemy, I reached the skirts of the mountain on the top of which the infidels had taken up their position in defiles and other strong places. I immediately gave orders to my valiant and experienced troops to ascend. Raising their war-cry and shouting the *takbīr,* they rushed to the attack... They all proved their zeal for Islam on the unbelieving foe, and having overpowered the infidels they put many of them to death and took possession of their fastnesses. Only a few of the enemy succeeded in sheltering themselves, wounded and worn out with fatigue, in their caverns. I sent Ak Sultan to them with the message that if they would consent to submit unconditionally and would all become Musulmans and repeat the creed, I grant them quarter, but otherwise I would exterminate them to a man... They all proffered submission, and

---

[52]A well-known sufi.
[53]Ibid., p. 398.
[54]A town in North-West Frontier Province.

repeating the necessary formula, embraced the Muhammadan faith...[55]

Blessings from Baba Farid

"I was informed that the blessed tomb of Hazrat Shaikh Farid Ganj-shakar (whom may Allah bless) was in this city [Ajodhan], upon which I immediately set out on pilgrimage to it. I repeated the *Fatiha*, and the other prayers, for assistance, etc., and prayed for victory from his blessed spirit, and distributed large sums in alms and charity among the attendants on the holy shrine.[56] I left Ajodhan on Wednesday, the 26th of the month on my march to Bhatnir.[57] The *raja* of that place was called Dul Chain. He had assembled a body of *Rajputs,* a class which supplies the most renowned soldiers of India, and with these he waited ready to do battle...[58]

Butchery at Bhatnir

"So in all directions the brave warriors of Islam attacked the infidels with lion-like fury, until at length by the grace of Allah, victory beamed upon the efforts of my soldiers. In a short space of time all the people in the fort were put to the sword, and in the course of one hour the heads of ten thousand infidels were cut off. The sword of Islam was washed in the blood of the infidels, and all the goods and effects, the treasure and the grain which for many a long year had been stored in the fort, became the spoil of my soldiers. They set fire to the houses and reduced them to ashes, and they razed the buildings and the fort to the ground. When this victory had been accomplished I returned to my tent. All the

---

[55]Ibid., pp. 403-05.

[56]No one from among the devotees of Baba Farid, the famous Chishtiyya sufi, is known to have disapproved of the crimes committed by Timur.

[57]Modern Hanumangarh in the Ganganagar district of Rajasthan.

[58]Ibid., pp. 421-22

princes and *amirs* waited upon me to congratulate me upon the conquest and upon the enormous booty which had fallen into my hands. It was all brought out and I distributed it among my brave *amirs* and soldiers.[59]

Slaughter at Sirsa

"When I made inquiries about the city of Sarsuti,[60] I was informed that the people of the place were strangers to the religion of Islam, and that they kept hogs in their houses and ate the flesh of those animals. When they heard of my arrival, they abandoned their city. I sent my cavalry in pursuit of them, and a great fight ensued. All these infidel Hindus were slain, their wives and children were made prisoners, and their property and goods became the spoil of the victors. The soldiers then returned, bringing with them several thousand Hindu women and children who became Muhammadans, and repeated the creed...[61]

Jihād against the Jats

"It was again brought to my knowledge that these turbulent *Jats* were as numerous as ants or locusts... They had now taken fright, and had gone into jungles and deserts hard to penetrate. My great object in invading Hindustan had been to wage a religious war against the infidel Hindus, and it now appeared to me that it was necessary for me to put down these *Jats*. On the 9th of the month I despatched the baggage from Tohana,[62] and on the same day I marched into the jungles and wilds, and slew 2,000 demon-like *Jats*. I made their wives and children captives, and plundered their cattle and property... On the same day a party of *saiyids*, who dwelt in the vicinity, came with courtesy and humility to wait

---

[59]Ibid., p. 427.
[60]The ancient name of Sirsa, now headquarters of a district in Haryana.
[61]Ibid., pp. 427-28.
[62]A town in Jind district of Haryana.

upon me and were very graciously received.[63] In my reverence for the race of the prophet, I treated their chiefs with great honour...[64]

Selective Slaughter and Pillage at Loni

"On the 29th I again marched and reached the river Jumna. On the other side of the river I descried a fort, and upon making inquiry about it, I was informed that it consisted of a town and fort, called Loni[65]...I determined to take that fort at once... Many of the *Rajputs* placed their wives and children in their houses and burned them, then they rushed to the battle and were killed. Other men of the garrison fought and were slain, and a great many were taken prisoners. Next day I gave orders that the Musalman prisoners should be separated and saved, but that the infidels should all be despatched to hell with the proselyting sword. I also ordered that the houses of the *saiyids, shaikhs* and learned Musulmans should be preserved but that all the other houses should be plundered and the fort destroyed. It was done as I directed and a great booty was obtained...[66]

A Hundred Thousand Hindus slaughtered in One Day

"Next day, Friday the 3rd of the month. I left the fort of Loni and marched to a position opposite to Jahan-numa[67] where I encamped... I now held a Court... At this Court Amir Jahan Shah and Amir Sulaiman Shah and other *amirs* of experience, brought to my notice that, from the time of entering Hindustan up to the present time, we had taken more than 100,000 infidels and Hindus prisoners, and that they were all in my camp. On the previous day,

---

[63]The *saiyids* had no sympathy with the Jats who were their neighbours; instead, they were delighted to witness their slaughter.

[64]Ibid., p. 429.

[65]A town opposite Delhi across the Jamuna.

[66]Ibid., pp. 432-33.

[67]Firoz Shah Tughlaq's palace on the Ridge, now Bara Hindu Rao Hospital.

when the enemy's forces made the attack upon us, the prisoners made signs of rejoicing, uttered imprecations against us, and were ready, as soon as they heard of the enemy's success, to form themselves into a body, break their bonds, plunder our tents, and then to go and join the enemy, and so increase his numbers and strength. I asked their advice about the prisoners, and they said that on the great day of battle these 100,000 prisoners could not be left with the baggage, and that it would be entirely opposed to the [Islamic] rules of war to set these idolaters and foes of Islam at liberty. In fact, no other course remained but that of making them all food for the sword. When I heard these words I found them in accordance with the rules of war, and I directly gave my command for the *tawāchis*[68] to proclaim throughout the camp that every man who had infidel prisoners was to put them to death and whoever neglected to do so should himself be executed and his property given to the informer. When this order became known to the *ghāzis* of Islam, they drew their swords and put their prisoners to death. 100,000 infidels, impious idolaters, were on that day slain. Maulana Nasiru-d-din 'Umar, a counsellor and man of learning, who, in all his life, had never killed a sparrow, now, in execution of my order, slew with his sword fifteen idolatrous Hindus,[69] who were his captives...[70]

Selective Slaughter and Pillage at Delhi

"On the 16th of the month some incidents occurred which led to the sack of the city of Delhi, and to the slaughter of many of the infidel inhabitants... The Hindus set fire to their houses with their own hands, burned their wives and children in them, and rushed into the fight and were killed... On that day, Thursday, and all the night of Friday, nearly 15,000 Turks were engaged in slaying, plundering, and destroying... The following day, Saturday, the 17th, all passed in the same way, and the spoil was so great that

---

[68]Drum-beaters.
[69]This speaks volumes about Maulanas produced by Islam.
[70]Ibid., pp. 435-36.

each man secured from fifty to a hundred prisoners — men, women, and children. There was no man who took less than twenty. The other booty was immense in rubies, diamonds, pearls and other gems; jewels of gold and silver, *ashrafis, tankas* of gold and silver of the celebrated 'Alai coinage; vessels of gold and silver; and brocades and silks of great value. Gold and silver ornaments of the Hindu[71] women were obtained in such quantities as to exceed all account. Excepting the quarter of the *saiyids*, the *'ulama* and the other Musulmans, the whole city was sacked...[72]

A *Mujāhid* knows no Rest

"I had been at Delhi fifteen days, which time I had passed in pleasure and enjoyment, holding royal Courts and giving great feasts. I then reflected that I had come to Hindustan to war against infidels, and my enterprise had been so blessed that wherever I had gone I had been victorious. I had triumphed over my adversaries. I had put to death some *lacs* of infidels and idolaters, and I had stained my proselyting sword with the blood of the enemies of the faith. Now this crowning victory had been won, and I felt that I ought not to indulge in ease but rather to exert myself in warring against the infidels of Hindustan...[73]

Jihād along the Jamuna

"On the 1st Jumada-l-awwal I placed the left wing of the army under the command of Amir Jahan Shah, with orders to march up the Jumna, to take every fort and town and village he came to, and to put all the infidels of the country to the sword. The *amir* led off his army to execute my commands... My brave fellows pursued

---

[71]The word "Hindu" in this citation has been left out in Mohammad Habib and K.A. Nizami (ed.), *A Comprehensive History of India*, Volume V, *The Sultanat*, published by the People's Publishing House, New Delhi, 1970, p. 122. Our "secular" historians are very honest indeed. Habib heads the list.

[72]Ibid., pp. 445-46

[73]Ibid., p. 448.

and killed many of them, made their wives and children prisoners, plundered their property and goods, and secured a vast number of cows and buffalos. When by the favour of Allah, I had secured this victory, I got off my horse and prostrated myself on the ground to pay my thanks...[74]

"Pressing on with all haste I passed the jungles and thickets, and arrived in front of the infidels [at Kutila].[75] After a slight resistance the enemy took flight, but many of them fell under the swords of my soldiers. All the wives and children of the infidels were made prisoners, and their property and goods, gold, money and grain, horses, camels (*shutur*), cows and buffaloes in countless numbers, fell as spoil into the hands of my soldiers. Satisfied with this rout of the enemy, I said the afternoon prayers in public in that desert, and I returned thanks to Allah...[76]

Slaughter at Hardwar

"My brave men displayed great courage and daring; they made their swords their banners, and exerted themselves in slaying the foe (during a bathing festival on the bank of the Ganges). They slaughtered many of the infidels, and pursued those who fled to the mountains. So many of them were killed that their blood ran down the mountains and plain, and thus (nearly) all were sent to hell. The few who escaped, wounded, weary, and half dead, sought refuge in the defiles of the hills. Their property and goods, which exceeded all computation, and their countless cows and buffaloes, fell as spoil into the hands of my victorious soldiers.[77]

Allah's Bloodlust Satisfied

"When I was satisfied with the destruction I had dealt out to the

---

[74]Ibid., pp. 451-54.
[75]A town on the east bank of the Jamuna.
[76]Ibid., pp. 457-58.
[77]Ibid., p. 459.

infidels, and the land was cleansed from the pollution of their existence, I turned back victorious and triumphant, laden with spoil. On that same day I crossed the Ganges, and said my mid-day prayers in the congregation, on the banks of that river. I prostrated myself in humble thanks to Allah, and afterwards again mounting my horse, marched five miles down the river and then encamped. It now occurred to my mind that I had marched as a conqueror from the river Sind to Delhi, the capital of the kings of India. I had put the infidels to the edge of the sword on both sides of my route, and had scoured the land... I had crossed the rivers Ganges and Jumna, and I had sent many of the abominable infidels to hell, and had purified the land from their foul existence. I rendered thanks to Almighty Allah that I had accomplished my undertaking, and had waged against the infidels that holy war I had resolved upon; then I determined to turn my course towards Samarkand, my capital and paradise.[78]

Plunder is Mothers' Milk to Musalmans

"Amir Sulaiman Shah... and other *amirs*... said : 'So long as we your servants, are able to move hand and foot, we will execute your orders... and (you) should now order us to march against the infidels of the Siwalik,[79] and to rout and destroy them.' I replied: 'My principal object in coming to Hindustan and in undergoing all this toil and hardship, has been to accomplish two things. The first was to war with the infidels, the enemies of the Muhammadan religion; and by this religious warfare to acquire some claim to reward in the life to come. The other was a worldly object; that the army of Islam might gain something by plundering the wealth and valuables of the infidels: plunder in war is as lawful as their mothers' milk to Musulmans who war for their faith, and the consuming of that which is lawful is a means of grace.[80]

---

[78]Ibid., pp. 459-60.
[79]Region round Dehradun and neighbouring districts of Himachal Pradesh
[80]Ibid., p. 461.

Sword of Islam in the Siwalik

"On the 10th Jumada-l-awwal I mounted my horse and drew my sword, determined on fighting the infidels of the Siwalik... The infidel *gabrs*[81] were dismayed at the sight, and took to flight. The holy warriors pursued them, and made heaps of slain. A few Hindus, in a wretched plight, wounded and half dead, escaped, and hid themselves in holes and caves. An immense spoil beyond all compute, in money, goods and articles, cows and buffaloes, fell into the hands of my soldiers. All the Hindu women and children in the valley were made prisoners.[82]

"On the following day, the 14th Jumada-I-awwal, I crossed the river Jumna with the baggage, and encamped in another part of the Siwalik hills. Here I learned that in this part of the Siwalik there was a *raja* of great rank and power, by name Ratan Sen... In the front of this valley Raja Ratan Sen had drawn out his forces. At the first onset, the Hindus broke and fled, and my victorious soldiers pursued, slashing their swords killing many of the fugitives, and sending them to hell. Only a few of them escaped, wounded and dispirited, and hiding themselves like foxes in the woods, thus saved their lives. When the soldiers gave up killing the infidels, they secured great plunder in goods and valuables, prisoners and cattle. No one of them had less than one or two hundred cows, and ten or twenty slaves — the other plunder exceeded all calculation.[83]

"Holy Warriors" at Kangra

"When I entered the valley on that side of the Siwalik, information was brought to me about the town (*shahr*) of Nagarkot,[84] which is a large and important town of Hindustan and situated in these mountains... I instantly ordered Amir Jahan Shah, whom I had sent to

---

[81]A term used for Zoroastrians of Iran to start with, it became a term of contempt for Hindu warriors, meaning vagabonds.

[82]Ibid., pp. 462-63.

[83]Ibid., pp. 463-64.

[84]Ancient name of Kangra, now a district headquarters in Himachal Pradesh.

the front with the forces of the left wing and the army of Khurasan, to attack the enemy. The *amir*, in obedience to my order, advanced and charged the enemy. At the very first charge the infidels were defeated and put to flight. The holy warriors, sword in hand, dashed among the fugitives, and made heaps of corpses. Great numbers were slain, and a vast booty in goods and valuables, and prisoners and cattle in countless numbers, fell into the hands of the victors who returned triumphant and loaded with spoil."[85]

BABUR (1519-1530 CE)

Babur, the founder of the Mughal dynasty of Islamic invaders in India, earned his title of a *mujāhid* when he stormed the small Hindu principality of Bajaur in the North-West Frontier Province at the start of his first invasion of India in 1519 CE. He describes the scene in his autobiography with great glee.

Drinking Party amidst Dead Bodies

"As the Bajauris were rebels and at enmity with the people of Islam, and as, by reason of the heathenish and hostile customs prevailing in their midst, the very name of Islam was rooted out from their tribe, they were put to general massacre and their wives and children were made captive. At a guess more than 3000 men went to their death; as the fight did not reach to the eastern side of the fort, a few got away there. The fort taken, we entered and inspected it. On the walls, in houses, streets and alleys, the dead lay, in what numbers! Comers and goers to and from were passing over the bodies... With mind easy about the important affairs of the Bajaur fort, we marched, on Tuesday the 9th of Muharram, one *kuroh* (2m) down the dale of Bajaur and ordered that a tower of heads should be set up on the rising ground.[86] On Wednesday the

---

[85]Ibid., pp. 465-66.
[86]In his *Glimpses of World History*, Pandit Jawaharlal Nehru has shown great fondness for Babur, including the latter's hobby of making towers of severed Hindu heads.

10th of Muharram, we rode out to visit the Bajaur fort. There was
a wine-party in Khawaja Kalan's house, several goat-skins of
wine having been brought."[87]

The Quran sustains the *Jihād* by Babur

The famous battle he fought in 1527 CE with the Rajput
Confederacy led by Maharana Sangram Singh of Mewar, was
hailed as a *jihād* by Babur. In his description of this contest, we
find him quoting copiously from the Quran.

"On Monday the 9th of the first Jumada, we got out of the
suburbs of Agra, on our journey (*safar*) for the Holy War, and
dismounted in the open country, where we remained three or four
days to collect our army and be its rallying-point...[88]

"On this occasion I received a secret inspiration and heard an
infallible voice say: '*Is not the time yet come unto those who
believe, that their hearts should humbly submit to the admonition
of Allah, and that truth which hath been revealed?*'[89] Thereupon
we set ourselves to extirpate the things of wickedness...[90]

"Above all, adequate thanks cannot be rendered for a benefit
than which none is greater in the world and nothing is more
blessed, in the world to come, to wit, victory over most powerful
infidels and dominion over wealthiest heretics, '*these are the
unbelievers, the wicked.*'[91] In the eyes of the judicious, no blessing
can be greater than this...[92]

"Previous to the rising in Hindustan of the Sun of dominion and
the emergence there of the light of the Shahansha's (i.e. Babur's)
Khalifate the authority of that execrated pagan (Sanga) — *at the
Judgment Day he shall have no friend*[93] — was such that not one

---

[87]*Babur-Nama*, translated into English by A.S. Beveridge, New Delhi reprint,
1979, pp. 370-71.
[88]Ibid., p. 547.
[89]Quran, 57.15.
[90]*Babur-Nama*, p. 554.
[91]Quran, 80.42.
[92]*Babur-Nama*, p. 560.
[93]Quran, 69.35.

of all the exalted sovereigns of this wide realm, such as the Sultan of Delhi, the Sultan of Gujarat and the Sultan of Mandu, could cope with this evil-dispositioned one, without the help of other pagans...[94]

"Ten powerful chiefs, each the leader of a pagan host, uprose in rebellion, as smoke rises, and linked themselves, as though enchained, to that perverse one (Sanga); and this infidel decade who, unlike the blessed ten, uplifted misery-freighted standards which *denounce unto them excruciating punishment,*[95] had many dependents, and troops, and wide-extended lands...[96]

"The protagonists of the royal forces fell, like divine destiny, on that one-eyed Dajjal who to understanding men, shewed the truth of the saying, *When Fate arrives, the eye becomes blind,* and setting before their eyes the scripture which saith, *whosoever striveth to promote the true religion, striveth for the good of his own soul,*[97] they acted on the precept to which obedience is due, *Fight against infidels and hypocrites*[98]...[99]

'The pagan right wing made repeated and desperate attack on the left wing of the army of Islam, falling furiously on the holy warriors, possessors of salvation, but each time was made to turn back or, smitten with the arrows of victory, was *made to descend into Hell, the house of perdition: they shall be thrown to burn therein, and an unhappy dwelling shall it be.*[100] Then the trusty amongst the nobles, Mumin Ataka and Rustam *Turkman* betook themselves to the rear of the host of darkened pagans...[101]

"At the moment when the holy warriors were heedlessly flinging away their lives, they heard a secret voice say, *Be not dismayed, neither be grieved, for, if ye believe, ye shall be exalted above the unbelievers,*[102] and from the infallible Informer heard

---

[94]*Babur-Nama*, p. 561.
[95]Quran, 3.20.
[96]*Babur-Nama*, p. 562.
[97]Quran, 29.5.
[98]Ibid., 66.9.
[99]*Babur-Nama*, p. 563.
[100]Quran, 14.33.
[101]*Babur-Nama*, p. 569.
[102]Quran, 3.133.

the joyful words, *Assistance is from Allah, and a speedy victory! And do thou bear glad tiding to true believers.*[103] Then they fought with such delight that the plaudits of the saints of the Holy Assembly reached them and the angels from near the Throne, fluttered round their heads like moths...[104]

Towers of Hindu Heads

"And victory the beautiful woman (*shāhid*) whose world-adornment of waving tresses was embellished by *Allah will aid you with a mighty aid,*[105] bestowed on us the good fortune that had been hidden behind a veil, and made it a reality. The absurd (*bātil*) Hindus, knowing their position perilous, *dispersed like carded wool before the wind,* and *like moths scattered abroad.*[106] Many fell dead on the field of battle; others, desisting from fighting, fled to the desert exile and became the food of crows and kites. Mounds were made of the bodies of the slain, pillars of their heads.[107]

Babur becomes a *Ghāzi*

"After this success, *Ghāzi* (Victor in a Holy-war) was written amongst the royal titles. Below the titles (*tughrā*) entered on the *Fath-nāma*, I wrote the following quatrain:

> For Islam's sake, I wandered in the wilds,
> Prepared for war with pagans and Hindus,
> Resolved myself to meet the martyr's death,
> Thanks be to Allah! a *ghāzi* I became."[108]

Babur shared a hobby with his ancestor, Timur. Both of them

---

[103]Ibid., 61.13.
[104]*Babu-Nama*, p. 572.
[105]Quran, 43.3.
[106]Ibid., 48.3.
[107]*Babur-Nama*, p. 572-73.
[108]Ibid., pp. 574-75

were mighty fond of raising towers of severed Hindu heads.

SHER SHAH SUR (1540-1545 CE)

"...Upon this, Sher Shāh turned again towards Kalinjar... The Rājā of Kalinjar, Kīrat Sing, did not come out to meet him. So he ordered the fort to be invested, and threw up mounds against it, and in a short time the mounds rose so high that they overtopped the fort. The men who were in the streets and houses were exposed, and the Afghāns shot them with their arrows and muskets from off the mounds. The cause of this tedious mode of capturing the fort was this. Among the women of Rājā Kīrat Sing was a Pātar slave-girl, that is a dancing-girl. The king had heard exceeding praise of her, and he considered how to get possession of her, for he feared lest if he stormed the fort, the Rājā Kīrat Sing would certainly make a *jauhar,* and would burn the girl.

"On Friday, the 9th of Rabī'u-l awwal, 952 A.H., when one watch and two hours of the day was over, Sher Shāh called for his breakfast, and ate with his '*ulamā* and priests, without whom he never breakfasted. In the midst of breakfast, Shaikh Nizām said, 'There is nothing equal to a religious war against the infidels. If you be slain you become a martyr, if you live you become a *ghāzi.*' When Sher Shāh had finished eating his breakfast, he ordered Daryā Khān to bring loaded shells, and went up to the top of a mound, and with his own hand shot off many arrows, and said, 'Daryā Khān comes not; he delays very long.' But when they were at last brought, Sher Shāh came down from the mound, and stood where they were placed. While the men were employed in discharging them, by the will of Allah Almighty, one shell full of gunpowder struck on the gate of the fort and broke, and came and fell where a great number of other shells were placed. Those which were loaded all began to explode. Shaikh Halīl, Shaikh Nizām, and other learned men, and most of the others escaped and were not burnt, but they brought out Sher Shāh partially burnt. A young princess who was standing by the rockets was burnt to death. When Sher Shāh was carried into his tent, all his nobles assembled in *darbār*; and he sent for 'Īsā Khān Hājib and Masnad Khān Kalkapūr, the son-in-law of 'Īsā Khān, and the paternal uncle of the author, to come into his tent, and ordered them to take the fort while he was yet alive. When 'Īsā Khān came out and told the chiefs that it was Sher Shāh's order that they should attack on every side and capture the fort, men came and swarmed out instantly on every side like ants and locusts; and by the time of afternoon prayers captured the fort, putting every one to the sword, and sending all the infidels to hell. About the hour of evening prayers, the intelligence of the victory reached Sher Shāh, and marks of joy and pleasure appeared on his countenance. Rājā Kīrat Sing, with seventy men, remained in a house. Kutb Khān the whole night long watched the house in person lest the Rājā should escape. Sher Shāh said to his sons that none of his nobles need watch the house, so that the Rājā escaped out of the house, and the labour and trouble of this long watching was lost. The next day at sunrise, however, they took the Rājā alive..."[109]

"It is related in the *Akbar Shāhī*, that when Sher Shāh rendered up his life to the angel of death in Kalinjar, Jalāl Khān, his youngest son, was in the town of Rewān, in the province of Bhata, and his eldest son 'Ādil Khān, the heir-apparent, in the fort of Runthūr (Ranthambhor). The nobles perceived that 'Ādil Khān would be unable to arrive with speed, and as the State required a head, they despatched a person to summon Jalāl Khān who was nearer. He reached Kalinjar in five days, and by the assistance of 'Īsā Hajjāb and other grandees, was raised to the throne near the fort of Kalinjar, on the 15th of the month Rabī'u-l awwal, 952 A.H. (25th May, 1545 CE). He assumed the title of Islām Shāh...

"After his accession, he ordered the Rājā of Kalinjar, who had been captured with seventy of his adherents, to be put to death, and directed that not one of them should be spared..."[110]

---

[109] *Tārīkh-i-Sher Shāhī* of Abbas Khan Sherwani in Elliot and Dowson, Volume IV, pp. 407-09.

[110] *Tārīkh-i-Dāūdī* of 'Abdullah in Elliot and Dowson, Volume IV, pp. 478-79.

JIHĀD AGAINST VIJAYANAGARA (1565 CE)

"Ally Adil Shah,[111] intent on adding to his dominions, and repairing the losses sustained by his father, entered into a close alliance with Ramraj; and on the occasion of the death of a son of that Prince, he had the boldness, attended only by one hundred horse, to go to Beejanuggur, to offer his condolence in person on that melancholy occasion. Ramraj received him with the greatest respect, and the King with the kindest persuasions, prevailed upon him to lay aside his mourning. The wife of Ramraj, on this occasion, adopted the King as her son; at the end of three days, which were spent in an interchange of friendly professions and presents, Ally Adil Shah took his leave...[112]

Islam Tramples upon Human Ties

"Ally Adil Shah resolved to curb his [Ramraj's] insolence and reduce his power by a league of the faithful against him; for which purpose he convened an assembly of his friends and confidential advisers. Kishwur Khan Lary and Shah Aboo Toorab Shirazy, whose abilities had often been experienced, represented, that the King's desire to humble the pride of the Ray of Beejanuggur was undoubtedly meritorious and highly politic, but could never be effected unless by the union of all the Mahomedan kings of the Deccan, as the revenues of Ramraj, collected from sixty seaports and numerous flourishing cities and districts, amounted to an immense sum; which enabled him to maintain a force, against which no single king of the Mussulmans could hope to contend with the smallest prospect of success. Ally Adil Shah commanded Kishwur Khan to take measures to effect the object of a general league; and an ambassador was accordingly despatched without

---

[111]Sultan of the Ādil Shāhi dynasty of Bijapur.

[112]*Tārīkh-i-Farishtah*, translated into English by John Briggs as *History of the Rise of the Mahomedan Power in India*, New Delhi reprint, 1981, Volume III, p. 71.

delay to sound Ibrahim Kootb Shah[113], and to open to him if prudent, the designed plan...[114]

Bickering Believers unite against Unbelievers

"Ibrahim Kootb Shah, who had been inwardly stung with indignation at the haughty insolence and the usurpations of Ramraj, eagerly acceded to the proposed alliance, and offered to mediate a union between Ally Adil Shah and Hoossein Nizam Shah,[115] and even promised to obtain for the former the fort of Sholapoor, which had been the original cause of their disagreement. With this view Ibrahim Kootb Shah despatched Moostufa Khan Ardistany, the most intelligent nobleman of his court, to Ally Adil Shah, with orders, if he should find him still sincere in his intentions towards the league, to proceed from thence to Ahmudnuggur, and conclude the alliance...[116]

"After some days it was agreed that Hoossein Nizam Shah should give his daughter Chand Beeby in marriage to Ally Adil Shah, with the fortress of Sholapoor as her dowry; and that he should receive the sister of that Prince, named Huddeea Sooltana, as a consort for his eldest son Moortuza; that a treaty of eternal friendship should be entered on between both states, and that they should unite sincerely to reduce the power of Ramraj; for which purpose it was resolved to march against him at the earliest practicable period. Hoossein Nizam Shah, Ally Adil Shah, Ibrahim Kootb Shah, and Ally Bereed Shah,[117] now began to make active preparations for the campaign against Ramraj...[118]

"In the year A.H. 972 (1564 CE), the four princes, at the head of their respective armies, met on the plains of Beejapoor, and on the 20th of Jumad-ool-Awul (Dec. 26) of the same year marched from

---

[113]Sultan of the Qutb Shāhī dynasty of Golkunda.
[114]Ibid., pp. 74-75.
[115]Sultan of the Nizām Shāhī dynasty of Ahmadnagar.
[116]Ibid., p. 75.
[117]Sultan of the Barīd Shāhi dynasty of Bidar.
[118]Ibid., p. 76.

that neighbourhood. After some days they arrived at Talikote, and the armies encamped near the banks of the Krishna; where, as the country on the north bank belonged to Ally Adil Shah he entertained his allies with great splendour, and sent strict orders to all the governors of his dominions to forward supplies of provisions from their districts regularly all to the camp."[119]

Islam enjoins Treachery towards Unbelievers

"The battle took place on Tuesday, 23 January, 1565. The Vijayanagara army commenced attack in right earnest and the right and left wings of the confederate army were thrown into such disorder that their commanders were almost prepared to retreat when the position was saved by Hussain who opposed the enemy with great valour. The fighting was then continued and the loss of life on both sides was heavy. But it did not last long and its fate was determined by the desertion of two Muhammadan commanders under Ramraja. Caesar Frederick, who visited Vijayanagara in 1567, said that each of these commanders had under him seventy to eighty thousand men and the defeat of Vijayanagara was due to their desertion. Ramaraja fell into enemy's hands and was beheaded on the order of Hussain."[120]

Slaughter, Plunder and Pillage

"The Hindoos, according to custom, when they saw their chief destroyed, fled in the utmost disorder from the field, and were pursued by the allies with such success, that the river was dyed red with their blood. It is computed, by the best authorities, that above one hundred thousand infidels were slain during the action and in the pursuit. The plunder was so great that every private man in the allied army became rich in gold, jewels tents, arms, horses, and

---

[119]Ibid., pp. 76-77.
[120]R.C. Majumdar (ed.), *The History and Culture of the Indian People*, Volume VII, *The Mughal Empire*, Bombay, 1973, p. 425.

slaves, the kings permitting every person to retain what he acquired, reserving the elephants only for their own use. Letters with accounts of this important victory were despatched to their several dominions, and to the neighbouring states, while the kings themselves, shortly after the battle, marched onwards into the country of Ramraj, as far as Anagoondy, and the advanced troops penetrated to Beejanuggur which they plundered, razed the chief buildings to the ground, and committed every species of excess."[121]

Destruction of the *Dār-ul-harb*

"The third day saw the beginning of the end. The victorious Mussulmans had halted on the field of battle for rest and refreshment, but now they had reached the capital, and from that time forward for a space of five months Vijayanagar knew no rest. The enemy had come to destroy, and they carried out their object relentlessly. They slaughtered the people without mercy; broke down the temples and palaces, and wreaked such savage vengeance on the abode of the Kings, that, with the exception of a few great stone-built temples and walls, nothing now remains but a heap of ruins to mark the spot where once stately buildings stood. They demolished the statues, and even succeeded in breaking the limbs of the huge Narasimha monolith. Nothing seemed to escape them. They broke up the pavilions standing on the huge platform from which the kings used to watch festivals, and overthrew all the carved work. They lit huge fires in the magnificently decorated buildings forming the temple of Vitthalaswami near the river, and smashed its exquisite stone sculptures. With fire and sword, with crowbars and axes, they carried on day after day their work of destruction. Never perhaps in the history of the world has such havoc been wrought, and wrought so suddenly, on so splendid a city; teeming with a wealthy and industrious population in the full plenitude of prosperity one day, and on the next seized, pillaged, and reduced to ruins, amid scenes of savage massacre and horrors

---

[121]*Tārīkh-i-Farishtah*, op. cit., p. 79.

beggaring description... The loot must have been enormous. Couto states that amongst other treasures was found a diamond as large as a hen's egg, which was kept by the Adil Shah."[122]

AKBAR (1556-1605 CE)

"Hīmūn was excessively arrogant on account of his troops and elephants. He advanced, fought, and routed the Mughals, whose heads lay in heaps, and whose blood flowed in streams. He thus at first vanquished the Mughal army; but as the brilliancy of the star of Prince Akbar's fortune was not destined to be diminished, it chanced that, by the decree of the Almighty, an arrow struck Hīmūn in the forehead. He told his elephant driver to take the elephant out of the field of battle...

"When Shāh Kulī Beg was told of what had occurred, he came up to the elephant, and brought it into the presence of Bairam Khān. Bairam Khān, after prostrating himself, and returning thanks, caused Hīmūn to descend from the elephant, after which he bound his hands, and took him before the young and fortunate Prince, and said, As this is our first success, let Your Highness's own august hand smite this infidel with the sword. The Prince, accordingly, struck him, and divided his head from his unclean body (Nov. 5, AD 1556)."[123]

"... The king struck Hemu with his sword and he won the title of Ghazi..."[124]

"Akbar was now informed that Hāji Khān, a *ghulām* of Sher Khān Afghān [Sher Shāh], a brave and able general, was setting up pretensions to rule in Alwar and that Hīmū's father and wife, and all his property and wealth, were in that country. So the Emperor sent Nāsiru-l Mulk [Pīr Muhammad Sarwāni] with a select force to attack him. Hāji Khān, in dread of the Imperial army, fled

---

[122]Robert Sewell, *A Forgotten Empire*, New Delhi reprint, 1962, pp. 199-200.

[123]*Tārīkh-i Salātin-i Afaghāna* of Ahmad Yadgar, translated in Elliot and Dowson, Volume V, pp. 65-66.

[124]*Tarikh-i-Akbari* of Muhammad Arif Qandhari, translated into English by Tanseem Ahmad, Delhi, 1993, p. 74.

before it arrived. Alwar and all the territory of Mewāt thus came into the Imperial power. The fugitives proceeded to Dewatī-mājarī, a strong place, which was Hīmū's family home. Much resistance and fighting followed. Hīmū's father was taken alive, and brought before Nāsiru-l Mulk, who tried to convert him to the faith; but the old man said, 'For eighty years I have worshipped God in the way of my own religion; how can I now forsake my faith? Shall I, through fear of death, embrace your religion without understanding it?' Maulāna Pīr Muhammad treated his question as unheard, but gave him an answer with the tongue of the sword. He then returned with much spoil and fifty elephants to the Emperor."[125]

Jihād at Chittor (1567-1568 CE)

"...The emperor prayed to the Almighty in the month of Ramzan/March of the same year saying 'O Allah thou should come to the help of the army of Muslims.' He further desired that the army should launch a sudden attack on the fort from all sides. The army came up like a huge pack of pigeons and, entered the fort by slaughtering those soldiers, who were guarding its gate. They pierced a group of the enemy by their arrows and killed them. Then they scaled the wall of the fort with much courage and jumped into it. Naturally the fire of battle blazed forth...

"Thus the emperor became the owner of the flag of battle, i.e. victorious and the rebels (Kafirs) became the prey of arrows. The breeze of the grace of Allah began to blow. The heart of enemy began to wreathe in pain. By the time of prayer the full volume of sound was blown and delivered the final attack on the Satans. Realizing their helpless condition that wretched race began to slaughter their women and children with their own hands, and set fire to them, reducing (them) to ashes.

"Despite all, there was only one victorious army and the

---

[125]*Akbar-Nāma* of Abul Fazl, translated in Elliot and Dowson, Volume VI, p. 21.

vanquished one were thousands. In short, many of the misguided persons were killed by swords. The number of the dead was about thirty thousand.

"As a result of this victory, most of the persons of the army became rich, and under the emperor's government (or in his kingdom) they became men of substance. Everyone achieved the desired object. Everybody got in his army his cherished ambition. Men of sport enjoyed the beautiful ladies. Those who were covetous of hoarding property, benefited themselves fully. Every one was very happy over the success and every soul got a fresh lease of life by this triumph...

"If proper attention is to be paid to understand the exceptional qualities and graces of the character of His Majesty, then it would become clear that the feelings and mind inside and outside are the mirror of Divine injunctions because on that day an extraordinary effect appeared from the limbs and organs of his body which is beyond comprehension. *His pure heart and noble mind were turned inwards and in consequence of this purity he made a pilgrimage to the tomb of Qutb-ul-Qutabi Khwaja Muinuddin Chishti* in his dream and he paid full attention and due reverence to that paradise like tomb. On Sunday, 26th of Ramazan/15th March, of the aforesaid year he went for the pilgrimage. He stayed there for ten days and then left for Agra."[126]

Fathnama-i-Chitor (March 1568)

Several *fathnamas* (letters of victory) issued by Akbar at various occasions include *Fathnama-i-Chitor* issued by Akbar after the conquest of Chitor. *It was issued from Ajmer, where he* stayed for some time en route to Agra, on Ramazan 10, 975/ March 9, 1568. The text of the aforesaid *Fathnama* follows:[127]

"Praise be to Allah who made good His promise, helped His servant, honoured His soldiers, defeated the confederates all

---

[126]*Tarikh-i-Akbari*, op. cit., pp.149-51. Emphasis added.
[127]*Proceedings of Indian History Congress*, New Delhi, 1972, translated and annotated by Ishtiaq Ahmed Zilli, pp. 350–61.

alone, and after whom there is nothing."[128] All Praise and thanks-giving behoves that great Opener (*fattah*) of forts and kingdoms, in whose grasp are the keys of the conquests of the just and religious *Sultans*, and with whose patent of favour and authority are decorated the *manshurs* of the *Khilafat* and sovereignty of the victorious emperors. The Merciful one (*Karim*) whose omnipotence has ensured the victory of the believers through the promise: "to help believers is incumbent upon us,"[129] the Omni-potent one who enjoined the task of destroying the wicked infidels on the dutiful *mujahids* through the blows of their thunder-like scimitars laid down: "Fight them! Allah will chastise them at your hands and He will lay them low and give you victory over them."[130] "Glorified is He, and High Exalted from what they say,"[131] "His sovereignty is not dependent on any friend and helper."

'Whereas the Sovereign one, universal be His bounty and exalted His glory, has, in conformity with "I am to appoint thee a leader of the mankind",[132] assigned to us government of the *mumalik* of Hindustan which is one of the biggest countries of the world, and the *Munshi* of the office (*diwan khana*) of munificence and the Supreme Sovereign has adorned the radiant mandate (*manshur*) of our *Khilafat* and monarchy with the *Parwana* "Surely we established him in the land"[133] and decorated it with the ornament of "That is the bounty of Allah, which He giveth unto whom He will".[134] All the people who are Allah's trusts, being in the security of Peace from the hardships and misfortunes of the age, are busy in discharging the obligations of obedience and worship of the Almighty under our benevolent Protection, we deem it our duty to render thanks and express gratitude for this

---

[128]Opening lines of the Prophet's speech after the Conquest of Mecca.
[129]Quran, 30.47.
[130]Ibid., 9.14.
[131]Ibid., 17.43.
[132]Ibid., 2.124.
[133]Ibid., 18.84.
[134]Ibid., 62.4.

great favour. In accordance with "Proceed whither you wish, you are victorious," in whatever direction we Proceed fortune and felicity come forward to greet us and whither we turn the reign of our resolution the success and victory hasten to our Presence. In conformity with the happy injunction — "This is of the grace of my Lord that He may try me whether I am grateful or ungrateful"[135] — we spend our precious time to the best of our ability in war (*ghiza*) and *Jihad* and with the help of Eternal Allah, who is the supporter of our ever-increasing empire, we are busy in subjugating the localities, habitations, forts and towns which are under the possession of the infidels, may Allah forsake and annihilate all of them, and thus raising the standard of Islam everywhere and removing the darkness of polytheism and violent sins by the use of sword. We destroy the places of worship of idols in those places and other parts of India. "The praise be to Allah, who hath guided us to this, and we would not have found the way had it not been that Allah had guided us."[136]

'The purport of the discourse is that during these victorious times, after the elimination of Ali Quli and (his) ungrateful faction we arrived at the Capital Agra like "the noble, victorious",[137] and with a view to augment the materials of our recreation of hunting of elephants we encamped in the confines of Sivi Supar and Gagrun which are on the border of the country of Chitor. There it was brought to our notice that Rana Udai Singh, may Allah annihilate him, from whom it was expected that he would come forward to welcome, pay respects and kiss the royal threshold or would send his son with *Peshkash*, has adopted, due to excessive pride and conceit, an obstinate and arrogant attitude. (He) is collecting provisions in the fort of Chitor which is his hereditary place of residence and is distinguished in the forts of India in strength and grandeur, with the intention of entrenching himself there. Since the thoughts of war (*ghiza*) and *Jihad* dominated the

---

[135]Ibid., 27.40.
[136]Ibid., 7.43.
[137]Ibid., 80.16.

enlightened mind, it (Rana's behaviour) made the King angry and increased (his) zeal for the divine religion. Despite the fact that most of the royal troops had returned to their *Jagirs* after the last victory and only a few, who happened to be present at the Capital, accompanied the royal cavalcade on this hunting (excursion), we turned our rein to suppress that infidel. Fearful of the approach of the imperial standards he left his uncle, Sahidas Jaimal and Udiban Patta who are renowned for their valour among the infidels, may Allah forsake them and lead them to the abode of perdition, and who are considered to be equal to a thousand horsemen in intrepidity and prowess, with five thousand chosen Rajputs, one thousand troops from his (Rana's) own contingent and ten thousand other men to guard the fort. (The Rana) himself hastened with his troops to Udaipur and Kombalmir which are located in the security of the mountains and jungles. When at the town of Rampur, which is one of the well-known towns attached to Chitor, it became known that he was entertaining such plans, the royal mind decided upon subjugating the fort (of Chitor) with the divine help and only then to take other steps that may appear feasible. In this way we arrived in front of the fort with the intention of besieging it on Thursday, 20 Rabi II/Oct. 24, 1567. A fort rose in view such as Alburz with all its majesty would appear an insignificant rock at its foot and Tur and Hindukush would fit as walls in its rampart. Its canopy vies with the Crystalline sphere in its height. Its circumference is about three *farsangs* and the calculators are unable to count its battlements.

'Though the siege of the fort looked impossible, but by the grace of Almighty and with the secret help of the accomplished people, any direction that we have taken we have achieved there what we have wished; the very same day we inspected the surroundings of the fort carefully, and entrusted each place to one of the courageous servants (*Khans, Sultans* and *Amirs*) of the exalted court who were present. The mountain traversing warriors, who brave the fields of battle and seek *Jihad* with all their heart and soul and consider martyrdom to be the greatest reward in this as well as the other world, sought permission to take themselves to the towers and fortifications and putting their trust in Allah and relying on the divine help, which is the source of strength to the imperial authority, carry out brave assaults and bring the fort under control by force. Since those ignoble people had collected such large quantities of weapons for defending the fort like mortars (*deg*), *zarbzan*, cannon (*top*), matchlock (*tufang*), catapult (*manjaniq*), *jarr-i saqil*, naphtha (*naft*) and *nawak* that would last for thirty years even if continuously used, and since they had great confidence in these weapons and in the strength of the fort as well as their own prowess, we did not let them (the royal officers) fight with a view to protecting the people of Islam, may Allah preserve them till the day of resurrection, lest some of them may get killed in rashness. (We) sent for the dragon-like *rads* (cannon), mortars and other pieces of artillery which were left at the capital. We also ordered the manufacture of cannon and mountain-breaking mortars in the camp and decided that tunnels be dug and after the arrival of battering ram (*sarkob*) and *sabat* (covered passage) an attack be launched. We appointed some troops of the left wing to sack, kill and (take) captives the people of Udaipur, and the troops and men of Rana who were there while he himself was perched at a distance of ten *Kos*. We sent another army to plunder and sack Rampur. The troops returned with immense booty after despatching many of the worthless infidels to the abode of perdition. After the arrival of the artillery (*topkhana*), completion of the covered passage (*sabat*), explosion of the mines causing conflagration and (the consequent) blowing up of the towers and battlements, we directed the troops to establish themselves at the foot of the rampart and surround the fort from every side. The doomed ones (Rajputs) being fully informed this time of the strength and prowess of the army of Islam and the asperity and haughtiness of their ruler they started imploring for intercession and respite with abject submission and some of the chiefs came out (with this petition). Notwithstanding the fact that they had caused death of many people of Islam, both nobles and common soldiers, with matchlock-fire, continuous showering of stones through the *manjaniq*, they sued (for peace) on such impossible terms which could not be conceded. They were permitted to return. Next day we went in person to the *sabat* of Muhammad Qasim Khad, *mir-i bahr*, which was nearest to the fort and issued orders for *Jang-i Sultani* to be launched.

'The armies of Islam placing their reliance in (the revelation) "Allah is sufficient for us and most excellent protector",[138] fearlessly and boldly commenced the assault. Within (the fort) the vigilant bands of jew-like infidels set ablaze the fire of conflict and brawl by discharging fire-raining *manjaniqs* and cannon (*top*) one after the other. The lions of the forest of intrepidity and the panthers of the mountain of bravery, in their extreme courage stretched their coveting hands to the Sash of the Constellation Orion and with great expedition snatched the diadem from the head of Bahram.

'In conformity with the commandment, "And prepare against them what force you can,"[139] the troops excelled each other and with complete unity betook themselves to the towers and the walls of the fort that were breached by the artillery fire. From that multitude, groups like the pigs hit by arrows rushed out of doors and blocked the entry of the combatants. In return they (the royal troops) fought back by throwing arrows and stones and scattered those retreating ones (the Rajputs). They sent a tremor through the ranks of the enemy with incessant and frightful cannonade setting fire to the harvest of their lives.

'Three days and nights passed in this manner. The two sides did not stop fighting even for a moment. All the attempts of these fox-like people at fraud and deception were frustrated by the lions of the jungle of intrepidity. At last on the night of Tuesday, 25th of Shaban, 975 A.H. (23 February 1568) in conformity with "...they shall not be able to ward off the fire from their faces nor from their backs, nor shall they be helped"[140] the continuous rain of fiery balls and cannonade became so intense in conformity with "Nay,

---

[138]Ibid., 8.62.

[139]Ibid., 8.60.

[140]Ibid., 21.39.

it shall come on them all of a sudden and cause them to be confounded"[141] that those condemned ones were no longer able to resist. The call from beyond — "If ye help Allah, He will help you and will make your foothold firm"[142] — was coming to the exalted hearing and every moment the Divine Inspirer made audible the good tidings: "Now surely Allah's help is nigh."[143] The revengeful warriors and the brave ones skilled in the use of daggers, deadly set against the enemy and drenched in the blood, delivered concerted assault and succeeded in removing the wooden planks with which those accursed ones had blocked the breaches. Seeing this, Jaimal, one of the three chiefs, who had taken the lead in the battle and was looking after the fort from the beginning to the end advanced with a body of men to stop the breach. In the meanwhile some artillery men belonging to that wretched band fired their guns one after the other (and in their flashes) Jaimal, and those accompanying him could be seen (from afar). As for the last three days and nights we have been present there (battery of Qasim Khan) often firing with muskets and arrows and since it was destined for Jaimal that he should hasten to the lowest parts of hell at our own Allah-worshipping hands, when he came in view the matchlock (*tufang*) we were holding, was ready as is said, "When Allah wills any-thing, He provides its means." No sooner he was seen and the gun discharged then the worthless infidel was struck in forehead and hearing the call, "where so ever you may be, death will overtake you, even though you were in lofty towers,"[144] proceeded to the abode of perdition. This caused great consternation among the high and low of that cattle-like community. (Subsequently) the other chiefs continued to resist but they could not repulse the brave from the openings. At the dawn, the excellent archers whose skill is such that they could pierce the eye of an ant at dark night and the lancers who could pick up the

[141]Ibid., 21.40.
[142]Ibid., 47.7.
[143]Ibid., 2.214.
[144]Ibid., 4.78.

crumbs of the breach from the ground, putting the elephants in front delivered another assault. (They) forced their entry into the fort through sheer bravery and prowess and started discharging arrows and fighting with lances.

'The hand of destiny had covered the deceitful eyes of that erroneous, arrogant and scanty host with the nocturnal blindness of ill-luck "And they thought that there would be no affliction and so they became blind and deaf"[145] and had blocked upon them the way of success and escape in accordance with "They could neither go forward nor turn back."[146] The people of Islam were busy praying: "Our lord! bestow on us endurance, make our foothold sure, and give us help against the disbelieving folk,"[147] and the refreshing message — "Help from Allah and present Victory. Give good tidings to believers"[148] — was coming to them from heaven. They advanced in groups against the wicked unbelievers to get hold of the opening. (They) stood in the foremost rank without flinching and got an upper hand. They felled them (the Rajputs) one upon the other with the strokes of (their) blood-thirsty sword, leaving all around heaps of the slain. Pursuing the remnant who were fleeing in different directions — "As they were frightened asses, fleeing from the lion"[149] — despatched them to the lowest part of the hell — when the star of success and good fortune rose from the horizon of the sublime message, "Victory comes only by the help of Allah, the Mighty, the Wise"[150] the whole victorious troop entered the fort. In accordance with the imperative Command "And kill the idolators all together,"[151] those defiant ones who were still offering resistance having formed themselves into knots of two to three hundred persons, were put to death and their women and children taken prisoners. According

---

[145]Ibid., 5.71.
[146]Ibid., 36.67.
[147]Ibid., 2.250.
[148]Ibid., 61.13.
[149]Ibid., 74.50-51.
[150]Ibid., 8.10.
[151]Ibid., 9.36.

to the promise, "Allah promised you many acquisitions which you will take,"[152] immense booty and spoils in cash and kind were acquired. "So the roots of the people who were unjust were cut off; and all praise is due to Allah, the Lord of the worlds."[153]

'The receptacle of nobility, the support of kingdom, the pillar of the mighty state, the prop of the magnificent empire, the confidant of the resplendent *Khilafat*, the foremost among the great *Khans* of the age, the climber of the ladder of authority and dignity, the devoted and sincere and the well-wishing one, the intrepid cavalier, the adorner of the ranks in the field of valour and bravery, Mubarizuddin Mir Mohammad Khan Bahadur, and the receptacle of nobility, the support of kingdom, the pillar of the mighty state, the prop of the magnificent empire, the best among the sinceres of the age, worthy of confidence and favour, the rider of the field of battle and valour, Qutbuddin Mohammad Khan Bahadur and the rest of the great *Khans* and noble *Sultans* alongwith the *Saiyids, Ulama, Mashaikh*, the *Ghazis* of *Shariat* and other dignitaries, residents, inhabitants, *Chaudhris, Qanoongos*, the *ri'aya* and peasants (*muzari'an*) of Sarkar Punjab respectively, being jubilant at the happy tidings carried by this auspicious *Fathnama*, which is, in fact, a foretaste of the victories to follow, should offer infinite thanks-givings. They should also pray in the auspicious moments, when the prayers are more likely to be granted, for the long life of our noble self, the perpetuity of the empire and for the grant of greater competence to us for fulfilling obligation of *Jihad*, divine worship and acts of piety. Further they should continuously be expecting that day after day doors of fresh victories and successes will be opened before us.

'Whereas after the management of the affairs of Chitor we have turned the reins of our determination towards the capital Agra,

> The horse beneath the thigh and overhead canopy of victory,
> The victory and success keeping company and divine help guiding the way.

---

[152]Ibid., 48.20.
[153]Ibid., 6.45.

'Allah willing within these few day we will reach the seat of the *Khilafat*. The pillar of the state knowing that our thoughts are directed towards the management of his affairs and the fulfilment of the hopes and aspirations of all the well-wishers may send regular reports about the development (in his region). Any request that he might like to make should be communicated (to the court) so that it may be granted. Written by the royal order (to be obeyed permanently) at Ajmer on 10th of the month of Ramzan 975 A.H., 9 March 1568."[154]

AHMAD SHAH ABDALI (1757 and 1761 CE)

Jihād at Mathura and Vrindavan (1757 CE)

"But the Jat peasantry were determined that it was over their corpses that the ravager should enter the sacred capital of Braja. ...eight miles north of Mathurā, Jawāhir Singh barred the invader's path with less than 10,000 men and offered a desperate resistance (28th February, 1757). From sunrise the battle raged for nine hours, and at the end of it 'ten to twelve thousand infantry lay dead on the two sides taken together, the wounded were beyond count'...[155]

The Hindu Bethlehem now lay utterly prostrate before the invaders. Early at dawn on 1st March the Afghān cavalry burst into the unwalled and unsuspecting city of Mathurā, and neither by their master's orders nor from the severe handling they received in yesterday's fight, were they in a mood to show mercy. For four

---

[154]See also Abul Fazl, *Akbar Nāma*, translated into English by H. Beveridge, Volume I and II Bound in One, New Delhi reprint, 1993, pp. 441-46 and 464-80. It is significant that this despicable lickspittle of Akbar does not even mention the *Fathnama* cited above. But his use of words like "martyrs", "holy warriors", and "*ghāzis*" for the Islamic gangsters and extremely abusive language for the Rajput warriors, leaves no doubt that he also viewed the sack of Chittor as a *jihād*.

[155]Jadunath Sarkar, *Fall of the Mughal Empire*, Volume II, Fourth Edition, New Delhi, 1991, p. 69.

hours there was an indiscriminate massacre and rape of the unresisting Hindu population — all of them non-combatants and many of them priests... 'Idols were broken and kicked about like polo-balls by the Islamic heroes.' [*Husain Shahi,* 39.] Houses were demolished in search of plunder and then wantonly set on fire. Glutted with the blood of three thousand men, Sardār Jahān Khan laid a contribution of one lakh on what remained of the population and marched away from the smoking ruins the same night.

"After the tiger came the jackal. 'When after the massacre Ahmad Shāh's troops marched onward from Mathurā, Najib and his army remained there for three days, plundered much money and buried treasure, and carried off many beautiful females as captives.' [Nur, 15 *b*.] The blue waves of the Jamunā gave eternal repose to such of her daughters as could flee to her outstretched arms; some other happy women found a nearer escape from dishonour by death in their household wells. But for those of their sisters who survived there was no escape from a fate worse than death. A Muslim eyewitness thus describes the scene in the ruined city a fortnight later. 'Everywhere in the lanes and bazaars lay the headless trunks of the slain and the whole city was burning. Many buildings had been knocked down. The water of the Jamunā flowing past was of a yellowish colour, as if polluted by blood. The man [a Muslim jeweller of the city, robbed of his all and fasting for several days] said that for seven days following the general slaughter the water had turned yellow. *At the edge of the stream I saw a number of huts of vairāgis and sannyāsis* [*i.e., Hindu ascetic*], *in each of which lay a severed head with the head of a dead cow applied to its mouth and tied to it with a rope round its neck.*'

"Issuing from the ruins of Mathurā, Jahān Khan roamed the country round, and plundering everywhere as directed. Vrindāvan, seven miles north of Mathurā, could not escape, as its wealth was indicated by its many temples. Here another general massacre was practised upon the inoffensive monks of the most pacific order of Vishnu's worshippers (*c.* 6th March). As the same Muhammadan diarist records after a visit to Vrindāvan: 'Wherever you gazed you beheld heaps of the slain; you could only pick your way with difficulty, owing to the quantity of bodies lying about and the amount of blood spilt. *At one place that we reached we saw about two hundred dead children lying in a heap.* Not one of the dead bodies had a head... The stench and effluvium in the air were such that it was painful to open your mouth or even to draw breath.'

Abdali's attack on Gokul

"Moving a fortnight behind his vanguard, the Abdāli king himself came upon the scene. He had stormed Ballabhgarh on 3rd March and halted there for two days. On 15th March he arrived near Mathurā, and wisely avoiding that reeking human shambles crossed over to the eastern bank of the Jamuna and encamped at Mahāvan, six miles south-east of the city. Two miles to his west lay Gokul, the seat of the pontiff of the rich Vallabhācharya sect. The Abdāli's policy of frightfulness had defeated his cupidity: dead men could not be held to ransom. The invader's unsatisfied need of money was pressing him; he sought the help of Imād's local knowledge as to the most promising sources of booty. A detachment from his camp was sent to plunder Gokul. But here the monks were martial Nāgā *sannyāsis* of upper India and Rajputāna. Four thousand of these naked ash-smeared warriors stood outside Gokul and fought the Afghāns, till half of their own number was killed after slaying an equal force of the enemy. Then at the entreaty of the Bengal *subahdār's* envoy (Jugalkishor) and his assurance that a hermitage of *faqirs* could not contain any money, the Abdāli recalled the detachment. 'All the *vairāgis* perished but Gokulnath [the deity of the city] was saved', as a Marāthi newsletter puts it." [Rajwade, i. 63.][156]

Describing Afghan atrocities at this time, Munshi Sadāsukh Dehlawī wrote, "I have myself seen the depredations of the Afghans round Dehli and Mattra. God defend us from them! It

---

[156]Ibid., pp. 70-71. Emphasis added.

makes the very hair of the body stand on end to think of them. Two hundred thousand men were destroyed in these massacres, and the hordes of the enemy were without number. *Such atrocities, forsooth, were perpetrated in compliance with their religion and law! What cared they for the religion, the law, the honour and reputation of the innocent sufferers? It was enough for such bigots that splendour accrued by their deeds to the faith of Muhammad and 'Ali!*"[157]

Jihād at Panipat (1761 CE)

"Next morning the sun revealed a horrid spectacle on the vast plain south of Pānipat. On the actual field of the combat thirty-one distinct heaps of the slain were counted, the number of bodies in each ranging from 500 upwards to 1000 and in four up to 1500 — a rough total of 28,000. In addition to these, the ditch round the ᵼ Marātha camp was full of dead bodies, partly the victims of disease and famine during the long siege and partly wounded men who had crawled out of the fighting to die there. West and south of Pānipat city, the jungle and the road in the line of Marātha retreat were littered with the remains of those who had fallen unresisting in the relentless Durrāni pursuit or from hunger and exhaustion. Their number — probably three-fourths non-combatants and one-fourth soldiers — could not have been far short of the vast total of those slain in the battlefield. 'The hundreds who lay down wounded, perished from the severity of the cold.'

"*After the havoc of combat followed massacre in cold blood.* Several hundreds of Marāthas had hidden themselves in the hostile city of Pānipat through folly or helplessness; and these were hunted out next day and put to the sword. According to one plausible account, the sons of Abdus Samad Khan and Mian Qutb received the Durrāni king's permission to avenge their father's death by an indiscriminate massacre of the Marāthas for one day,

---

[157]*Muntakhāb-ut-Tawārīkh*, translated in Elliot and Dowson, Volume VIII, pp. 405-06. Emphasis added.

and in this way nearly nine thousand men perished [*Bhau Bakhar*, 123.]; these were evidently non-combatants. The eyewitness Kashiraj Pandit thus describes the scene: '*Every Durrāni soldier brought away a hundred or two of prisoners and slew them in the outskirts of their camp, crying out, When I started from our country, my mother, father, sister and wife told me to slay so may kāfirs for their sake after we had gained the victory in this holy war, so that the religious merit of this act [of infidel slaying] might accrue to them.* In this way, thousands of soldiers and other persons were massacred. In the Shāh's camp, except the quarters of himself and his nobles, every tent had a heap of severed heads before it. One may say that it was verily doomsday for the Marātha people.'

Spoils of the Victors

'"The booty captured within the entrenchment was beyond calculation and the regiments of Khans [i.e. 8000 troopers of Abdāli clansmen] did not, as far as possible, allow other troops like the Irānis and the Turānis to share in the plunder; they took possession of everything themselves, but sold to the Indian soldiers handsome Brahman women for one *tuman* and good horses for two *tumans* each.' [Nur, 50 *b*.] The Deccani prisoners, male and female reduced to slavery by the victorious army numbered 22,000, many of them being the sons and other relatives of the *sardārs* or middle class men. Among them 'rose-limbed slave girls' are mentioned... Besides these 22,000 unhappy captives, some four hundred officers and 6000 men fled for refuge to Shujā-ud-daulah's camp, and were sent back to the Deccan with monetary help by that nawab, at the request of his Hindu officers. The total loss of the Marāthas after the battle is put at 50,000 horses, captured either by the Afghān army or the villagers along the route of flight, two hundred thousand draught cattle, some thousands of camels, five hundred elephants, besides cash and jewellery. 'Every trooper of the Shāh brought away ten, and some-times twenty camels laden with money. The captured horses were beyond count but none of them was of value; they came like droves of sheep in their thousands.'"[158]

The Key is held by the Quran

The *mujāhids* who mounted the various *jihāds* in India lived in different centuries — from the first quarter of the 8th to the second half of the 16th (CE).

They belonged to different races and came from different countries — Arabia, Turkistan, Iran, Afghanistan, India (in case of Hindu converts to Islam).

They spoke different languages — Arabic, Turkish, Persian, Pushto.

Yet, they used the same self-righteous language for the Hindus, and enacted similar sanguinary scenes.

Again, the Muslim historians, who described these *jihāds* with abundant admiration, also functioned at different times and places. They wrote in two different languages — the earlier ones in Arabic and the later ones in Persian. Babur wrote in Turkish.

Yet, their accounts follow the same pattern. The accounts read as if the historians have only filled the blanks in a prescribed proforma. Or, to change the metaphor, the different stories read like varied scripts of the same drama staged by different directors. Only the *dramatis personae* change from performance to performance.

How do we account for this repetition of the repertoire?

The key is held by the Quran. That is the only thing which all *mujāhids* and their historians, have shared in common.

The same logic leads to another and a very ominous conclusion. *Jihād* cannot be regarded as something which happened only in the past. On the contrary, it is an ever-present possibility in India. The Quran will create a *jihād* whenever and wherever the "infidels" provide an opportunity. Pious Muslims in every place and at all times, are taught to see, or seek, or provoke situations in which solutions prescribed by the Quran can be practised.

---

[158]*Fall of the Mughal Empire*, op. cit., Volume II, pp. 210-11. Emphasis added.

Chapter 7

Doctrine of the Islamic State

The doctrine of *jihād,* which is the whole of the Quran, deals primarily with the performance of the militarized Muslim Ummah till the time an "infidel land" is conquered and Muslim hold is consolidated over it by terrorising its people through slaughter and pillage. The operations of the same military machine after the conquest are dealt with by another department of Islamic theology — doctrine of the Islamic state. A very clear exposition of this doctrine is provided by Professor Jadunath Sarkar who had spent a life-time in studying the theology and history of Islam. We reproduce below what he stated in 1928. Once again we have replaced the word "God" by the word "Allah".

Islamic State is an Agency for Spreading the Faith

"By the theory of its origin the Muslim State is a theocracy. Its true king is Allah, and earthly rulers are merely His agents, bound to enforce His law on all. Civil Law is completely subordinated to Religious Law and, indeed, merges its existence in the latter. The civil authorities exist solely to spread and enforce the true faith. In such a State, infidelity is logically equivalent to treason, because the infidel repudiates the authority of the true king and pays homage to His rivals, the false gods and goddesses. All the resources of the State, all the forces under the political authorities, are in strict legality at the disposal of the missionary propaganda of the true faith.

Tolerance towards Infidels is Tantamount to Sin

"Therefore, the toleration of any sect outside the fold of orthodox Islam is no better than compounding with sin. And the worst form of sin is polytheism, the belief that the one true Allah has partners in the form of other deities. Such a belief is the rankest ingratitude (*kufr*) to him who gives us our life and daily bread...

"The conversion of the entire population to Islam and the extinction of every form of dissent, is the ideal of the Muslim State. If any infidel is suffered to exist in the community, it is as a necessary evil, and for a transitional period only. Political and social disabilities must be imposed on him, bribes offered to him from the public funds to hasten the day of his spiritual enlighten-ment and the addition of his name to the roll of true believers. The growth of the infidel population in number or wealth would, therefore, defeat the very end of the State...

Status of Non-Muslims in an Islamic State

"A non-Muslim, therefore, cannot be a citizen of the State; he is a member of a depressed class; his status is a modified form of slavery. He lives under a contract (*zimma*) with the State: for the life and property that are grudgingly spared to him by the Commander of the Faithful. He must undergo political and social disabilities, and pay commutation-money (*jaziya*). In short, his continued existence in the State after the conquest of his country by the Muslims is conditional upon his person and property being made subservient to the cause of Islam.

"He must pay a tax for his land (*kharaj*), from which the early Muslims were exempt; he must pay other exactions for the maintenance of the army, in which he cannot enlist even if he offers to render personal service instead of paying the poll-tax;

and he must show by humility of dress and behaviour that he belongs to a subject class. No non-Muslim (*zimmi*) can wear fine dresses, ride on horseback or carry arms; he must behave respectfully and submissively to every member of the dominant sect...

"In addition to the poll-tax and public degradation in dress and demeanour imposed on them, the non-Muslims were subjected to various hopes and fears. Rewards in the form of money and public employment were offered to apostates from Hinduism. The leaders of Hindu religion and society were systematically repressed, to deprive the sect of spiritual instruction, and their religious gatherings and processions were forbidden in order to prevent the growth of solidity and a sense of communal strength among them. No new temple was allowed to be built nor any old one to be repaired, so that the total disappearance of all places of Hindu worship was to be merely a question of time. But even this delay, this slow operation of Time, was intolerable to many of the more fiery spirits of Islam, who tried to hasten the abolition of 'infidelity' by anticipating the destructive hand of Time and forcibly pulling down temples."[1]

Earlier Conclusions Confirmed

Professor Jadunath Sarkar confirmed his earlier conclusions after a further and deeper study of Islam. In an article published in the 1950 Pooja Number of the *Hindustan Standard*, Calcutta, he observed:

"The poison lay in the very core of Islamic theocracy. Under it there can be only one faith, one people and one all overriding authority. The State is a religious trust administered solely by His people (the faithful) acting in obedience to the Commander of the Faithful, who was in theory, and very often in practice too, the supreme General of the Army of militant Islam (*Janud*). There could be no place for non-believers. Even Jews and Christians

---

[1] Jadunath Sarkar, *History of Aurangzib*, Volume III, Calcutta, 1928, pp. 164-67.

could not be full citizens of it, though they somewhat approached the Muslims by reason of their being 'People of the Book' or believers in the Bible, which the Prophet of Islam accepted as revealed.

"As for the Hindus and Zoroastrians, they had no place in such a political system. If their existence was tolerated, it was only to use them as hewers of wood and drawers of water, as tax-payers, '*Khiraj-guzar*', for the benefit of the dominant sect of the Faithful. They were called *Zimmis* or people under a contract of protection by the Muslim State on condition of certain services to be rendered by them and certain political and civil disabilities to be borne by them to prevent them from growing strong. The very term *Zimmi* is an insulting title. It connotes political inferiority and helplessness like the status of a minor proprietor perpetually under a guardian; such protected people could not claim equality with the citizens of the Muslim theocracy.

"The *Zimmi* is under certain legal disabilities with regard to testimony in law courts, protection under criminal law, and marriage. The State, as the other party in the contract (*zimma*), guarantees to him security of life and property and a modified protection in the exercise of his religion: he cannot erect new temples, and has to avoid any offensive publicity in the exercise of his faith. But everything short of open physical persecution, — everything that would not be a flagrant breach of the contract of protection, can be legitimately practised by the Muslim ruler to reduce the number of the undesirable alien sect...

"*Thus by the basic conception of the Muslim State all non-Muslims are its enemies, and it is in the interest of the State to curb their growth in number and power. The ideal aim was to exterminate them totally*, as Hindus, Zoroastrians and Christian nationals have been liquidated (sometimes totally, sometimes leaving a negligible remnant behind) in Afghanistan, Persia and the Near East."[2]

---

[2]Cited in R.C. Majumdar (ed.), *The History of the Indian People and Culture*, Volume VI, *The Delhi Sultanate*, Bombay, 1960, pp. 617-18. Emphasis added.

Hindus should be grateful to Imam Hanifa

Hindus should be grateful to Imam Hanifa for some mercy shown to them. He had recommended that Hindus, though idolaters, could be accepted as a "People of the Book" like the Jews, the Christians and the Zoroastrians, and granted the status of *zimmis*. The Muslim swordsmen and theologians in India happened to follow his school of Islamic law. That enabled them to "upgrade" the "crow-faced infidels"[3] of this country to the status of *zimmis*. Hindus could save their lives and some of their properties, though not their honour and places of worship and pilgrimage, by paying *jizyah* and agreeing to live under highly discriminative disabilities. The only choice which the other great Imams of Islam — Mālik, Shāfii and Hanbal — gave to the Hindus was between Islam and death.

Alauddin Khilji had consulted the most learned Maulana of his realm — Qazi Mughis-ud-din of Bayana — on this point. The Qazi pronounced the correct position as follows: "The Hindus are designated in the law as 'payers of tribute' (*kharaj-guzar*); and when the revenue officer demands silver from them, they should, without question and with all humility and respect, tender gold. If the officer throws dirt into their mouths, they must without reluctance open their mouths wide to receive it. By these acts of degradation are shown the extreme obedience of the *zimmi*, the glorification of the true faith of Islam, and the abasement of false faiths. Allah himself orders them to be humiliated, as He says, 'till they pay (*jaziya*) with the hand and are humbled.' ... *The Prophet has commanded us to slay them, plunder them and make them captive.* No other religious authority except the great Imam (Hanifa) whose faith we follow, has sanctioned the imposition of the *jaziya* on Hindus. According to all other theologians, the rule for Hindus is 'Either death or Islam'."[4]

---

[3]A term which Amir Khusru frequently used for Hindus.
[4]Cited in Jadunath Sarkar, *History of Aurangzib*, Volume III, Calcutta, 1928, p. 166. Emphasis addded.

Imam Hanifa criticized by Amir Khusru

Amir Khusru was a contemporary of Qazi Mughis-ud-din. He is presented by the "modern" Muslims and lionised by the "educated" Hindus as the "pioneer of secularism in India". He had, however, something very specific to say on the status of Hindus vis-à-vis the Islamic state. "Happy Hindūstān", he wrote, "the splendour of Religion, where the Law finds perfect honour and security. In learning Dehli can now compete with Bokhārā, for Islām has been made manifest by its kings. The whole country, by means of the sword of our holy warriors, has become like a forest denuded of its thorns by fire. The land has been saturated with the water of the sword, and the vapours of infidelity have been dispersed. The strong men of Hind have been trodden under foot, and all are ready to pay tribute. Islām is triumphant, idolatry is subdued. *Had not the law* [of Imam Hanifa] *granted exemption from death by the payment of poll-tax, the very name of Hind, root and branch, would have been extinguished.* From Ghaznī to the shore of the ocean you see all under the domination of Islām. Cawing crows[5] see no arrows pointed at them; nor is the *Tarsā* (Christian) there, who does not fear *(taras)* to render the servant equal with Allah; nor the Jew who dares to exalt the Pentateuch to a level with the Kurān; nor the *Magh* who is delighted with the worship of fire, but of whom the fire complains with its hundred tongues. The four sects of Musulmāns are at amity and the very fish are Sunnīs."[6]

It has to be remembered that Amir Khusru was one of the foremost disciples of Nizam-ud-din Awliya of Delhi who is counted among the five great sufis of the Chishtiyya school. He is himself regarded as an outstanding sufi on whose *mazār* in Delhi *urs* is held every year. His Hindi verses are cited as a proof positive of his love for the land of his birth. But what the Amir

---

[5]Another term of contempt used by Amir Khusru for Hindus.

[6]*Ashiqā* of Amir Khusru, translated in Elliot and Dowson, Volume III, pp. 545-46. Emphasis added.

says about Hindustan and Hindus speaks volumes about sufis and Sufism. The few "educated" Hindus who admit that Prophetic Islam is "somewhat fanatic", believe that Sufistic Islam is "large-hearted and liberal". The Chishtiyya school of Sufism in particular is supposed to have "built bridges between the two communities".

True Face of Sufism

But the evidence that is available points towards a contrary conclusion. The Chishtiyya school was foisted on India by Muin-ud-din who had settled down in Ajmer before the Second Battle of Tarain. According to the sufi lore, he had made a few converts from among the local Hindus and started issuing orders to Prithivi Raj Chauhan, the Hindu king, for the benefit of these converts. When the king ignored him, he invited Muhammad Ghuri to invade the Chauhan Kingdom. *Sir-ul-Awliya*, the most famous history of the Chishtiyya school written by Khwaja Amir Khurd, another disciple of Nizam-ud-din Awliya, tells the following story: "His [Muin-ud-din's] blessed tongue uttered spontaneously, 'We have handed over Pithora alive to the army of Islam.' In those very days, Sultan Muiz-ud-din Sam arrived in Ajmer from Ghazni. Pithora had to face the army of Islam. He was captured alive by Sultan Muiz-ud-din... The Khwaja [Muinud-din] was a worker of great wonders. Before he reached Hindustan, all its cities right upto the point of sunrise were sunk in tumult and infidelity and were involved with idols and idolatry. Everyone among the rabble [Gods] of Hindustan claimed to be the great God and a co-sharer in the divinity of Allah. The people paid homage to stones, sods of clay, trees, quadrupeds, cows and bulls and their dung. The darkness of infidelism had made still more firm the seals on their hearts... Muin-ud-din was indeed the very sun of the true faith. As a result of his arrival, the darkness that had spread over this country was dispelled. It became bright and glowed in the light of Islam... Anyone who has become a Musalman in this country will stay a Musalman till the Day of Dissolution. His progeny will also remain Musalman... The people [of Hindustan] will be brought out of *dār-ul-harb* into *dār-ul-Islām* by means of many wars."[7] There is plenty of primary literature available in Arabic and Persian regarding the rise, development, and doings of numerous sufi *silsilas* in India. Some of this literature has been translated into Urdu and English as well. A study of this literature leaves little doubt that sufis were the most fanatic and fundamentalist elements in the Islamic establishment in medieval times. Hindus should go to this literature rather than fall for latter-day Islamic propaganda. The ruin of Hindus and Hinduism in Kashmir in particular, can be safely credited to sufis who functioned there from the early thirteenth century onwards.

---

[7]Amir Khurd, *Siyar-ul-Awliya*, New Delhi, 1985, pp. 111-12. The passage cited has been translated from the Urdu version. Saiyid Athar Abbas Rizvi has presented a lot of primary material on Sufism in his *A History of Sufism in India*, New Delhi, Volume I, 1978 and Volume II, 1983

Chapter 8

Muslim *Ummah* is a Military Machine

The teeming tomes on orthodox Islamic theology devote plenty of space to non-warlike subjects, such as faith, purification, prayers, alms, fasting, pilgrimage, marriage, divorce, business transactions, inheritance, gifts, bequests, vows, oaths, crime, punishment, government, hunting, food, drink, dress, decoration, greetings, magic, poetry, visions, dreams, virtue, last day, repentance, etc. But the rules laid down for every Muslim, everywhere and at all times, are the same. In the final analysis this uniform pattern of belief and behaviour erases the individual in man and turns him into a member of a close-knit collective, the *Ummah*.

The *Ummah*, however, acquires an altogether new colour when juxtaposed with *jihād*, on which subject also the tomes wax no less eloquent. It looks too much like a military machine to pass as a peaceful society. The rules laid down by the Shariat read like a manual compiled for use in military barracks — waking up every morning to the call of a bugle, rolling up the bed, sweeping the floor, pressing the uniform, polishing the shoes, rushing for a bath, moving the body in different ways in mass drills, sharing meals in the mess-hall, drinking from a common canteen and, finally, facing the court martial for mistakes made in any part. One is amazed as well as amused when this mechanical conformity to a set pattern of external exercises is presented by the spokesmen of Islam as the very essence of universal spirituality and morality.

Prayers of Military Parade?

D.S. Margoliouth cites several early Muslim sources regarding what the Muslim ranks looked like on the eve of the Battle of Badr: "Of the battle that followed we have no clear or detailed account: but we know at least some of the factors which brought about the result. The discipline of the *salat* or 'prayer', in which the Moslems were arranged in rows, and had to perform after a leader certain bodily exercises, and falling out of line was threatened with divine punishment, had served as a rough sort of drill, and Mohammed before the battle discharged the duty of making the troops fall into line. The Meccan general 'Utbah, son of Rabiah, was struck with their appearance; they were keeling on their knees, silent as though they were dumb, and stretching out their tongues like snakes. They were all subject to the single will of their Prophet, who was aware that the general should not risk his life; for him therefore in the rear of the army a hut was built, where attended by his most trusted counsellors, he could issue orders; and to which camels were tied ready to be used by the leaders for flight in case of disaster."[1]

Observations of Count Keyserling

This militarization of everyday Muslim life was noticed with keen interest by Count Keyserling (1880-1946 CE) during his travels in Islamic countries. He summed up his over-all impression in his *The Travel Diary of a Philosopher.* "Islam is a religion," he wrote, "of absolute surrender and submissiveness to God — but to a God of a certain character — a War-Lord who is entitled to do with us as he will and who bids us stand ever in line of battle against the foe... The ritual of this belief embodies the idea of

---

[1]*Mohammed and the Rise of Islam,* op. cit., pp. 258-59. He also says that the Pagan Arabs, on the other hand, "were unacquainted with the rudiments of military science", that they "fought in no order, with no leadership", and that "of the hundred or more technical terms which the warfare of Islam evolved, the Arabs of the Ignorance had no knowledge" (Ibid., pp. 259-60).

discipline. When the true believers every day at fixed hours perform their prayers in serried ranks in the mosque, all going through the same gestures at the same moment, this is not, as in Hinduism, done as a method of self-realization, but in the spirit in which the Prussian soldier defiled before his Kaiser. This military basis of Islam explains all the essential virtues of the Musalman. It also explains his fundamental defects — his unprogressiveness, his incapacity to adapt himself, his lack of invention. The soldier has simply to obey orders. All the rest is the affair of Allah."[2]

Congregational or Friday Prayers

"In the early days of Islam", writes Professor K.S. Lal, "the main features of the Friday service were prayers in congregation with worshippers standing in straight linear rows. Attendance was compulsory and military discipline was maintained. The sermon was like the order of the day; it comprised advice, reprimand and directions on religious and political obligations of the faithful. A sense of awe pervaded — raising the number of worshippers..."[3] Small wonder that great importance is attached to congregational or Friday prayers in Islam. "The *ahadis* declare that namaz said in congregation is twenty-five times superior to namaz said alone at home. Muhammad was very strict about attendance in congregational prayer."[4] The Prophet is reported to have said that he felt like burning down the houses of those who did not attend the Friday prayers. In the history of Islam in India, Friday "sermons result in working up the feelings of the *namazis*, and sabre-rattling and street riots generally take place on Friday after the afternoon prayers".[5]

---

[2]Cited by Jadunath Sarkar, *History of Aurangzib*, Volume III, Calcutta, 1928, p. 171.
[3]*Theory and Practice of Muslim State in India*, op. cit., pp. 83-84.
[4]Ibid., p. 82.
[5]Ibid., p. 93.

Islam divides the Human Family

The picture becomes perfectly clear when we contemplate the thought-categories which form the very foundations of Islamic theology. The thought-categories are derived from the Quran which the theologians quote at every turn and on every subject. Islamic theology divides the human family into two incompatible factions. There are the *mu'mins* (believers) on the one hand. They are Allah's favourites to whom he has promised victory in this world and paradise hereafter. On the other hand, there are the *kāfirs* (unbelievers) whose lives, liberties, properties and honour Allah has forfeited in favour of the faithful. *Mu'mins* can have a clean conscience when they slaughter and plunder and enslave the *kāfirs* by every means and in every way. They are only fulfilling Allah's inexorable Will.

Islam polarises the Inhabited World

The same theology divides the inhabited world into two irreconcilable camps. On the one hand, there is the *dār-ul-Islām,* the lands held by Muslims where the Shariat rules. This is the base from which the *mu'mins* operate. On the other hand, there is the *dār-ul-harb,* the lands in which *kāfirs* live and which the *mu'mins* should subject to non-stop war. The *mu'mins* should spare neither their persons nor their properties in the effort to convert every *dār-ul-harb* into a *dār-ul-Islām.*

Islam bifurcates Human History

Again, Islamic theology bifurcates human history into two sharply defined periods. The period before the proclamation of Muhammad's prophethood is the Age of Ignorance (*jāhiliya*), and the period that follows is the Age of Illumination (*ilm*). Everything that prevailed in the Age of Ignorance is to be destroyed outright or to be converted in such a manner that it looks as if it came into existence after the dawn of the Age of Illumination. The norms of ignorance and illumination are determined not by any objective or comparative criteria, but by dictums of the Quran and Hadis.

Believers are Better Human Beings

It is nowhere stated in Islamic theology that the *mu'mins* have to be better human beings in terms of mind or morals. They have only to swear by a certain phantom named Allah and a certain historical person called Rasūl (prophet), and they become qualified to kill all those who refuse to swear in the same manner. They are exempted from prayers, fasting, pilgrimage and the rest and all their sins and crimes stand pardoned, if they engage themselves in killing the *kāfirs*.

Islam incompatible with Peace

Mahatma Gandhi was no specialist of Islamic theology. He accepted the modern Muslim apologist's interpretation that Islam means peace. But he saw no sign of Muslim adherence to this interpretation. "Islam was born," he observed, "in an environment where the sword was and still remains the supreme law... The sword is yet too much in evidence among Mussalmans. It must be sheathed if Islam is to be what it means — peace."[6]

Professor Jadunath Sarkar, on the other hand, had devoted a life-time to the study of Islam in theory and practice. He could not avoid reaching a very grim conclusion. "The murder of infidels (*kafir-kushi*)," he wrote, "is counted a merit in a Muslim. It is not necessary that he should tame his own passions or mortify his flesh; it is not necessary for him to grow a rich growth of spirituality. He has only to slay a certain class of his fellow beings or plunder their lands and wealth, and this act in itself would raise his soul to heaven. A religion whose followers are taught to regard robbery and murder as a religious duty, is incompatible with the progress of mankind or with the peace of the world."[7]

If the aforesaid authorities on Islam, including the great savant and historian from Bengal, had been brought to the notice of Justice Basak before he pronounced that the Quran "is not prejudicial to the maintenance of harmony between different religions" and that "Because of the Quran no public tranquility has been disturbed upto now and there is no reason to apprehend any likelihood of such disturbance in future", his verdict might well have been different. The whole history of Islam, particularly in India, runs counter to this pronouncement. The people of Bengal know it in their bones what the Quran stands for. The stream of refugees from Bangladesh (erstwhile East Pakistan) has not yet ceased to flow.

---

[7]Jadunath Sarkar, *History of Aurangzib*, Calcutta, 1928, Volume III, pp. 168-69.

Chapter 9

The Petition has served a Great Purpose

By filing the Writ Petition for a ban on the Quran, Chandmal Chopra has invited attention to a subject which Hindus have neglected for long and at great cost to themselves. They have yet to examine critically the claim of the Quran as a sacred scripture and of Islam as a religion. If Hindus now take up this study in all seriousness and educate themselves about the character of Islam, the Petition will have served its purpose.

Mahatma Gandhi on Hindu Psychology

The panic shown by the State and Union governments in the face of violent Muslim mobs, points towards a psychology from which Hindus have yet to free themselves. "The thirteen hundred years of imperialistic expansion," wrote Mahatma Gandhi, "has made the Mussalmans fighters as a class. They are, therefore, aggressive. Bullying is the natural excrescence of an aggressive spirit. The Hindu has an age-old civilization. He is essentially non-violent... Predominance of the non-violent spirit has restricted the use of arms to a small minority; not knowing their [arms'] use nor having an aptitude for them, they [Hindus] have become docile to the point of timidity or cowardice."[1]

---

[1]*Young India*, 30 December 1927.

He was convinced that Muslims will not stop being bullies so long as Hindus continue to be cowards. He saw no hope for a healthy relationship between the two communities till this imbalance was corrected. "But my own experience," he observed "confirms the opinion that the Mussalman as a rule is a bully and the Hindu as a rule is a coward... If the Hindus wish to convert the Mussalman bully into a respecting friend, they have to learn to die in the face of the heaviest odds... Hindus must cease to fear the Mussalman bully."[2]

How the Quran became a "Holy Book" for Hindus

The story of how Hindus came to accept the Quran as a "holy book" is long and painful. There are very few Hindus now who know the story. Generation after generation of Hindus has been brainwashed by slogans of secularism and *sarva-dharma-samabhāva* to believe that they have always revered the Quran, and accepted Islam as a *dharma*.

But history is a witness that during the centuries of Islamic invasions and rule, Hindus hated Islam as barbarism and fought the Muslim marauders tooth and nail. They had, however, also to live for several centuries as terrorized subjects of Islamic military states which ruled in most parts of India at one time or the other. Under the Islamic "law" that prevailed, it was a crime punishable with death to question the final prophethood of Muhammad, the divinity of the Quran, and the monopoly of Islam as a religion. Medieval Muslim historians have mentioned in passing some prominent instances of Hindus attracting the supreme penalty for committing one or the other of these "crimes". Many more cases must have remained unmentioned. Small wonder that Hindus under Muslim domination, had to pretend all the time that they harboured nothing but the highest sentiments for the Quran. Pretension tended to become belief as it was passed down by one generation to another.

---

[2]Ibid., 5 June 1924.

Pioneering Work of Swami Dayananda

Some Hindus did try to have a close look at the Quran when the nightmare of Muslim rule was over. The pride of place in this respect goes to Swami Dayananda, the founder of the Arya Samaj. He tore through the theology of the Quran and brought up to the surface the criminal psychology camouflaged by it. At the same time, he made an appeal to the Muslims to reflect upon how they would feel if the *kāfirs* started doing to them what the Quran has prescribed for the *kāfirs*. Some subsequent scholars of the Arya Samaj followed the lead given by Swamiji and did commendable work. Hindus started waking up and wondering whether the Quran was at all worthy of the reverence expected from them.

Political Expediency triumphs over Truth

But it proved to be a passing phase. The leaders of the Freedom Movement against British rule which was surging forward and which aroused emotions deeper than the "controversy about the Quran", were eager to draw the "Muslim minority" into the national struggle in order to be in a better position to bargain with the British. They thought they could win over the Muslims by praising the Prophet, by holding up the Quran as a holy book, by espousing Pan-Islamic causes, and by looking the other way when faced with facts of history. Starting with the Swadeshi Movement in Bengal, this flattering of Muslims by praising Islam culminated in Mahatma Gandhi's *sarva-dharma-samabhāva* — the opiate which lulled the Hindus into a deep slumber such as they had never known vis-à-vis Muslim aggression.

Some national leaders even made a bold bid to revise medieval Indian history. Muslim heroes were presented as national heroes. On the other hand, Hindu heroes who had fought against Islamic imperialism were "cut to size". Lala Lajpat Rai propagated the proposition that "the Hindus and Muslims have coalesced into an Indian people, very much the same way as the Angles, Saxons,

Danes and Normans formed the English people of to-day" and that "the Muslim rule in India was not a foreign rule."[3] These were leaders of great stature. They had made great sacrifices. Their words carried a weight which specialists of the subject like Professor Jadunath Sarkar could not command. Thus the atmosphere became highly discouraging for any serious and comparative study of religions. On the other hand, puerile nonsense like the *Essential Unity of All Religions* by Dr. Bhagwan Das became very popular. Anyone who questioned the pious proposition that the Quran was as good as the Vedas and the Puranas, ran the risk of being nailed down as an "enemy of communal harmony". There were quite a few casualties in the public life of India caused by this euphoria for the Quran.

Blinded by the Make-Beliefs

The experiment was a stupendous failure as it was bound to be, based as it was on no more than mere make-beliefs. Every concession made to the "Muslim minority" helped only to whet its appetite for more. It staged street riots whenever the "Hindu majority" showed some resistance to its mounting demands. In the event, it opted for a separate nationhood and established another Islamic state on the soil of India.

But instead of laying the blame where it really belonged, the political leadership blamed British imperialism for creating the "communal divide" and "Hindu communalism" for "deepening the crisis" which culminated in Partition. This Big Lie was sold on a large scale after independence when political power passed into the hands of self-alienated Hindus who paraded themselves as "progressive", "leftist", "revolutionary" etc., and who harboured an incurable animus against everything native and national. Once again, the Quran came out quite unscathed.

---

[3]Cited by R.C. Majumdar (ed.), *The History and Culture of the Indian People*, Preface to Volume VII, *The Mughal Empire*, Bombay, 1974, p. xii.

Muslims start the Game Again

That part of the "Muslim minority" which had voted for Pakistan but had chosen to stay in India, restarted the old game when India was proclaimed a secular state pledged to freedom of propagation for all religions. It revived its tried and tested trick of masquerading as a "poor and persecuted minority". It cooked up any number of Pirpur Reports.[4] The wail went up that the "lives, liberties and honour of the Muslims were not safe" in India, in spite of India's "secular pretensions". At the same time, street riots were staged on every possible pretext. The "communal situation" started becoming critical once again.

History to be Re-written

And once again, the political leadership came out with a make-belief. The big-wigs from all political parties were collected in a "National Integration Council". It was pointed out by the leftist professors that the major cause of "communal trouble" was the "bad habit" of living in the past on the part of "our people". Most of the politicians knew no history and no religion for that matter. They all agreed with one voice that Indian history, particularly that of the "medieval Muslim period", should be re-written. That, they pleaded, was the royal road to "national integration".

Muslim History is the best Commentary on the Quran

Hindus who had suffered from the Islamic onslaught in medieval times had written no history of what they went through. It was only the medieval Muslim historians who had preserved with meticulous care and great glee the record of what the *ghāzis*

---

[4]A report prepared by the Muslim League in 1938 listing "atrocities heaped on Muslims" by the Congress Ministries which ruled in seven Province from 1937, onwards.

had done to the *kāfirs* and *mushriks*, again and again. Historians like Zia-ud-din Barani[5] believed that the treatment meted out to the Hindus by the Muslim swordsmen was a part the divine plan which was unfolding according to promises Allah had made in the Quran. Thus the best and the most honest commentaries which the Hindus could read on the Quran, were the histories written by medieval Muslim historians.

A determined effort was now launched by Stalinist professors, particularly of the Jawaharlal Nehru University (JNU) in New Delhi, to keep away these commentaries from the Hindus. Muslim historians, particularly of the Aligarh school, came forward to lend whole-hearted cooperation. If the Quran could be divorced from the history it had created in the past, it could retain intact the hallow which Hindus accorded to it in the present. Professional historians in most places fell into line. It was too bad to become known as a "Hindus communalist" in the All India History Congress which had, meanwhile, been captured by the Stalinist and Muslim "historians".

Warning from a Veteran Historian

The only voice which was heard against this nation-wide exercise in *suppressio veri suggestio falsi* in the field of medieval Indian history, was that of the veteran historian, R.C. Majumdar. For him, this "national integration" based on a wilful blindness to recorded history of the havoc wrought by Islam in India, could lead only to national suicide. He tried his best to arrest the trend by presenting Islamic imperialism in medieval India as it was, and not as the politicians in league with Stalinist and Muslim historians were tailoring it to become.

"Political necessities of the Indians during the last phase of British rule," he wrote in 1960, "underlined the importance of alliance between the two communities, and this was sought to be

---

[5]Another disciple and contemporary of Nizam-ud-din Awliya.

smoothly brought about by glossing over the differences and creating an imaginary history of the past in order to depict the relations between the two in a much more favourable light than it actually was. Eminent Hindu political leaders even went so far as to proclaim that the Hindus were not at all a subject race during the Muslim rule. These absurd notions, which would have been laughed at by Indian leaders at the beginning of the nineteenth century, passed current as history owing to the exigencies of the political complications at the end of that century. Unfortunately slogans and beliefs die hard, and even today, for more or less the same reasons as before, many Indians, specially Hindus, are peculiarly sensitive to any comments or observations even made in course of historical writings, touching upon the communal relations in any way. *A fear of wounding the susceptibilities of the sister community haunts the minds of Hindu politicians and historians, and not only prevents them from speaking out the truth, but also brings down their wrath upon those who have the courage to do so.* But history is no respecter of persons or communities, and must always strive to tell the truth, so far as it can be deduced from reliable evidence. This great academic principle has a bearing upon actual life, for ignorance seldom proves to be a real bliss either to an individual or to a nation. In the particular case under consideration, ignorance of the actual relation between the Hindus and the Muslims throughout the course of history — an ignorance deliberately encouraged by some — may ultimately be found to have been the most important single factor which led to the partition of India. The real and effective means of solving a problem is to know and understand the facts that gave rise to it, and not to ignore them by hiding the head, ostrich-like, into sands of fiction."[6]

A Voice in the Wilderness

But his voice remained a voice in the wilderness. Fourteen years

---

[6]R.C. Majumdar (ed.), *The History and Culture of the Indian People*, Volume VI, *The Delhi Sultanate*, Bombay, 1960, p. xxix. Emphasis added.

later, he had to return to the theme and give specific instances of falsification. *"It is very sad,"* he observed, *"that the spirit of perverting history to suit political views is no longer confined to politicians, but has definitely spread even among professional historians... It is painful to mention though impossible to ignore, the fact that there is a distinct and conscious attempt to rewrite the whole chapter of the bigotry and intolerance of the Muslim rulers towards Hindu religion.* This was originally prompted by the political motive of bringing together the Hindus and Musalmans in a common fight against the British but has continued ever since. A history written under the auspices of the Indian National Congress sought to repudiate the charge that the Muslim rulers broke Hindu temples, and asserted that they were the most tolerant in matters of religion. Following in its footsteps, a noted historian has sought to exonerate Mahmud of Ghazni's bigotry and fanaticism, and several writers in India have come forward to defend Aurangzeb against Jadunath Sarkar's charge of religious intolerance. It is interesting to note that in the revised edition of the *Encyclopaedia of Islam*, one of them, while re-writing the article on Aurangzeb originally written by William Irvine, has expressed the view that the charge of breaking Hindu temples brought against Aurangzeb is a disputed point. Alas for poor Jadunath Sarkar, who must have turned in his grave if he were buried. For, after reading his *History of Aurangzib*, one would be tempted to ask, if the temple-breaking policy of Aurangzeb is a disputed point, is there a single fact in the whole recorded history of mankind which may be taken as undisputed? A noted historian has sought to prove that the Hindu population was better off under the Muslims than under the Hindu tributaries or independent rulers."[7]

Falsification of History becomes State Policy

This caravan loaded with synthetic merchandise has, however, continued to move forward. Eight years later (1982), it was

---

[7] R.C. Majumdar (ed.), Ibid., Volume VII, Preface to *The Mughal Empire*, Bombay, 1974, p. xii. Emphasis added.

reported that "History and Language textbooks for schools all over India will soon be revised radically. In collaboration with various state governments the Ministry of Education has begun a phased programme to weed out undesirable textbooks and remove matter which is prejudicial to national integration and unity and which does not promote social cohesion. The Ministry of Education's decision to re-evaluate textbooks was taken in the light of the recommendations of the National Integration Council of which the Prime Minister [Indira Gandhi] is Chairman. The Ministry's view was that history had often been used to serve narrow, sectarian and chauvinistic ends."[8]

Feeding people on such palpable falsehoods can sometimes produce a complete collapse of their mental and moral faculties. An instance is provided by Shalini Saran's article, *Akbar, The Great Unifier,* published in *Readers Digest* (Indian edition) of October, 1985. She hails Akbar by asserting that "Centuries before his time, this versatile emperor helped make us one nation". One of her strong arguments in support of this thesis is that "Akbar could be ruthless in his drive for unity: after the fall of Chitor, he ordered all its 30,000 inhabitants massacred."

It did not occur to her that Akbar had arrived in India only 14 years before he invested Chittor in 1568. He was at that time too much of a foreigner to fancy any idea of an Indian nation. His invasion of Mewar was a copy-book exercise of earlier Islamic invasions — a *jihād* as depicted in Chapter 6 above. Every Islamic imperialist from Alauddin Khilji onwards had tried to reduce this defiant Rajput state to slavery.

She is also blissfully oblivious of what Akbar's contemporaries have recorded as his reason for slaughtering so many non-combatants in cold blood. Abul Fazl and Badayuni have not tried to hide the truth that Akbar was inspired by the time-honoured

---

[8]*Indian Express*, New Delhi, 17 January 1982. See Sita Ram Goel, *The Story of Islamic Imperialism in India,* Voice of India (1982), Second Revised Edition, 1994, for full discussion of the guidelines laid down by the Ministry of Education in this context. Also, Arun Shourie, *Eminent Historians: Their Technology, Their Line, Their Fraud,* New Delhi, 1998.

tenets of *jihād* which enjoin a total destruction of "infidels" after they have been defeated. The "infidels" in this instance had also aroused Akbar's ire by offering a very stiff resistance.

Shalini Saran's eulogy of Akbar will make the most blatant apologist of Islamic imperialism blush with embarrassment. But she is not alone. She represents a whole tribe who depend entirely upon their ideological predilections for concocting India's history. Only they do not extend that bias to the British period. Holding the British responsible for everything that went wrong, is still the progressive platform.

Though, by the logic of this tribe, the best promoters of India's unity were the British. They did far more and succeeded to a much greater extent in imposing a unity on India. By that logic, General Dyer of the Jallianwala Bagh fame comes out with flying colours as the foremost builder of an Indian nation. He was also very ruthless in gunning down unarmed people who were not impressed by the "benefits of the British Raj".

The Fundamental Failure

These perverse efforts to re-write medieval Muslim history in India are bound to fail in solving the "communal problem" because the psyche which created that history continues to pulsate in the Quran. *The Quran cannot be re-written by re-writing that history.* On the other hand, an honest presentation of that history can help immensely an understanding of the Muslim behaviour pattern which is shaped by the Quran. Let there be no mistake that Hindus will never be able to tackle the "Muslim minority" unless they understand the source of its behaviour pattern.

But Hindus have so far failed to study the Quran with any seriousness whatsoever. That is why they have readily conceded the Muslim claim that the Quran is a "religious scripture full of lofty messages, moral and spiritual". They have confused the language of the Quran with the language of Hindu spirituality so that Allah passes for the *Parmātman* and the Prophet for the *Purushottama*. They feel puzzled when Muslims "fail" to live upto their expectations. But they never care to examine the assumptions on which those expectations are based. On the contrary, they appeal to the Muslims in the name of the Quran. Muslims cannot be blamed if they feel amused at this presumptuousness on the part of "accursed infidels".

It is high time for Hindu scholarship to come forward and make a serious study of the Quran with the help of Islamic theology and history. It is high time for Hindus to have a close look at the character of Allah which is the seed from which everything else in Islam has sprouted. The results will be very rewarding.

"Hindus have fought Muslim invaders," writes Ram Swarup, "and locally established Muslim dynasties but neglected to study the religious and ideological motives of the invaders. Hindu learning, or whatever remained of its earlier glory, followed the old grooves and its texts and speculations remained unmindful of the new phenomenon in their midst. For example, even as late as the thirteenth century, when Malik Kafur was attacking areas in the far South, in the vicinity of the seat of Sri Ramanujacharya, the scholarly dissertations of the disciples of the great teacher show no awareness of this fact."

He continues: "Hindus were masters of many spiritual disciplines; they had many Yogas and they had a developed science of inner exploration. There had been a continuing discussion whether the ultimate reality was *dvaita* or *advaita.* It would have been very interesting and instructive to find out if any of these savants of Yoga ever met, on their inner journey, a Quranic being, Allah (or its original, Jehovah of the Bible), who is jealous of other Gods, who claims sole sovereignty and yet whom no one knows except through a pet go-between, who appoints a favourite emissary and uses the latter's mouth to publish his decrees, who proclaims crusades and *jihad,* who teaches to kill the unbelievers and to destroy their shrines and temples and to levy permanent tribute on them and to convert them into *zimmis,* into hewers of wood and drawers of water. Even today, the question retains its importance. Is the Allah of the Quran a spiritual being? Or, is he some sort of a mental and vital formation, a hegemonistic idea? Does he represent man's own deepest truth and reside in his innermost being? Or, is he a projection of a less edifying source in man's psyche? Is he discovered when a man's heart is tranquil, desireless and pure? Or, does he originate in a fevered state of the mind? Is his source the Samadhi of the Yogic *bhumi* or some sort of a trance of a non-Yogic *bhumi*? In the *Yoga-darshana*, this distinction is fundamental but it is not much remembered these days."[9]

Hindus should Appeal to a Higher Court

The "law" which prohibits Hindus from having a public discussion on the Quran, embodies a disability which was once imposed upon them at the point of the sword. The law courts cannot be helpful so long as that lawless law remains on the statute book. Its repeal is a task to be undertaken by an informed public opinion. India is a democracy in which the sword of Islam is not supposed to have any sway.

There is, however, a court higher than the Calcutta High Court or the Supreme Court of India. That is the court of human reason, of human values, of human conscience, of human aspiration for a purer and loftier life. The Quran should be brought before that court. The devotees of the Quran should be invited to defend it in that court rather than in the streets.

It was not so long ago that the Bible enjoyed a stranglehold similar to that of the Quran over vast populations in the West. The theocracies propped up by the Bible in Europe and America had enacted similar sagas of slaughter and pillage for several centuries. But a sustained Western scholarship showed up the Bible for what it was. "It would be more consistent," proclaimed Thomas Pain, "that we call it [the Bible] the work of a demon than the word of God." The spell of Jehovah was broken. The god of the Bible, according to Thomas Jefferson, "is cruel, vindictive,

---

[9]Introduction to *Mohammed and the Rise of Islam* by D.S. Margoliouth, Voice of India reprint, New Delhi, 1985, pp. xvii-xviii.

capricious and unjust". The rest is history. Christianity is now seeking a refuge in countries like India where its rout in the West remains unknown.

A similar scholarship will not only put the Quran and its Allah in their proper place but also restore the image of Hindu spirituality which has suffered due to an adulteration of religious language by the gibberish of the biblical or prophetic creeds. The Muslim mullah and the Christian missionary had an upper hand so long as Islamic and Christian-Western imperialism prevailed in this country. A class of Hindu scholars learnt from them how to process Hindu spirituality and culture in terms of Islamic and Christian monolatries. It is that class which still passes for what is known as India's "intellectual elite". In fact, that class has grown stupendously in numbers as well as influence, after India attained independence; it had been created by a system of education which we have chosen to continue.

Islamic and Christian imperialisms have been defeated and dispelled from the greater part of the ancient Hindu homeland. There is no reason why aggressive and inhuman ideologies brought in by those imperialisms should continue to flourish. They shall stand exposed as soon as Hindus evolve appropriate methods for processing those ideologies in terms of their own spirituality and culture.

"Hitherto," observes Ram Swarup, "we have looked at Hinduism through the eyes of Islam and Christianity. Let us now learn to look at these ideologies from the vantage point of Hindu spirituality — they are no more than ideologies, lacking as they are in the integrality and inwardness of true religion and spirituality. Such an exercise would also throw light on the self-destructiveness of the modern ideologies of Communism and Imperialism, inheritors of the prophetic mission or 'burden' in its secularized version, of Christianity and Islam. The perspective gained will be a great corrective and will add a new liberating dimension; it will help not only India and Hinduism but the whole world."

He concludes: "A fateful thing has been happening. The East is waking up from its slumber. The wisdom of Hinduism, Buddhism, Taoism and Confucianism is becoming available to the world. Already, it is having a transforming effect on the minds of the people, particularly in countries where there is freedom to seek and express. Dogmas are under a cloud; claims on behalf of Last Prophethood and Only Sonship, hitherto enforced through great intellectual conditioning, brow-beating, and the big stick, are becoming unacceptable. Religions of proxy are in retreat. More and more men and women now seek authentic experience. Borrowed creed will not do. Men and women are ceasing to be obedient believers and are becoming seekers. They no longer want to be anybody's sheep, now that they know they can be their own shepherds. An external authority, even when it is called God in certain scriptures, threatening and promising alternately, is increasingly making less and less impression; people now realize that Godhead is their own true, secret status and they seek it in the depth of their own being. All this is in keeping with the wisdom of the East."[10]

---

[10]Ibid., pp. xix-xx.

Chapter 10

A Close Look at Allah of the Quran

The one name which Muslims hate and fear most is that of Chengiz Khan. He is a spectre which has haunted Muslim historians for centuries. He swept like a tornado over the then most powerful and extensive Islamic empire of Khwarazm. In a' short span of five years (1219-1224 CE), he slaughtered millions of Muslims, forced many others including women and children into slavery, and razed to the ground quite a few of the most populous and prosperous cities of the Muslim world at that time.

Muslim and Mongol historians have preserved a record of Chengiz Khan's doings in region after region and city after city. We present some of that record in order to point out how closely it resembles the record of *jihāds* waged by Muslim swordsmen in India and elsewhere.

Cities on the Jaxartes Frontier

"There was no army to dispute the passage of the Jaxartes with Chengiz. He despatched Juji against *Jund;* his second and third sons, Chaghatai and Ogtai, against *Otrar;* and his other officers against *Khojend, Fanakat*, etc.; while he personally proceeded against *Samarqand* and *Bukhara. Otrar* was defended by Ghayir Khan with an army of 60,000; the city resisted for five months after which Ghayir's subordinate, Qaracha, surrendered with his men in the hope of mercy but was put to death. The inhabitants, 'both wearers of the veil and those who wore *kulah* (hat) and turbans' were taken out of the city, while the Mongols plundered their houses. Young men were picked up for the levy *(hashr)* and the artisans for service. Ghayir Khan retreated into the *ark* with 20,000 soldiers. They held out for another month and died fighting. No other city in Trans-Oxiana was able to hold out for so long. Juji sent a Muslim merchant, Haji Hasan, who had long been in Chengiz's service, to ask the citizens of *Sughnaq* to submit. But some persons attacked Haji with cries of *Allah-O-Akbar* and put him to death. In retaliation for this, the Mongols slaughtered the whole population in seven days.[1]

"*Fanakat*: The garrison led by Iltegu Malik fought for three days and then asked for quarter. All soldiers were put to death but the civil population, apart from the artisans and the young men required for the levy, was spared. *Khojend*: Timur Malik, the commander, fortified himself in an island and then escaped to the Khwarazm Shah after a series of heroic exploits, but *Khojend* shared the fate of other cities and its young men were drafted into the *hashr* (levy). Here the number of the levy is given as 50,000 while the Mongol army was 20,000.[2]

Bukhara and Samarqand

"Though Samarqand was nearer, Chengiz decided to proceed first against Bukhara by way of Zarnaq and Nur. Both cities surrendered and were treated in the usual Mongol manner... The citadel of Bukhara was in charge of Kok Khan, a Mongol who had fled from Chengiz and taken service with the Sultan. Kok decided to fight to the bitter end, but the citizens preferred to submit and sent their religious representatives to invite Chengiz into the town...[3]

---

[1]Mohammad Habib and Khaliq Ahmad Nizami (ed.), *A Comprehensive History of India*, New Delhi, 1970, Volume V, *The Sultanat*, First Reprint, 1982, p. 73.
[2]Ibid., pp. 73-74,
[3]Ibid., p. 74.

"But the problem of Kok Khan and the garrison in the *ark* remained. They were fighting to sell their lives as dear as possible and sallied forth against the Mongols both day and night. Now the houses of Bukhara were made entirely of wood, apart from the Juma mosque and a few palaces; consequently, when Chengiz ordered the houses near the *ark* to be set on fire, the whole city was consumed by the flames. Ultimately the *ark* was captured and all soldiers were put to death. Further, as to the Qanqali Turks, all male children who stood higher than the butt of a whip, were put to death, and more than thirty thousand corpses were counted, 'while their smaller children and the children of their notables and their women-folk, slender as the cypress, were reduced to slavery.' All the civil inhabitants of Bukhara, male and female, were brought out to the plain of Musalla, outside the city; the young and the middle-aged, who were fit for service in the levy against Samarqand were picked up, and the rest were spared. When Chengiz left the place, 'Bukhara was level plain.'[4]

"The Sultan had thrown a garrison of 60,000 Turks and 50,000 Tajiks into Samarqand and strengthened its defence. It was thought that 'Samarqand could stand a siege of some years'; so Chengiz decided to subdue the country round Samarqand first, and when he had finished doing so, the fate of Samarqand was sealed. Chengiz did not fight for two days after he had encircled the city; on the third and fourth day there was some fighting; on the fifth day the civil population sent its Qazi and Shaikhul Islam to offer its submission. The city-ramparts were pulled down and next day the citadel was captured between the morning and afternoon prayers. About thirty thousand Qanqalis and Turks with some twenty high amirs of the Sultan were put to death; but some fifty thousand people whom the Qazi and the Shikhul Islam had taken under their protection were left unmolested. The rest of the population was taken out and counted, while their houses were plundered. Some thirty thousand men were selected for their craftsmanship and an equal number for the levy...

---

[4] Ibid., pp. 74-75.

Khwarazm

"The citizens refused to submit. 'They opposed the Mongols in all the streets and quarters of the town; in every lane they engaged in battle and in every *cul-de-sac* they resisted stoutly... The greater part of the town was destroyed; the houses with their goods and treasures were but mounds of earth and the Mongols despaired of benefiting from the stores of their wealth.' When the Mongols succeeded in capturing the town, which now lay in shambles, they drove the people into the open; more than a hundred thousand craftsmen were selected and sent to the countries of the east; the children and young women were taken away as captives. Order was given for the rest to be slaughtered; every Mongol soldier had to execute twenty-four persons...[5]

Campaign by Yeme and Subetai

"The mission of these two brothers was to capture the Sultan [of Khwarazm] alive; in this they failed. But Subetai succeeded in capturing Turkan Khatun and the Sultan's *haram* in the Mazendaran castle of Ilal along with his wazir, Nasiruddin. When they were brought before Chengiz at Taliqan, he had Nasiruddin tortured and all the male sons of the Sultan put to death... Their army of 30,000 was really insufficient for the conquest of the region, and very often Yeme and Subetai had to march separately. They resorted to massacres wherever they could, in order to create an atmosphere of terror in which provisions may be forthcoming...[6]

Merv

"All the inhabitants of Merv, both men and women, were brought out, kept on the plain for four days and nights and then

[5]Ibid., p. 75.
[6]Ibid., p. 76.

ordered to be put to death. Every Mongol soldier had to execute three to four hundred persons. One Saiyyid Izzuddin Nasseba, along with some friends who had escaped the massacre, passed thirteen days and nights in counting such corpses as they could easily discover. The total came to one million and three hundred thousand (February 1221). This does not seem to be an exaggerated figure in view of the fertility of the Merv valley. But people collected in the city again and again and were repeatedly destroyed...[7]

Naishapur

"While Tului was attacking Merv, Toghachar Kurgen, a son-in-law of Chengiz, appeared before Naishapur with an army of 10,000. He was shot dead by a stray arrow and apologists for Mongol misdeeds have found in this a justification for the complete destruction of Naishapur. While waiting for Tului's arrival, Toghachar's army withdrew to attack smaller towns. Sabzwar (also called Baihaq) was captured after three days of severe fighting, a general massacre was ordered and 70,000 corpses were counted. Two other cities, Nuqan and Qar, were also conquered and their inhabitants slaughtered. Tului on his arrival refused to accept the submission of Naishapur. So the battle commenced on Wednesday (7 April 1221) and by Saturday the city-ramparts were in Mongol hands. All the inhabitants were brought out and slaughtered; Toghachar's wife then entered the city with her escort and slew those who had survived. Even cats and dogs were not spared. 'The only inhabitants of Naishapur left alive were forty artisans, who were taken to Turkistan on account of their skill. For seven days and nights water was flown into the city so that barley may be sown there. It is said in some histories that the dead were counted for twelve days and that there were one million and forty thousand corpses, apart from the corpses of women and children...'[8]

---

[7]Ibid., pp. 76-77.
[8]Ibid., p. 77.

Herat

"Ilchikdai succeeded in reducing Herat after a siege of six months and seventeen days and forced his way into the city on a Friday morning (AD 1222). 'For seven days the Mongols devoted themselves exclusively to killing, burning and destroying the buildings. A little less than one million and six hundred thousand of the inhabitants were martyred.' Ilchikdai then proceeded against the fort of Kaliwayan, but he sent back a Mongol contingent of 10,000, who put to death about a hundred thousand Musalmans who had collected at Herat again."[9]

Commandments of Il Tengiri

We are not mentioning here the horrors heaped by Halaku Khan, the grandson and successor of Chengiz, who inherited the Mongol empire west of the Jaxartes. He sacked many more cities in Iran, Iraq and Syria, destroyed the hideout of the assassins at Almut, killed the last Abbasid Caliph in the most cruel manner, and levelled with the ground the holy city of Baghdad which had been the capital of Islamdom for five hundred years. The story is far more blood-soaked than that enacted by Chengiz Khan.

Few people, Muslim or non-Muslim, apart from specialists of Mongol theology and history, suspect that Chengiz Khan did what he did not, "on his own" but "on orders" from his "One God whom they called *Tengiri* or *Il Tengiri*."[10] Professor Mohammad Habib, who has studied Mongolian lore on the subject, sums up the situation. "Chengiz Khan," he writes, "who sincerely believed that *Il Tengiri* had given him and his family and his officers the commission to dominate the world for all time and that defiance of him was resistance to a clear order of *Il Tengiri,* must have been delighted when he heard that he would have to face no field-force and that the enormous Khwarazmian army had been divided and sealed up in the inner citadels of cities or put on the top of

---

[9]Ibid., p. 78.
[10]Ibid., p. 56.

inaccessible hill forts."[11] We come across similar sentiments in medieval Muslim historians when they thank Allah for having bottled up the Hindu rajas in fortified cites or citadels.

Professor Habib adds: "Chengiz Khan was prepared to kill as many Musalmans as may be necessary and, to be on the safe side, a lot more. In any case, it was *Il Tengiri's* order; consequently, Chengiz in clear conscience was not responsible. This reign of terror through wholesale massacres was warning to all mankind; there was nothing secret about it. Chengiz and his successors wanted it to be advertised to the whole world. Consequently, the official historians of the Mongols, like Juwayni and Rashiduddin, while justifying these massacres as due to 'disobedience and revolt', are careful in explaining their exact character and extent."[12] Chengiz Khan himself told the Muslim magnates of Bukhara that "I am the punishment of God; if you had not committed great sins, God would not have sent a punishment like me upon you."[13]

Mongol Historians vis-à-vis Muslim Historians

It may be pointed out that medieval Muslim historians such as Al-Utbi, Hasan Nizami, Abdullah Wassaf, Amir Khusru and Muhammad Qasim Firishtah, from all of whom we have quoted, belong to the same blood-thirsty tribe as the Mongol historians. They wrote glowing accounts of *jihād*, not so much out of admiration for their heroes as in order to proclaim to the world the fate that awaited those who did not worship Allah of the Quran. These historians also use expressions such as "disobedience and revolt (*sarkashi*)" for which Allah was punishing the "accursed *kāfirs*" of Hindustan. We do not find a trace of pity or sorrow or sympathy in these historians while they dilate on stories of

---

[11]Ibid., p. 69.
[12]Ibid., p. 70.
[13]Ibid., p. 74.

slaughter, pillage, plunder and the plight of women and children. On the contrary, they derive immense satisfaction from describing the most dreadful scenes of death and devastation. Timur and his lineal as well as spiritual descendant, Babur, were convinced that they could not leave to mere court scribes the sacred task of recording what the sweep of their swords did in the service of Allah. So they themselves took time from their crowded schedules and wrote or dictated the record with considerable relish. As one reads these royal historians describing the scenes of bloodshed and rapine they enacted, one can almost see them licking their lips as if after a hearty meal following upon a keen appetite.

How Chengiz Khan communicated with Il Tengiri

Minhajus Siraj, the famous historian who wrote in the middle of the thirteenth century, was in his teens when Chengiz Khan let loose his blood-thirsty hordes on the Muslim world. Later in life, he met persons who had seen from close quarters the performance of the Mongol conqueror. His religious predisposition led Minhaj to believe that "some satans had become his [Chengiz Khan's] friends."[14] But in spite of this strong prejudice, he has left for posterity a faithful pen-portrait of Chengiz Khan receiving "revelations" from Il Tengiri. He writes in his *Tabqāt-i-Nāsiri*: "After every few days he would have a fit and during his unconsciousness he would say all sorts of things. It was like this. When he had his first fit and the satans, after overpowering his mind, informed him of his forthcoming victory, he put the clothes and the cloak he was then wearing in a sealed bag and carried it about with him. Whenever this fit was about to overpower him, (he would put on these clothes) and talk about every event, victory, campaign, the appearance of his enemies, and the conquest of the territories he wanted. Someone would write down all he said, put (the papers) in a bag and seal them. When Chengiz

---

[14]Cited in Ibid., p. 68.

246 / THE CALCUTTA QURAN PETITION

recovered consciousness, everything was read out to him and he acted accordingly. Generally, in fact always, his designs were successful."[15]

Chengiz Khan's *"Fit"* compared with Muhammad's *"Wahy"*

Chengiz Khan's *"fit"* for getting into contact with Il Tengiri resembles, rather too closely to be missed, the *"wahy"* in which Allah communicated the Quran to the prophet of Islam. One wonders what it would have read like if Chengiz Khan or his followers had cared to compile in a Book all that Il Tengiri told him before he breathed his last in 1227 CE at the age of 63. For all we know, it might have been another version of the Quran, at least so far as it concerns aggression against other people's lands, cutting the heads of those who resist the aggression, plundering their properties, destroying their dwelling places, and selling their women and children into concubinage and slavery.

Another Quran, but...

It is only in one respect that the *Quran* revealed by Il Tengiri might have differed from the *Quran* revealed by Allah. It seems that, quite unlike Allah, Il Tengiri was not intolerant towards revelations other than his own. Professor Habib writes: "The Musalmans, whom Chengiz Khan murdered in such enormous numbers, were surprised at his belief in *his* God and at his undoubted tolerance in religious matters. Having no priests of their own, the leaders of steppe society were remarkably tolerant to the priests of all other cults — Muslim, Christian, Taoist, Buddhist ... they were expected to pray in their own way... Lastly, the Mongols had no objection to intermarriage, and even Chengiz Khan gave one of his daughters in marriage to a Muslim chief, Arsalan Khan of Kayaliq."[16] Again: "In the precincts of

---

[15]Cited in Ibid., p. 69.
[16]Ibid., p. 57.

Samarqand he [Chengiz Khan] is said to have had discussions with two Muslim scholars and expressed his agreement with the Islamic belief in Allah and all its four rites except the Haj. 'God is everywhere, and you can find him everywhere'."[17]

This was definitely an improvement on the decrees of Allah who has commanded his faithful to go out first for the priests and religious places of other people; who has forbidden on pain of death the marriage of a Muslim to a non-Muslim unless the latter is first converted to the "only true faith", and who has stated in so many words his marked partiality for the mosque at Mecca (Ka'ba).

On the other hands, Il Tengiri was as particular as Allah that the mutual relations among the Mongols should be guided by a stern code of conduct. Minhajus Siraj records: "The justice of Chengiz Khan was so severe that no one except the owner had the courage to pick up a whip that had fallen by the road-side. Lying and theft were things quite unknown in his army and no one could find any trace of them."[18] We are reminded of the strict rules which Allah has laid down in the Quran regarding the conduct of one Muslim towards another.

And that brings us to the crucial and quintessential question.

Evaluation of Allah

Should we cite *only* the stern code which the Mongols observed among themselves and proclaim that Il Tengiri stood for stark honesty and straight truth in human relations? Should we ignore or overlook the gruesome fate which Il Tengiri had decreed for the Muslims, their lives, their honour, their women and children, their cities and their properties? Should we proclaim that Il Tengiri was something divine and that Chengiz Khan who carried out his commandments quite faithfully should be hailed as a hero?

Yet that is exactly what the votaries of Allah do themselves and

---

[17]Cited in Ibid., p. 81.
[18]Cited in Ibid., p. 69.

want us to do. They cite certain rules which Allah had revealed regarding sharing of plunder among the Muslims or pertaining to their participation in congregational prayers, and want us to believe that Allah stands for social equality and human brotherhood! At the same time, we are advised not even to notice the barbarities which Allah wants the Muslims to heap on the non-Muslims. And if we fail to respond positively and try to judge Allah not in terms of isolated *āyats* but on the basis of the Quran as a whole, we run the risk of being run down as bigots, as lacking in respect for the religion of a sister community! The logic which declares Il Tengiri to be a satan and denounces Chengiz Khan as an archcriminal but which, in the same breath, proclaims Allah as divine and hails the Ghaznavis, Ghuris, Timurs and Baburs as heroes, is, to the say the least, worse than casuistry.

The Quran can claim to be derived from a "divine source" only if we concede Allah's claim to be divine. But the Quran itself provides ample evidence that its Allah is quite a questionable character even by ordinary ethical standards, not to speak of spiritual standards. Theologians of Islam have got away with the plea that the Quran has a "divine source" simply because its Allah has not yet been subjected to the scrutiny he deserves on account of his role in human history. He will continue to torment mankind till he is found out for what he is, and exorcised from minds on which he has acquired a stranglehold.

Failure in Finding Out Allah of the Quran

Christian scholars of Islam have failed to nail down Allah of the Quran because he is the re-incarnation, under another name, of Jehovah whom we meet in the Bible. They only reject Muhammad as a prophet and call him an impostor, which is quite dishonest if we keep in mind the biblical prophets, particularly Moses.

The scholars of European Enlightenment who were influenced by Hindu, Chinese, Greek and Roman traditions of spirituality and culture, have judged Jehovah quite correctly and identified him as the main source of darkness which prevailed in Europe during the

Middle Ages. But they have so far neglected Allah of the Quran and not weighed him in the same balance of rationalism, humanism and universalism on which Jehovah was weighed and found wanting.

Hindus have been the worst in their neglect of Allah of the Quran who has plagued them for more than thirteen hundred years. Hindu scholars and saints have been equating him with *Paramātman,* even with *Parabrahma,* without finding out, in the first place, whether Allah of the Quran is at all equal to the comparison. As a corollary, they have been hailing the Quran as a "divine revelation" and Islam as a *"dharma".* They feel perplexed only by the Muslim behaviour pattern which does not square with the expectations they have built round these eulogies. Hindu politicians have continued to cherish the fond belief that they can manage the Muslims and draw them into the national mainstream by fawning upon the Quran and glorifying its Allah. But that Allah has so far frustrated all their hopes.

The story of Il Tengiri we have cited may help Hindus in general and Hindu scholars, saints and politicians in particular, to see the prototype and start having a close look at Allah of the Quran. It may also help them to see the truth about revelatory or prophetic or biblical creeds. The biblical prophets have revealed nothing divine, nothing derived from a supracosmic or super-human source. They have only revealed themselves, that is, the ordinary human nature which is brimful of dark drives. In fact, the ordinary man has always been more honest about his animal appetites. The biblical prophets, on the other hand, start by deceiving themselves and end by deceiving others when they dress up the same appetites in pretentious language and pass them off as impersonal revelations.

Section II

THE PETITION AND THE JUDGEMENT

(1)

Himangshu Kishore's Letter

From:
Himangshu Kishore Chakraborty, M.A., (Cal.),
12/A/4, Pashupati Bhattacharya Road,
Behala,
Calcutta - 34.

Dated 20th July, 1984.

To,
The Secretary,
Department of Home,
Government of West Bengal,
Writers' Building,
Calcutta - 1.

Dear Sir,

Sub: Request for proscription of 'Koran'.

As you may be aware, the Islamic religious book, Koran, also spelt as 'Qur'an', said to be a collection of revelations made through the angel Gabriel by the almighty Allah to the Prophet Muhammad, containing numerous sayings, repeated in the book over and over again, which on grounds of religion promote disharmony, feeling of enmity, hatred and ill-will between different religious communities and incite people to commit violence and disturb public tranquility, and though most of the events which had occasioned those sayings have now lost all historical significance, the book is still published in the unabridged form, with persistence, and clearly with the deliberate and malicious intention of outraging or insulting other religions and the religious feelings of other communities in India which is apparent from the fact that all the publishers of the book know very well that the various sayings of the book are offensive in this sense.

Some of these sayings are reproduced for your ready reference in the three annexures enclosed to this letter.

As the publication of the book is thus an offence punishable under Sections 153A and 295A of the Indian Penal Code, each copy of the book, whether in the original Arabic or in its translation in Urdu, Bengali, Hindi, English or in any other language, is liable, in terms of Section 95 of the Code of Criminal Procedure, 1973, to be declared to be forfeited to the Government.

You are, therefore, requested to proscribe the book and, in the interest of the public at large, to do so promptly.

Yours faithfully,
Sd/-
Enclo: As stated above.   (Himangshu Kishore Chakraborty)

ANNEXURE 'A'

Sayings of 'Koran' which Preach Cruelty, Incite Violence and Disturb Public Tranquility

1. **Surah 2: ayat 193.**
   Fight against them until idolatry is no more and Allah's religion reigns supreme.

2. **Surah 8: ayat 39.**
   Make war on them until idolatry is no more and Allah's religion reigns supreme.

3. **Surah 2: ayat 216.**
   Fighting is obligatory for you, much as you dislike it. But you may hate a thing although it is good for you, and love a thing although it is bad for you. Allah knows, but you do not.

4. **Surah 9: ayat 41.**
   Whether unarmed or well-equipped, march on and fight for the cause of Allah, with your wealth and your persons. This will be best for you, if you but knew it,

5. **Surah 9: ayat 123.**
   Believers! make war on the infidels who dwell around you. Let them find harshness in you.

6. **Surah 66: ayat 9.**
   O Prophet! make war on the unbelievers and the hypocrites and deal sternly with them. Hell shall be their home, evil their fate.

7. **Surah 9: ayat 73**
   O Prophet! Make war on the unbelievers and the hypocrites. Be harsh with them. Their ultimate abode is Hell, a hapless journey's end.

8. **Surah 8: ayat 65.**
   O Prophet! Exhort the believers to fight. If there are twenty

steadfast men among you, they shall vanquish two hundred; and if there are a hundred, they shall rout a thousand unbelievers, for they are devoid of understanding.

9. **Surah 8: ayat 66.**
Now hath Allah lightened your burden, for He knoweth that there is weakness in you. So if there be of you a steadfast hundred they shall vanquish two hundred, and if there be of you a thousand steadfast they shall vanquish two thousand by permission of Allah. Allah is with the steadfast.

10. **Surah 47: ayats 4-15.**
When you meet the unbelievers in the battlefield strike off their heads and when you have laid them low, bind your captives firmly. Then grant them their freedom or take ransom from them, until war shall lay down her armour. Thus shall you do. Had Allah willed, He could Himself have punished them (without your help); but He has ordained it thus that He might test you, the one by the other. As for those who are slain in the cause of Allah, He will not allow their works to perish. He will vouchsafe them guidance and ennoble their state; He will admit them to the Paradise He has made known to them.

Believers! if you help Allah, Allah will help you and make you strong. But the unbelievers shall be consigned to perdition. He will bring their deeds to nothing. Because they have opposed His revelations, He will frustrate their works... Allah is the protector of the faithful; unbelievers have no protector. Allah will admit those who embrace the true faith to gardens watered by running streams. The unbelievers take their full of pleasure and eat as the beasts eat; but Hell shall be their home... They shall abide in Hell for ever and drink scalding water which will tear their bowels.

11. **Surah 8: ayat 12.**
I shall cast terror into the hearts of the infidels. Strike off their heads, maim them in every limb.

12. **Surah 69: ayats 30-33.**
We shall say, 'Lay hold of him and bind him. Burn him in the fire of Hell, then fasten him with a chain seventy cubits long. For he did not believe in Allah, the Most High.

13. **Surah 8: ayats 15-18.**
Believers! when you encounter the armies of the infidels do not turn your backs to them in flight. If anyone on that day turns his back to them, except it be for tactical reasons, or to join another band, he shall incur the wrath of Allah and Hell shall be his home: an evil fate.

It was not you, but Allah, who slew them. It was not you who smote them; Allah smote them so that He might richly reward the faithful. He hears all and knows all. He will surely thwart the designs of the unbelievers.

14. **Surah 25: ayat 52.**
Do not yield to the unbelievers, but fight them strenuously with this Koran.

15. **Surah 9: ayat 39.**
If you do not fight He will punish you sternly and replace you by other men...

16. **Surah 9: ayat 111,**
Allah has purchased of the faithful their lives and worldly goods and in return has promised them the Garden. They will fight for His cause, slay and be slain. Such is the true pledge which He has made them in the Torah, the Gospel and the Koran. And who is more true to His promise than Allah? Rejoice then in the bargain you have made. That is the supreme triumph.

17. **Surah 3: ayats 169-171.**
You must not think that those who were slain in the cause of Allah are dead. They are alive, and well provided for by their

Lord; pleased with His gifts and rejoicing that those whom they left behind and who have not yet joined them have nothing to fear or to regret; rejoicing in Allah's grace and bounty. Allah will not deny the faithful their reward.

18. **Surah 4: ayat 100.**
He that flies his homeland for the cause of Allah shall find numerous places of refuge in the land and great abundance. He that leaves his dwelling to fight for Allah and His apostle and is then overtaken by death, shall be rewarded by Allah. Allah is forgiving and merciful.

19. **Surah 48: ayat 29.**
Muhammad is Allah's apostle. Those who follow him are ruthless to the unbelievers but merciful to one another... Through them Allah seeks to enrage the unbelievers.

20. **Surah 49: ayat 15.**
The true believers are those that have faith in Allah and His apostle and never doubt; and who fight for His cause with their wealth and persons. Such are those whose faith is true.

21. **Surah 2: ayat 154.**
Do not say that those who were slain in the cause of Allah are dead; they are alive, although you are not aware of them.

22. **Surah 3: ayats 157-158.**
If you should die or be slain in the cause of Allah, His forgiveness and His mercy would surely be better than all the riches they amass. If you should die or be slain, before Him you shall all be gathered.

23. **Surah 8: ayats 59-60.**
Let the unbelievers not think that they will escape Us. They have not the power to do so. Muster against them all the men and cavalry at your disposal, so that you may strike terror into the enemies of Allah and the faithful, and others besides them. All that you give for the cause of Allah shall be repaid you. You shall not be wronged.

4. **Surah 9: ayats 2-3.**

...Allah will humble the unbelievers... Allah and His apostle are free from obligation to the idol-worshippers... Proclaim a woeful punishment to the unbelievers.

5. **Surah 9: ayat 29.**

Fight against such of those to whom the Scriptures were given as believe neither in Allah nor the Last Day, who do not forbid what Allah and His apostle have forbidden, and do not embrace the true faith, until they pay tribute out of hand and are utterly subdued.

26. **Surah 8: ayat 67.**

It is not for any Prophet to have captives until he has made slaughter in the land...

27. **Surah 4: ayat 84.**

So fight for the cause of Allah. You are accountable for none but yourself. Rouse the faithful; perchance Allah will defeat the unbelievers. He is mightier and more truculent than they.

28. **Surah 29: ayat 6.**

He that fights for Allah's cause fights for himself...

29. **Surah 29: ayat 69.**

Those that fight for Our cause We will surely guide to our own paths. Allah is with the righteous.

30. **Surah 61: ayats 9-13.**

It is He who has sent His messenger with the guidance and the Religion of Truth, so that He may make it the conqueror of all religions, much as the idol-worshippers may dislike it.

Believers! Shall I point out to you a profitable course that will save you from a woeful scourge? Have faith in Allah and His apostle and fight for His cause with your wealth and your persons. That would be best for you, if you but knew it. He will forgive you your sins and admit you to gardens watered by running streams; He will lodge you in pleasant mansions in the gardens of Eden. That is the supreme triumph.

31. **Surah 9: ayat 36.**
Allah ordained the months twelve in number when He created the Heavens and the earth. Of these four (Dhi-Qa'ada, Dhul-Hajja, Muharram and Rajab) are sacred according to the true faith. Therefore do not sin against yourselves by violating them. But you may fight against the idolaters in all these months since they themselves fight against you in all of them. Know that Allah is with the righteous.

32. **Surah 9: ayat 5.**
When the sacred months are over slay the idol-worshippers wherever you find them. Arrest them, besiege them, and lie in ambush everywhere for them. If they repent and take to prayer and pay the alms-tax, let them go their way. Allah is forgiving and merciful.

33. **Surah 9: ayat 14.**
Fight them! Allah will chastise them at your hands, and He will lay them low and give you victory over them, and He will heal the breasts of folk who are believers.

34. **Surah 9: ayats 20-22.**
Those that have embraced the faith and fled their homes and fought for Allah's cause with their wealth and their persons are held in higher regard by Allah. It is they who shall triumph. Their Lord has promised them joy and mercy, and gardens of eternal pleasures where they shall dwell for ever. Allah's reward is great indeed.

35. **Surah 4: ayats 95-96.**
The believers who stay at home — apart from those that suffer from a grave impediment — are not equal to those who fight for the cause of Allah with their goods and their persons. Allah has given those that fight with their goods and their persons a higher rank than those who stay at home. He has promised all a good reward: but far richer is the recompense of those who

fight for Him: rank of His own bestowal, forgiveness, and mercy. Allah is forgiving and merciful.

36. **Surah 8: ayats 72-74.**

Those that have embraced the faith and fled their homes, fought for the cause of Allah with their wealth and their persons; and those that sheltered them and helped them, shall be friends to each other ... they are the true believers. They shall receive mercy and generous provision.

37. **Surah 3: ayat 142.**

Did you suppose that you would enter Paradise before Allah has proved the men who fought for Him and endured with fortitude?

ANNEXURE 'B'

Sayings of 'Koran' which Promote, on Grounds of Religion, Feeling of Enmity, Hatred and Ill-Will between different Religious Communities in India

1. **Surah 4: ayat 101.**
   It is not offence for you to shorten your prayers when travelling the road if you fear that the unbelievers may attack you. The unbelievers are your sworn enemies.

2. **Surah 60: ayat 4.**
   ...We renounce you (i.e. the idolaters): enmity and hate shall reign between us until you believe in Allah only...

3. **Surah 58: ayat 23.**
   You shall find no believers in Allah and the Last Day on friendly terms with those who oppose Allah and His apostle, even though they be their fathers, their sons, their brothers, or their nearest kindred...

4. **Surah 9: ayat 7.**
   Allah and His apostle repose no trust in idolaters...

5. **Surah 8: ayats 13-14.**
   Thus We punished them because they defied Allah and His apostle. He that defies Allah and His apostle shall be sternly punished. We said to them, 'Feel Our scourge. Hell-fire awaits the unbelievers.'

6. **Surah 8: ayat 55.**
   The basest creatures in the sight of Allah are the faithless who will not believe...

7. **Surah 25: ayat 55.**
   Yet the unbelievers worship idols which can neither help nor harm them. Surely the unbeliever is his Lord's enemy.

8. **Surah 5: ayat 72.**
...He that worships other Gods besides Allah shall be forbidden Paradise and shall be cast into the fire of Hell. None shall help the evil-doers.

9. **Surah 9: ayat 23.**
Believers! do not befriend your fathers or your brothers if they choose unbelief in preference to faith. Wrong-doers are those that befriend them.

10. **Surah 9: ayat 28.**
Believers! know that the idolaters are unclean...

11. **Surah 3: ayat 28.**
Let believers not make friends with infidels in preference to the faithful; he that does this has nothing to hope for from Allah — except in self-defence. Allah admonishes you to fear Him; for to Him you shall all return.

12. **Surah 3: ayat 118.**
Believers! do not make friends with any men other than your own people. They will spare no pains to corrupt you. They desire nothing but your ruin. Their hatred is clear from what they say, but more violent is the hatred which their breasts conceal...

13. **Surah 4 ayat 144.**
Believers! do not choose the infidels rather than the faithful for your friends. Would you give Allah a clear proof against yourselves?

14. **Surah 5: ayat 14.**
...Therefore, We stirred among them (i.e. the Christians) enmity and hatred, which shall endure till the Day of Resurrection, when Allah will declare to them all that they have done.

15. **Surah 5: ayat 64.**

    ...That which Allah has revealed to you will surely increase
    the wickedness and unbelief of many of them (i.e. the Jews).
    We have stirred among them (i.e. the Jews) enmity and hatred,
    which will endure till the Day of Resurrection...

16. **Surah 5: ayat 18.**

    The Jews and the Christians say, 'We are the children of Allah
    and His loved ones.' Say: 'Why then does He punish you for
    your sins?'...

17. **Surah 5: ayat 51.**

    Believers! take neither Jews nor Christians for your friends.
    They are friends with one another. Whoever of you seeks their
    friendship shall become one of their number. Allah does not
    guide the wrong-doers.

ANNEXURE 'C'

Sayings of 'Koran' which Insult other Religions as also the Religious Beliefs of other Communities in India

1. **Surah 5: ayat 17.**
Unbelievers are those who declare: 'Allah is the Messiah (i.e. Christ), the son of Mary.' Say: 'Who could prevent Allah from destroying the Messiah (i.e. Christ), the son of Mary, together with his mother and all the people of the earth?'...

2. **Surah 4: ayat 157.**
They denied the truth and uttered a monstrous falsehood against Mary. They declared: 'We have put to death the Messiah Jesus, the son of Mary, the apostle of Allah.' They did not kill him, nor did they crucify him, but they thought they did.

3. **Surah 5: ayats 116-118.**
Then Allah will say, 'Jesus, son of Mary, did you ever say to mankind: "Worship me and my mother as Gods beside Allah?' 'Glory to You,' he will answer, 'how could I say that to which I have no right? If I had ever said so, You would have surely known it. You know what is in my mind, but I cannot tell what is in Yours. You alone know what is hidden. I spoke to them of nothing except what You bade me. I said, "Serve Allah, my Lord and your Lord." I watched over them whilst living in their midst, and ever since You took me to You, You Yourself have been watching over them. You are the witness of all things. They are Your own bondsmen: it is for You to punish or to forgive them. You are the Mighty, the Wise one.'

4. **Surah 98: ayat 6.**
The unbelievers among the people of the Book (i.e. Christians and Jews) and the pagans shall burn for ever in the fire of Hell. They are the vilest of all creatures.

5. **Surah 68: ayats 8-13.**
Give no heed to the disbelievers: they desire you to overlook their doings that they may overlook yours. Nor yield to the wretch of many oaths, the mischief-making slanderer, the opponent of good, the wicked transgressor, the bully who is of doubtful birth to boot.

6. **Surah 38: ayats 55-57.**
...But doleful shall be the return of the transgressors. They shall burn in the fire of Hell, a dismal resting-place. There let them taste their drink: scalding water, festering blood and other putrid things.

7. **Surah 22: ayats 19-21.**
...Garments of fire have been prepared for unbelievers. Scalding water shall be poured upon their heads, melting their skins and that which is in their bellies. They shall be lashed with red iron.

8. **Surah 22: ayats 56-57.**
...Those that have embraced the true faith and done good works shall enter the gardens of delight, but the unbelievers who have denied Our revelations shall receive an ignominious punishment.

9. **Surah 5: ayats 36.**
As for the unbelievers, if they offered all that the earth contains and as much besides to redeem themselves from the torment of the Day of Resurrection it shall not be accepted from them. Theirs shall be a woeful punishment.

10. **Surah 15: ayats 2.**
The day will surely come when the unbelievers will wish that they were Muslims.

11. **Surah 72: ayats 14-15.**
Some of us are Muslims and some are wrong-doers. Those that embrace Islam pursue the right path; but those that do wrong (of not embracing Islam) shall become the fuel of fire.

12. **Surah 41: ayat 33.**

And who speaks better than he who calls others to the service of Allah, does what is right, and says: 'I am a Muslim?'

13. **Surah: 4 ayat 125.**

And who has a nobler religion than the man who surrenders himself to Allah?...

14. **Surah 25: ayats 27-29.**

On that day the wrong-doer will bite his hands and say, 'Would that I had walked in the Apostle's path. Oh, would that I had never chosen so-and-so for my companion: It was he that made me disbelieve in Allah's warning after it had reached me.' Satan is ever treacherous to man.

15. **Surah 26: ayats 96-99.**

"By Allah", they will say to their idols, as they contend with them, "we erred indeed when we made you equals with the Lord of the Creation. It was the evil-doers who led us astray."

16. **Surah 3: ayat 85.**

He that chooses a religion other than Islam, it will not be accepted from him and in the world to come he will be one of the lost.

17. **Surah 8: ayat 38.**

Tell the unbelievers that if they mend their ways (i.e. embrace Islam) their past shall be forgiven: but if they persist in sin (i.e. idol-worshipping) let them reflect upon the fate of their forefathers.

18. **Surah 31: ayat 13.**

Luqman admonished his son. 'My son', he said, 'serve no other God instead of Allah, for idolatry is an abominable sin.'

19. **Surah 29: ayats 41-42.**

The false Gods which the idolaters serve besides Allah may be compared to the spider's cobweb. Surely, the spider's is the frailest of all dwellings, if they but know it. Allah knows what they invoke besides Him; He is the Mighty, the Wise one.

20. **Surah 37: ayats 22-25.**
But We shall say: 'Call the sinners, their wives, and the idols which they worshipped besides Allah and lead them to the path of Hell. Keep them there for questioning — But what has come over you that you cannot help one another?'

21. **Surah 37: ayats 26-32.**
On that day they will all submit to Allah. They will reproach each other, saying: 'You have imposed upon us. It was you who would not be believers. We had no power over you; you were sinners all. Just is the verdict which our Lord has passed upon us, we shall surely taste His punishment. We misled you, but we ourselves have been misled.'

22. **Surah 25: ayats 17-19.**
On that day when He assembles them with all their idols, He will say: 'Was it you who misled My servants, or did they wilfully go astray?' They will answer: 'Allah forbid that we should choose other guardians besides You. You gave them and their fathers the good things of life, so that they forgot Your warnings and thus incurred destruction.' Then to the idolaters Allah will say: 'Your idols have denied your charges. They cannot avert your doom, nor can they help you. Those of you who have done wrong shall be sternly punished.'

23. **Surah 7: ayat 173.**
'Our forefathers were indeed, idolaters; but will You destroy us, their descendants, on account of what the followers of falsehood did?'

24. **Surah 21: ayats 66-67.**
He (Abraham) answered: 'Would you then worship that, instead of Allah, which can neither help nor harm you? Shame on you and on your idols: Have you no sense?'

25. **Surah 21: ayats 98-100.**
You and all your idols shall be the fuel of Hell: therein you shall all go down. Were they true Gods, yours idols would not

go there: but in it they shall abide for ever. They shall groan
with pain and be bereft of hearing.

26. **Surah 16: ayats 20-21.**

But the false Gods which infidels invoke create nothing: they
are themselves created. They are dead, not living, nor do they
know when they will be raised to life.

27. **Surah 6: ayats 22-23.**

On that day when We gather them all together We shall say to
the idolaters: 'Where are your idols now, those whom you
supposed to be your Gods?' They will not argue, but will say:
'By Allah, our Lord, we have never worshipped idols.'

28. **Surah 6: ayats 40-41.**

Say: 'When Allah's scourge smites you and the Hour of Doom
suddenly overtakes you, will you call on any but Allah to help
you? Answer me, if you are men of truth: No, on Him alone
you will call; and if He please, He will relieve your affliction.
Then you will forget your idols.'

29. **Surah 6: ayat 148:**

...The idolaters will say: "Had Allah pleased neither we nor
our fathers would have served other Gods besides Him.'...

30. **Surah 2: ayat 221.**

You shall not wed pagan women, unless they embrace the
faith. A believing slave-girl is better than an idolatress,
although she may please you. Nor shall you wed idolaters
unless they embrace the faith. A believing slave is better than
an idolater, although he may please you. These call you to
Hell-fire, but Allah calls you, by His will, to paradise and to
forgiveness. He makes plain His revelations to mankind, so
that they may take heed.

31. **Surah 24: ayat 3.**

The adulterer may marry only an adulteress or an idolatress;
and adulteress may marry only an adulterer or an idolater.
True believers are forbidden such marriages.

(2)

Himangshu Kishore's Reminder

From:
Himangshu Kishore Chakraborty, M.A.,(Cal.),
12/A/4, Pashupati Bhattacharya Road,
Behala,
Calcutta - 34.

14th August, 1984.

To
The Secretary,
Department of Home,
Government of West Bengal,
Writers' Building,
Calcutta - 1.

Dear Sir,

Sub: Request for proscription of 'Koran'.

Please refer to my letter dated 20th July, 1984, (delivered in your office on the same date) in which I had made a request for forfeiture of the Islamic book, Koran, for the reason that it contains numerous sayings of Prophet Muhammad which on ground of religion promote disharmony, feeling of enmity, hatred and ill-will between different religious communities; incite people to commit violence and disturb public tranquility and outrage or insult other religions and the religious feelings of other communities in India, which render the book liable to be forfeited to the Government in terms of Section 95 of the Code of Criminal Procedure, 1973, read with Sections 153A and 295A of the Indian Penal Code.

I had also enclosed some three annexures to my said letter wherein I had reproduced some of those sayings of the book.

Since you do not seem to have given due consideration to my letter, I would request you, once again, to attend to this matter early.

A copy of my said letter dated 20th July, 1984, is enclosed for your ready reference.

Yours faithfully,
Sd/-
Enclo: As above.   (Himangshu Kishore Chakraborty)

Notice from Chandmal Chopra

From:
C.M. Chopra.

25, Burtolla Street,
Calcutta - 7.
16th March, 1985.

To
The Secretary,
Department of Home,
Government of West Bengal,
Writers' Building,
Calcutta - 1.

Dear Sir,

Sub: The Islamic book — Koran — forfeiture of — request for

In terms of Section 95 Cr. P.C. read with Sections 153A and 295A I.P.C. every copy of a book is liable to be forfeited to the Government if the book contains words or sayings which promote, on ground of religion, disharmony, enmity, hatred or ill-will between different religious communities or which outrage the religious feelings of any class of citizens of India or insult the religion or religious beliefs of that class of people. This is so whether the book is classic or epic, religious or temporal, old or new,

Now the Islamic religious book, Koran (or Qur'an), which is available throughout India, whether in the original Arabic or in its translations in Urdu, Bengali, Hindi, English or any other language, is blatantly guilty of each one of the above offences and thus squarely deserves to be declared forfeited to the Government in terms of the above provisions of law.

For example, the Koran incites violence by saying, "Believers! make war on the infidels who dwell around you. Let them find harshness in you" (Surah 9: ayat 123) or by saying, "Do not yield to the unbelievers, but fight them strenuously with this Koran" (Surah 25: ayat 52) or by saying, "If you do not fight He will punish you sternly and replace you by other men" (Surah 9: ayat 39) or by saying, "When the sacred months are over, slay the idol-worshippers, wherever you find them. Arrest them, besiege them and lie in ambush everywhere for them" (Surah 9: ayat 5).

Similarly this book promotes religious enmity, hatred and ill-will when it says, "Believers! know that idolaters are unclean" (Surah 9: ayat 28) or when it says, "Therefore We stirred among them, i.e. the Christians, enmity and hatred which shall endure till the Day of Resurrection" (Surah 5: ayat 14) or when it says, "Believers! take neither Jews nor Christians for your friends. They are friends with one another. Whoever of you seeks their friendship shall become one of their number. Allah does not guide the wrong-doers" (Surah 5: ayat 51).

The above are but a few examples. Actually, the Koran abounds, or overflows with such offensive sayings, some more of which were set out in some three annexures to the letter dated 20th July, 1984, addressed to you in this behalf by a fellow citizen, Sri Himangshu Kishore Chakraborty, M.A., (Cal.) of 12/A/4, Pashupati Bhattacharya, Road, Behala, Calcutta - 34.

It is a matter of regret that inspite of being a blatantly offensive book, the book is still being widely circulated and has not been declared as forfeited to the Government by you inspite of Mr. Chakraborty's request in the said letter dated 20th July, 1984 and his reminder dated 14th August, 1984

Now you are finally requested to take necessary steps in this behalf within 7 days of the receipt hereof, failing which such legal steps will be taken as may be advised to us. This may please be treated as notice demanding justice.

Yours faithfully,
Sd/-
(C.M. Chopra)

(4)

The Writ Application

MATTER NO. 227 OF 1985
IN THE HIGH COURT AT CALCUTTA.
Constitution Writ Jurisdiction.
(ORIGINAL SIDE)

In the Matter of
An application Under Article 226 of
the Constitution of India and Writs,
directions and orders thereunder.

A N D

In the Matter of
Section 95 of the Code of Criminal
Procedure, 1973.

A N D

In the Matter of
Sections 153A and 295A Indian Penal
Code.

A N D

In the Matter of
The Koran, an Islamic book, published
and sold in India in the original Arabic

and in its translations in Urdu, Bengali, Hindi, English, etc.

A N D

In the Matter of

1. Chandmal Chopra, son of late Tikam Chand Chopra, aged 53, at present residing at 25, Burtolla Street, Calcutta - 7, and

2. Sital Singh, son of late Lal Singh at present residing at No. 1, Munshi Sadruddin Lane, Calcutta - 7.

—PETITIONERS

Versus

The State of West Bengal, represented by the Secretary, Department of Home, Government of West Bengal, having his office at Writers' Building, Calcutta - 1.

—RESPONDENT.

To

The Hon'ble Mr. Tarun Kumar Basu, the Acting Chief Justice and His Companion Justices of the said Hon'ble Court.

The humble petition of the petitioners abovenamed most respectfully

S H E W E T H :

1. The petitioners are the citizens of India and are engaged in various types of social work.

2. The respondent is a public authority having in terms of Section 95 Criminal Procedure Code, 1973, read with Sections 153A and 295A Indian Penal Code, a public duty to forfeit to the Government every copy of a book which incites violence,

disturbs public tranquility, promotes, on ground of religion, feelings of enmity, hatred and ill-will between different religious communities and insults other religions or religious beliefs of other communities in India.

3. The Koran, also spelt as 'Qur'an', the so-called religious book of the Muslims the world over, written originally in the Arabic and available throughout India in the original Arabic or in its translation in Urdu, Bengali, Hindi, English, etc., is *ex facie* guilty of each one of the above offences.

4. For example, in Surah 9, ayat 5, the book says, "When the sacred months are over, slay the idolaters wherever you find them. Arrest them, besiege them and lie in ambush everywhere for them."

In Surah 48, ayat 29, it says, "Muhammad is Allah's apostle. Those who follow him are ruthless to the unbelievers but merciful to one another... Through them Allah seeks to enrage the unbelievers."

In surah 49, ayat 15, it says, "The true believers are those who have faith in Allah and His apostle and never doubt; and who fight for His cause with their wealth and persons."

In surah 8, ayat 39, it says, "Make war on them (idol-worshippers) until idolatry is no more and Allah's religion reigns supreme."

In surah 2, ayat 193, it again says, "Fight against them until idolatry is no more and Allah's religion reigns supreme."

In surah 2, ayat 216, it has made fighting "obligatory" for every Muslim. In surah 9, ayat 41, it exhorts Muslims to "march on and fight for the cause of Allah", whether unarmed or well-equipped.

In surah 9, ayat 123, exhorting Muslims to make war on infidels "who dwell around you", it says, "Let them find harshness in you."

In surah 66, ayat 9, an exhortation is given to the prophet to make war on the unbelievers and "deal sternly with them."

In surah 9, ayat 73, it again exhorts the prophet to "make war" on the unbelievers and to be "harsh" with them.

In surah 8, ayat 65, it asks the prophet to exhort the Muslims to fight, saying, "If there are twenty steadfast men among you, they shall rout a thousand unbelievers." More or less the same thing is repeated in ayat 66 of the same surah 8.

In surah 47, ayats 4 to 15, the Koran calls upon the Muslims to "strike off" the heads of the non-Muslims when the two meet in the battlefield, without minding risking their own lives, for if any of them are killed fighting in the name of Allah they are assured of admission in the paradise.

In surah 8, ayat 12, the Koran exhorts the Muslims to "strike off" the heads of the non-Muslims and to "maim them in every limb."

In surah 69, ayats 30 to 37, the Muslims are asked to capture non-Muslims and burn them in hell-fire after fastening them with chains.

In surah 8, ayats 15 to 18, the Muslims are exhorted not to run away while fighting the non-Muslims and thus incur the wrath of Allah.

In surah 25, ayat 52, the Muslims are exhorted not to yield to the non-Muslims but to fight them strenuously, while according to surah 9, ayat 39, if anybody does not fight, he will be punished by Allah sternly.

In surah 9, ayat 111, the Koran exhorts the Muslims to kill and be killed because, it says that Allah in exchange of promise of heavenly garden has already purchased the lives and the worldly belongings of the Muslims.

In surah 3, ayats 157 and 158 a believer is told that if he is killed while fighting the unbelievers, he will get Allah's mercy all the more.

In surah 8, ayats 59 and 60, the believers are told to muster all the men and the entire cavalry against the unbelievers so that it may strike terror into non-believers.

In surah 9, ayats 2 and 3, the believers are exhorted to proclaim a woeful punishment to the unbelievers.

In surah 9, ayat 29, the Muslims are exhorted to fight the Christians and the Jews until they embrace the true faith, that is, Islam.

In surah 4, ayat 66, it is stated that the prophet does not take people captives; he simply kills them.

In surah 4, ayat 84, the believers are roused to fight. In surah 29, ayat 6, it says, "He that fights for Allah's cause fights for himself."

In surah 9, ayat 14, it exhorts the believers to "fight them. Allah will chastise them at your hands, and He will lay them low and give you victory over them..."

In surah 9, ayats 20 and 21, the believers are assured that "those that have embraced the faith and fled their homes and fought for Allah's cause with their wealth and their persons are held in higher regard by Allah. It is they who shall triumph. Their Lord has promised them joy and mercy, and gardens of eternal pleasure where they shall dwell for ever."

In surah 3, ayat 142, a dangerous statement is made in the interrogative, "Did you suppose that you would enter paradise before Allah has proved the men who fought for him and endured with fortitude?"

5. The book promotes religious enmity, hatred and ill-will between different religious communities in India.

For example, in surah 60, ayat 4, it says, "We renounce you (i.e. idol-worshippers); enmity and hate shall reign between us until you believe in Allah only."

In surah 58, ayat 22, it says, "You shall find no believers in Allah and the Last Day on friendly terms with those who oppose Allah and His apostle, even though they may be their fathers, their sons, their brothers, or their nearest kindred."

In surah 9, ayat 23, it says "Believers! do not befriend your fathers or your brothers, if they choose unbelief in preference to faith. Wrong-doers are those that befriend them."

In surah 3, ayat 28, it says, "Let believers not make friends with infidels in preference to the faithful; he that does this has nothing to hope for from Allah."

In surah 3, ayat 118, it says, "Believers! do not make friends with any men other than your own people."

In surah 4, ayat 144, it says, "Believers! do not choose the infidels rather than the faithful for your friends. Would you give Allah a clear proof against yourself?"

In surah 9, ayat 7, it says, "Allah and His apostle repose no trust in idolaters." In surah 8, ayat 55, It says, "The basest creatures in the sight of Allah are the faithless who will not believe."

In surah 25, ayat 55, it says, "Yet the unbelievers worship idols which can neither help nor harm them. Surely the unbeliever is his Lord's enemy."

In surah 5, ayat 72, it says, "He that worships other Gods besides Allah shall be forbidden Paradise and shall be cast into the fire of Hell. None shall help the evil-doers."

In surah 9, ayat 28, it says, "Believers! know that the idolaters are unclean."

In surah 5, ayat 14, it says, "Therefore, we stirred among them (i.e. the Christians) enmity and hatred, which shall endure till the Day of Resurrection"

In surah 5, ayat 64, it says, "That which Allah has revealed to you will surely increase the wickedness and unbelief of many of them (i.e. the Jews). We have stirred among them, (i.e. the Christians) enmity and hatred, which shall endure till the Day of Resurrection..."

In surah 5, ayat 18, it says. "The Jews and the Christians say, 'We are the children of Allah and His loved ones.' Say, 'Why then does He punish you for your sins'?"

In surah 5, ayat 51, it says, "Believers! take neither Jews nor Christians for your friends. They are friends with one another. Whoever of you seeks their friendship shall become one of their members. Allah does not guide the wrong-doers."

6. The book insults other religions or religious beliefs of other communities in India.

For example, in surah 5 ayat 17, it says, "Unbelievers are those who declare, 'Allah is the Messiah (i.e. the Christ), the son of Mary.' Say, 'Who could prevent Allah from destroying the Messiah, the son of Mary, together with his mother and all the people of the earth'?"

In surah 4, ayat 157, it says, "They denied the truth and uttered a monstrous falsehood against Mary. They declared, 'We have put to death the Messiah Jesus, the son of Mary, the apostle of Allah.' They did not kill him nor did they crucify him but they thought they did."

In surah 98, ayat 6, it says, "The unbelievers among the people of the Book (i.e. the Christians and the Jews) and the pagans shall burn for ever in the fire of Hell. They are the vilest of all creatures."

In surah 68, ayats 10 to 13, it says, "Give no heed to the

disbelievers; they desire you to overlook their doings that they may overlook yours. Nor yield to the wretch of many oaths, the mischief-making slanderer, the opponent of good, the wicked transgressor, the bully who is of doubtful birth to boot."

In surah 22, ayats 19 to 22, it says. "Garments of fire have been prepared for unbelievers. Scalding water shall be poured upon their heads, melting their skins and that which is in their bellies. They shall be lashed with rods of iron."

In surah 22, ayats 56 and 57, it says, "Those that have embraced the true faith and done good work shall enter the gardens of delight, but the unbelievers who have denied Our revelations shall receive an ignominious punishment."

In surah 5, ayats 36 and 37, it says, "As for the unbelievers, if they offered all that the earth contains and as much besides to redeem themselves from the torment of the Day of Resurrection, it shall not be accepted from them. Theirs shall be a woeful punishment."

In surah 15, ayat 2, it says, "The day will surely come when the unbelievers will wish that they were Muslims."

In surah 72, ayats 14 and 15, it says, "Some of us are Muslims and some are wrong-doers. Those that embrace Islam pursue the right path, but those that do wrong shall become the fuel of fire."

In surah 41, ayat 33, it says. "And who speaks better than he who calls others to the service of Allah, does what is right, and says, 'I am a Muslim'?"

In surah 4, ayat 125, it says, "And who has a nobler religion than the one who surrenders himself to Allah?"

In surah 3, ayat 85, it says, "He that chooses a religion other than Islam, it will not be accepted from him and in the world to come, he will be one of the last."

In surah 8, ayat 38, it says, "Tell the unbelievers that if they

THE WRIT APPLICATION / 283

mend their ways (i.e. embrace Islam) their past will be forgiven but if they persist in sin (i.e. idol-worshipping) let them reflect upon the fate of their forefathers."

In surah 31, ayat 13, it says, "Luqman admonished his son. 'My son', he said, 'serve no other God instead of Allah, for idolatry is an abominable sin'."

In surah 29, ayat 41, it says, "The false Gods which the idolaters serve besides Allah may be compared to the spider's cobweb. Surely the spider's is the frailest of all dwellings if they but know it."

In surah 37, ayats 22 to 25, it says, "But We shall say, 'Call the sinners, their wives and the idols which they worshipped besides Allah, and lead them to the path of Hell. Keep them there for questioning — But what has come over you that you cannot help one another'?"

In surah 7, ayat 173, it makes the Muslims say, "Our forefathers were indeed idol-worshippers, but will you destroy us, their descendants, on account of what the followers of falsehood did?"

In surah 21, ayats 66 and 67, it says, "He answered, 'Would you then worship that, instead of Allah, which can neither help nor harm you? Shame on you and on your idols! Have you no sense?'"

In surah 21, ayats 98 to 100, it says, "You and all your idols shall be the fuel of Hell; therein you shall all go down. Were they true Gods, your idols would not go there; but in it they shall abide for ever. They shall groan with pain and be bereft of hearing."

In surah 6, ayats 22 and 23, it says. "On that day when We gather them all together, We shall say to the idolaters: 'Where are your idols now, those whom you supposed to be your Gods?' They will not argue, but will say, 'By Allah, our Lord, we have never worshipped idols'."

In surah 6, ayats 40 and 41, it makes the believers say, "Say, 'When Allah's scourge smites you and the Hour of Doom suddenly overtakes you, will you call on any but Allah to help you? Answer me, if you are men of truth. No, on Him alone you will call, and if He pleases, He will relieve your affliction. Then you will forget your idols'."

In surah 6, ayat 149 it says, "The idolaters will say, 'Had Allah pleased, neither we nor our fathers would have served other Gods besides Him'."

In surah 2, ayat 221, it says, "You shall not wed pagan women, unless they embrace the faith. A believing slave-girl is better than an idolatress, although she may please you. Nor shall you wed idolaters, unless they embrace the faith. A believing slave is better than an idolater, although he may please you. These call you to Hell-fire, but Allah calls you, by His will, to Paradise and to forgiveness."

In surah 24, ayat 3, it says, "The adulterer may marry only an adulteress or an idolatress, and the adulteress may marry an adulterer or an idolater."

In surah 5, ayats 116 to 118, there is given this imaginary dialogue between Allah and Jesus Christ, which is highly insulting to the Christians: "Then Allah will say, 'Jesus, son of Mary, did you ever say to mankind, worship me and my mother as Gods besides Allah?' 'Glory to You,' he will answer, 'How could I say that to which I have no right? If I had ever said so, You would have surely known it. You know what is in my mind, but I cannot tell what is in Yours. You alone know what is hidden. I spoke to them of nothing except what You bade me. I say, Serve Allah, my Lord and your Lord. I watched over them whilst living in their midst, and ever since You took me to You, You Yourself have been watching over them. You are the witness of all things. They are Your own bondsmen. It is for You to punish or to forgive them. You are the Mighty, the Wise one'."

In surah 25, ayats 17 to 19, there is given another imaginary conversation, this time between Allah, the idols and the idol-worshippers, which is highly insulting to Christians, Buddhists, Hindus, etc. "On the day when He assembles them with all their idols, He will say: 'Was it you who misled My servants, or did they wilfully go astray?' They will answer: 'Allah forbid that we should choose other guardians besides You. You gave them and their fathers the good things of life, so that they forgot Your warnings and thus incurred destruction.' Then to the idolaters Allah will say: 'Your idols have denied your charges. They cannot avert your doom, nor can they help you. Those of you who have done wrong shall be sternly punished'."

7. While the Koran abounds with saying which incite violence, insult the religious beliefs of other communities and even exhort the Muslims to kill and murder non-Muslims, the problem is aggravated by yet another fact which has been true in the past and is universally true in our own times that unlike other communities Muslims are, and even fresh converts tend to become, highly orthodox people and follow the sayings of the book with a fanatical zeal with the result that whichever country has their sizable number amongst its population can never have peace on its soil. The examples of communal strifes and conflicts in most European states have not yet passed into history. What is happening in Lebanon is very much in our perception. An example of orthodoxy is Pakistan whose Hindu population has been obliterated through murder or through forcible conversion. Even Ahmediyas are being persecuted there because they regard Mirza Ghulam Ahmed (1839-1908 AD), the founder of their religion, as another prophet along with Muhammad which is contrary to Koran because according to the Koran Muhammad is the last prophet. Baha'i religion, even though a Muslim sect and founded by Baha-ul-lah in Iran in the nineteenth century and which has some one million followers in India along with some 400,000 in Iran, has been banned in Indonesia on the ground that it stresses men's spiritual unity, which is unconformable with Koranic preachings. In Iran, Baha'is are being subjected to worst per-secution; many have been executed, many more jailed without

trial. Even Baha'i students have been expelled from schools and colleges in Iran. Another example of orthodoxy or religious intolerance is furnished by Iran and Iraq, both Muslim countries but both of which are out to fight tooth and nail with each other because one happens to be a Shia nation while the other a Sunni nation. In our country, violent conflict resulting in numerous deaths between Shias and Sunnis is almost an annual ritual. Another example of religious fanaticism is provided by the fact that the Muslim countries the world over have ganged up together to crush Israel, because it happens to be a Jewish state and as already stated in para 5 above, the Koran makes most uncharitable remarks about the Jews.

8. The offending expressions contained in the Koran and quoted in paragraphs 4, 5 and 6 above are not so offensive in their translation in which they are so quoted as they are in the original verses in Arabic or in Urdu, the very sound of whose inimitable symphony not only sends the Muslims to tears and ecstasy but arouses in them the worst communal passions and religious fanaticism which have manifested themselves in murder, slaughter, loot, arson, rape and destruction or desecration of holy places in historical times as also in contemporary period not only in India but almost all over the world.

9. In this way, the publication of the Koran in the original Arabic as well as in its translations in various languages including Urdu, Hindi, Bengali, English, etc., amounts to commission of offences punishable u/s 153A and 295A of the Indian Penal Code and accordingly each copy of the book must be declared as forfeited by the respondent u/s 95 of the Code of Criminal Procedure, 1973.

10. By letter dated 16th March, 1985, the petitioner No. 1, requested the respondent to declare each copy of the Koran, whether in the original Arabic or in its translation in any of the languages, as forfeited to the Government within seven days of the receipt of the letter. By the same letter the respondent was also

requested to treat the letter as notice demanding justice. A copy of this letter is annexed hereto marked 'A'.

11. The respondent, however, has not complied with the said request.

12. Being aggrieved by the failure of the respondent to accede to the said request, your petitioners beg to move this petition before this Hon'ble Court on the following

GROUND

The respondent, by not declaring, inspite of a specific request, copies of the 'Koran' to be forfeited to the Government, even though its publication amounts to commission of offences punishable under Sections 153A and 295A, Indian Penal Code, has failed to discharge its statutory duty as enshrined in Section 95 of the Code of Criminal Procedure, 1973.

13. There is no other adequate, efficacious and alternative remedy available to your petitioners and the reliefs prayed for herein, if granted, will afford complete and efficacious remedy to your petitioners.

14. The petition is being made bonafide and in the interest of the public.

In the circumstances aforesaid your petitioners humbly pray to your Lordships for

A. A rule nisi on the respondent to show cause as to why a writ of mandamus be not issued to it directing it to declare each copy of the Koran, whether in the original Arabic or in its translation in any of the languages as forfeited to the Government.

B. The rule issued in terms of prayer 'A' above be made absolute.

C. Such further or other order and/or orders be made and/or directions be given as may be deemed fit and proper.

And your petitioners as in duty bound shall ever pray.

Sd/- Chandmal Chopra.
Sd/- Sital Singh

29th March, 1985.

(5)

Affidavit in Opposition

Government of West Bengal
Office of the Advocate-on-Record,
5, K.S. Ray Road, (2nd floor)
Calcutta - 1

No. AGR/985/85.   Dated the 29th April 1985.

From: Shri R.C. Deb,
     Advocate-on-Record, West Bengal.

To: Shri Chandmal Chopra,
     25, Burtolla Street,
     Calcutta - 7.

Matter No. 297 of 1985
Chandmal Chopra & Anr.
– vs –
State of West Bengal

- - -

Dear Sir,

Enclosed please find a copy of the affidavit in opposition to be filed on behalf of the respondent.

Yours faithfully,
Sd/-
(R.C. DEB).

Enclo: As stated.
RCD/SP.

In the Matter of an application under Article 226 of the Constitution of India and Writs, directions and orders thereunder.

AND

In the Matter of Section 95 of the Code of Criminal Procedure, 1973.

AND

In the Matter of Sections 153A and 295A, Indian Penal Code.

AND

In the Matter of the Koran, an Islamic book, published and sold in India in the original Arabic and in its translations in Urdu, Bengali, Hindi, English, etc.

AND

In the Matter of:
1.   Chandmal Chopra, son of late Tikam Chand Chopra, aged 53, at present residing at 25, Burtolla Street, Calcutta - 7 and
2.   Sital Singh, son of late Lal Singh at present residing at No.1, Munshi Sadruddin Lane, Calcutta - 7.

... Petitioners

– Vs –

The State of West Bengal, represented by Secretary, Department of Home, Government of West Bengal, having his office at Writers' Building, Calcutta - 1.

...   ...   *Respondent*

I, **TIMIR HARAN SEN GUPTA,** Deputy Secretary, Home Department, Government of West Bengal, residing at Saptarany Flat 9, 11/3 Old Ballygunge, 2nd Lane, Calcutta - 19, solemnly affirm and say as follows:

1. I am competent enough and have been duly authorised to affirm the affidavit.

1a. I state that according to the Islamic belief the Holy Quran is a Divine Book. It contains the words of God Almighty revealed at His last Prophet Muhammad. The verses of the Holy Quran were revealed on the happenings of particular events and its each and every verse has a connotation of its own and on different and separate background.

2. I further state that as the Holy Quran is a Divine Book, no earthly power can sit upon judgment on it and no Court of law has jurisdiction to adjudicate it. The Holy Books like the Quran, the Bible, the Geeta, the Granth Sahib, etc., or their translations cannot be the subject-matters of adjudication in a court of law. All Holy Scriptures are immune from judicial scrutiny.

3. I submit that this Hon'ble Court has no jurisdiction to pronounce a judgment on the Quran, the Holy Scripture of the Muslims all over the world, each and every word of which, according to the Islamic belief, is unalterable.

4. There is, as far as known to me, no country in the world where there are no Muslims practising their religion, not to mention the countries where the whole population believe in Islam

and the Holy Quran. From the time of British Rule and since Independence, inspite of the Indian Penal Code being in existence, there has never been such an application in any court in India.

In view of the aforesaid submission I am not dealing with any of the allegations in the said petition.

5. The instant Writ application has been filed with malafide and ulterior motives and should be dismissed with costs.

6. That the statements contained in paragraphs 1, 1a, 2, 3, 4 and 5 hereof are submissions to this Hon'ble Court.

Sd/-
(Timir Haran Sen Gupta).

(6)

The Judgement

BIMAL CHANDRA BASAK
May 17   85.
Chandmal Chopra & Anr.
Versus
State of West Bengal

The Court: I have heard and disposed of this application on the 13th of May 1985 when I indicated that I shall give my reasons later.

Facts:

2. This is an application under Article 226 of the Constitution of India praying for a Writ of Mandamus directing the State of West Bengal to declare each copy of the Koran, whether in the original Arabic or in its translation in any of the languages, as forfeited to the Government.

3. This application was first moved before Khastgir J. The learned Judge entertained the application, gave directions for notice and for affidavits. Thereafter for some reason or other the learned Judge chose not to proceed in this matter any further and released this matter from her list. Such reason cannot be found out from the records of this case though the learned Judge had chosen to take an unprecedented step by giving an interview to the Press

regarding the same of which I cannot and do not take any notice. The Chief Justice thereafter assigned this matter to me. As the learned Judge after giving directions has chosen not to hear this matter any further and as this matter has been assigned to me, I have recalled all the earlier orders and/or directions passed and heard the matter afresh as Court Application on the question of issue of the Rule nisi, if any. Accordingly the petitioner no.1 who is appearing in person made submissions and prayed for issue of a Rule.

4. The learned Advocate General has appeared for the State and with the leave of this Court the learned Attorney General has made submissions on behalf of Union of India.

5. The petitioners have, in this petition, quoted some passages from the English translation of Koran and thereafter made the following averments:

The offending expressions contained in the Koran and quoted in paragraphs 4, 5 and 6 above are not so offensive in their translation in which they are so quoted as they are in the original verses in Arabic or in Urdu, the very sound of whose inimitable symphony not only sends the Muslims to tears and ecstasy but arouses in them the worst communal passions and religious fanaticism, which have manifested themselves in murder, slaughter, loot, arson, rape and destruction or desecration of holy places in historical times as also in contemporary period not only in India but almost all over the world. (paragraph 8).

In this way, the publication of the Koran in the original Arabic as well as in its translations in various languages including Urdu, Hindi, Bengali, English, etc., amounts to commission of offences punishable u/s 153A and 295A of the Indian Penal Code and accordingly each copy of the book must be declared as forfeited by the respondent u/s 95 of the Code of Criminal Procedure, 1973. (paragraph 9).

Submissions — Petitioner

6. The petitioner in his submission has repeated what has been stated in the petition. He has submitted that the provisions of Sections 153A and 295A of the Indian Penal Code are attached and accordingly the respondent should be directed to take action under Section 95 of the Criminal Procedure Code. He has submitted that Koran seeks to destroy idols. It encourages crime and invites violence. It is also against morality. It outrages the religious feelings of non-Muslims. It insults all religions excepting Islam. It encourages hatred, disharmony, feelings of enmity between different religious communities in India.

7. The relevant provisions of Section 95 of the Criminal Procedure Code (hereinafter referred to as Cr. P.C.) and Sections 153A, 295 and 295A of the Indian Penal Code (hereinafter referred to as I.P.C.), are set out hereinbelow:

Cr. P.C. – Sec. 95: "(1) Where (a) any newspaper, or book (b) any document, wherever printed, appears to the State Government to contain any matter the publication of which is punishable under section 124A or section 153A or section 153B or section 292 or section 293 or section 295A of the Indian Penal Code (45 of 1860), the State Government may, by notification, stating the grounds of its opinion, declare every copy of the issue of the newspaper containing such matter, and every copy of such book or other document to be forfeited to Government, and thereupon any police officer may seize the same wherever found in India and any Magistrate may by warrant authorise any police officer not below the rank of sub-inspector to enter upon and search for the same in any premises where any copy of such issue or any such book or other document may be or may be reasonably suspected to be.

(2) In this section and in section 96

(a) newspaper and book have the same meaning as in the Press and Registration of Book Act, 1867 (25 of 1867).

(b) document includes any painting, drawing or photograph or other visible representation.

(3) No order passed or action taken under this section shall be called in question in any court otherwise than in accordance with the provisions of section 96."

I.P.C. – Sec. 153A: "Whoever by words, either spoken or written or by visible representations, or otherwise, promotes or attempts to promote feelings of enmity or hatred between different classes of Her Majesty's subjects, shall be punished with imprisonment which may extend to two years, or with fine or with both."

I.P.C. – Section 295: "Whoever destroys, damages or defiles any place of worship, or any object held sacred by any class of persons with the intention of thereby insulting the religion of any class of persons or with the knowledge that any class of persons is likely to consider such destruction, damage or defilement as an insult to their religion, shall be punished with imprisonment of either description for a term which may extend to two years, or with fine, or with both."

Section 295A: "Whoever, with deliberate and malicious intention of outraging the religious feelings of any class of His Majesty's subjects, by words, either spoken or written, or by visible representations insults or attempts to insult the religion or the religious beliefs of that class, shall be punished with imprisonment of either description for a term which may extend to two years, or with fine, or with both."

8. The petitioner no.1 has addressed the Court in person and placed the petition and drawn my attention to the relevant provisions of the Act referred to above and has submitted that it is a fit and proper case where such an order is to be passed against the Government directing them to take action under Section 95 of the Code of Criminal Procedure.

Submission — State

9. The learned Advocate General appearing on behalf of the State has placed before me Section 295 of the Indian Penal Code which I have set out above.

10. The learned Advocate General has submitted that the Koran is a sacred book of the Muslim community and making an order of the nature as prayed for would amount to abolition of this religion. Such a prayer offends the provisions of Section 295 of the I.P.C. and, therefore, the question of invoking jurisdiction of this Court in respect of Section 295A of the I.P.C. cannot and does not arise. In this connection he has relied on a decision of the Supreme Court in the case of *Veerabadram Chettiar – vs – V. Ramaswami Naicker & Ors.* reported in A.I.R. 1958 S.C. 1032 at page 1035, paragraph 7. The relevant passage is set out hereinbelow:

"The learned Judge in the court below, has given much too restricted a meaning to the words 'any object held sacred by any class of persons,' by holding that only idols in temples or idols carried in processions on festival occasions, are meant to be included within those words. There are no such express words of limitation in S. 295 of the Indian Penal Code and in our opinion the learned Judge has clearly misdirected himself in importing those words of limitation. Idols are only illustrative of those words. A sacred book, like the Bible, or the Koran, or the Granth Saheb, is clearly within the ambit of those general words. If the courts below were right in their interpretation of the crucial words in S. 295 the burning or otherwise destroying or defiling such sacred books, will not come within the purview of the penal statute. In our opinion, placing such a restricted interpretation on the words of such general import, is against all established canons of construction. Any object however trivial or destitute of real value in itself, if regarded as sacred by any class of persons would come within the meaning of the penal section. Nor is it absolutely necessary that the object, in order to be held sacred should have been actually worshipped. An object may be held sacred by a class of persons without being worshipped by them. It is clear, therefore, that the courts below were rather cynical in so lightly brushing aside the religious susceptibilities of that class of persons to which the complainant claims to belong. The section has been intended to respect the religious susceptibilities of persons of different religious persuasions or creeds. Courts have got to be very circumspect in such matters, and to pay due regard to the feelings and religious emotions of different classes of persons with different beliefs, irrespective of the consideration whether or not they share those beliefs, or whether they are rational or otherwise, in the opinion of the court."

Mr. Advocate General has submitted that the Koran has been in existence for a long time. No grievance has been made at any point of time by any one to the effect as the petitioner is seeking to do before this Court. He has submitted that this Court is not entitled to go into this matter as this relates to a question of religion itself. He has further submitted that this is a motivated application with the intention of destroying communal harmony.

He has relied on a decision in the case of *Public Prosecutor – vs – P. Ramaswami* reported in 1966 (1) C.L.J., 672.

Submission — Union of India.

12. Mr. Attorney General appearing on behalf of Union of India assisted by M.K. Banerjee Additional Solicitor General has adopted the submission of Mr. Advocate General and further added as follows:

He has referred to a passage from the Encyclopaedia Britannica at pages 444 and 445. He has submitted that the Koran is a basic text. It is the basis and foundation of the Muslim religion. This cannot be made justiciable in a court of law. The challenge of the petitioner amounts to not only an insult to the Muslim religion as such but against all other religions also. He has further submitted that certain passages taken out of context cannot be referred to for invoking the writ jurisdiction of this Court. He has also relied on a passage from *The Life and Letters of Raja Rammohan Roy* written by Collet.

13. He has also relied on a decision in the case of *Krishna Singh – vs – Mathura & Ors.* reported in A.I.R. 1980 S.C. 707 at page 712 paragraph 17.

14. He has also relied on several passages from Fyzee and Mulla's 18th Edition on Mohammedan Law.

15. He has also relied on a decision in the case of *Ramjilal Modi – vs – State of U.P.* reported in A.I.R. 1957 S.C. 620, paragraph 9.

16. Next. Mr. Attorney General has drawn my attention to the Preamble of the Constitution of India and Article 25 thereof which are set out hereinbelow:

Preamble : WE, THE PEOPLE OF INDIA, having solemnly resolved to constitute India into a SOVEREIGN SOCIALIST SECULAR DEMOCRATIC RE-PUBLIC and to secure to all its citizens Liberty of thought, expression, belief, faith and worship.

Art. 25: (1) Subject to public order, morality and health and to the other provisions of this Part, all persons are equally entitled to freedom of conscience and the right freely to profess, practise and propagate religion.

17. He has submitted that in view of such provisions of the Constitution the Court has no such power to give any such direction.

18. He has further relied on a passage from Halsbury's Laws of England (4th Edition, Vol. 18, paragraphs 1692 and 1693).

19. He has further submitted that this is supposed to be a public interest litigation and this Court should be very cautious about the same. In this connection he has drawn my attention to the decision of the Supreme Court in *Bandhu Mukti Morcha – vs – Union of*

India and others reported in 1984(3) S.C. 161 at 231 paragraphs 59 to 67.

Reply

20. The petitioner in his reply repeated his submissions.

Decision

21. Before examining the scope of the contention of the petitioners, it is necessary to ascertain the scope and importance of the Koran as such. It is the basic text of the Muslim religion. Like all other religions it proceeds on the basis that it is the only true religion and that those who do not follow that religion are not the true devotees of God.

22. As observed by the Supreme Court in the case of S. Veerabadram Chettiar – vs – V. Ramaswami Naicker (supra), as followed in the Madras decision of Public Prosecutor vs. Ramaswami (supra) the Koran, like the Bible and the Granth Saheb is a sacred book. It is an object held sacred by Muslims. Allah is considered as the God.

23. As pointed out in the Encyclopaedia Britannica, the Koran is the sacred scripture of the religion of Islam. It is a book in the Arabic language containing about 80,000 words. It is composed of 114 suras, or chapters, of varying size. The first sura, entitled "The Opening", is in the form of a short devotional prayer; it is constantly so used, ceremonially and otherwise, and by comparativists has been called "the Lord's Prayer of the Muslims". It is addressed to God. The remainder of the Koran is in the form of an address from God, he either speaking himself, sometimes in the first person, or else, through the imperative *ul*, "say" which introduces many verses and passages and some suras, ordering that the words that follow be proclaimed. The subject matter is varied; passages of one or several verses, or of an entire sura, deal in diverse ways with many topics. It speaks about

oneness and omniscience and supreme majesty of God. The style at time fiery, is powerful, the general tone deeply moralist and theocentric; the whole reverberates with a passionate demand for obedience to the will of a transcendent but near and mightily active God.

24. In the faith of Muslims, and according to the theory propounded in the book itself, the Koran is the revealed word of God. This postulates God, and indeed the kind of God who has something to say to us and who takes the initiative in saying it. Religion in this view is not a human searching after God; it is God who acts, and is known because and insofar as, and only as, he chooses to disclose himself.

25. In the Muslim view, God created the universe, ordaining its processes and controlling them. He prescribed a pattern or order, which nature must obey. For man also he obtained a pattern of behaviour, but unlike the rest of the natural world, man was made conscious and free, to choose whether or not he will conform to God's decrees. There is for mankind a right way to live; it is the Koran that seeks to make this known.

26. For Muslims the Koran is the *ipsissima verba* of God himself. It is God speaking to man not merely in 7th century Arabia to Mohammed but from all eternity to every man throughout the world including the individual Muslim as he reads it or devoutly holds it. It is eternal breaking through into time, the unknowable disclosed, the transcendent entering history and remaining here, available to mortals to handle and to appropriate, the divine become apparent. To memorise it, as many Muslims have ceremonially done, and perhaps even to quote from it, as every Muslim does daily in his formal prayers and otherwise, is to enter into some sort of communion with ultimate reality.

27. There is another aspect of this matter. There are various interpretations of different verses of the Koran. As pointed out by S.D. Collet in *The Life and Letters of Raja Rammohan Roy* two verses of the Koran quoted by Raja Rammohan Roy are

interpreted differently by some modern scholars. So far as verse of the Koran under IX.5. is concerned according to a scholar, it does not refer to general massacre of all polytheists and idolaters, that is all non-Muslims, but it speaks only of those non-Muslims who were waging war at the time with the Muslims treacherously by breaking previous agreement.

28. According to the *Mulla on Mohammedan Law* there are four sources of Islamic Law, one of which is the 'Koran'. The word 'Islam' means peace and submission. In its religious sense it denotes submission to the will of God and in its secular sense the establishment of peace. The word 'Muslim' in Arabic is the active participle of 'As-salam' which is acceptance of the faith and of which the noun of action is 'Islam'. In English the word 'Muslim' is used both as a Noun and an Adjective and denotes both the persons professing faith and something peculiar to Muslims, such as law, culture, etc. The Muslims believe in the divine origin of their holy book which according to their belief was revealed to the prophet by the angel Gabriel. The 'Koran' is Al-furcan, i.e., one showing truth from falsehood and right from wrong. The Koran contains about 6000 verses but not more than 200 verses deal with legal principles. The portion which was revealed to the prophet at Mecca is, singularly free of legal matter and contains the philosophy of life and religion and particularly 'Islam'. As the Koran is of divine origin, so are the religion and its tenets and the philosophy and the legal principles which the Koran inculcates. The Koran has no earthly source. It was compiled from memory after the prophet's death from the version of Osman the third Caliph.

29. It is in the light of the above that one should approach to examine the said book. Some passages containing interpretation of some chapters of the Koran quoted out of context cannot be allowed to dominate or influence the main aim and object of this book. It is dangerous for any court to pass its judgement on such a book by merely looking at certain passages out of context.

30. In my opinion the Koran being a sacred Book and "an object held sacred by a class of persons" within meaning of Section 295 of Indian Penal Code, against such book no action can be taken under Section 295A. Section 295A is not attracted in such a case. Section 295A has no application in respect of a sacred book which is protected under Section 295 of I.P.C. Any other interpretation would lead to absurdity. If any offence, within the meaning of Section 295 is committed, in respect of Koran then it is punishable. Such Book gets protection in view of Section 295A. At the same time if it is open to take any such action under Section 295A against such Book, then the protection given under Section 295 will become nugatory and meaningless.

31. Further, as pointed out by the Supreme Court in the case of *Ramji Lal Modi – vs – State of U.P.* (supra) Section 295A does not penalise any and every act of insult or attempt to insult the religion or the religious beliefs of a class of citizens, which are not perpetrated with the deliberate and malicious intention of outraging the religious feelings of that class. Insults to religion offered unwittingly or carelessly or without any deliberate or malicious intention of outraging the religious feelings of that class do not come within the scope of the section. It only punishes the aggravated form of insult to religion when it is perpetrated with deliberate and malicious intention of outraging the religious feelings of that class. I have set out the aim and object of the Koran. In my opinion it cannot be said that Koran offers any insult to any other religion. It does not reflect any deliberate or malicious intention of outraging the religious feelings of non-Muslims. Isolated passages picked out from here and there and read out of context cannot change the position.

32. The Attorney General is right in his contention that such a construction as suggested cannot be given as this would amount to violation of the Constitution. I have already set out the Preamble to and Article 25 of the Constitution.

33. Preamble to the Constitution is a part of the Constitution. *Keshavananda – vs – Kerala*, A.I.R. 1973 S.C. 1461. Accordingly, it is open to the Court to keep the same in mind while considering any provision of the Constitution of India.

34. In my opinion passing of such order as prayed for would go against the Preamble of the Constitution and would violate the provisions of Article 25 thereof. The Preamble proclaims India to be a secular State. It means that each and every religion is to be treated equally. No preference is to be given to any particular religion. No religion is to be belittled. Liberty of thought, expression, belief, faith and worship are assured. Koran, which is the basic text book of Mohammedans, occupies a unique position to the believers of that faith as Bible is to the Christians and Gita, Ramayana and Mahabharata to the Hindus. In my opinion, if such an order is passed, it would take away the secularity of India and it would deprive a section of people of their right of thought, expression, belief, faith and worship. This would also amount to infringement of Article 25 which provides that all persons shall be equally entitled to freedom of conscience and the right freely to profess, practise and to propagate religion. Banning or forfeiture of Koran would infringe that right. Such action would amount to abolition of the Muslim religion itself. Muslim religion cannot exist without Koran. The proposed action would take away the freedom of conscience of the people of that faith and their right to profess, practise and propagate the said religion. Such action is unthinkable. The Court cannot sit in judgment on a holy book like Koran, Bible, Geeta and Granth Saheb.

35. As pointed out in Halsbury 4th Ed. Vol. 18 on "Foreign Relations Law", right of freedom of thought, conscience and religion includes freedom, alone or with or in community with others, and in public or private, to manifest religion or belief in worship, teaching, practice and observance. In my opinion, the action proposed will deprive a class of persons of their human rights.

36. There is another aspect of the matter. This sacred book has been in existence for a number of years with its different interpretations and translations. Upto now no one has chosen to challenge the same.

37. For similar reasons I also hold that Section 153A of the Indian Penal Code has no application in the facts of the present case. Apart from anything else, there is no question of forfeiture or banning of the said book on the grounds of disharmony or feelings of enmity or hatred or ill-will between different religions or communities. This book is not prejudicial to the maintenance of harmony between different religions. Because of the Koran no public tranquility has been disturbed upto now and there is no reason to apprehend any likehood of such disturbance in future. On the other hand the action of the petitioners may be said to have attempted to promote, on the grounds of religion, disharmony or feelings of enmity, hatred or ill-will between different religions, i.e., between Muslims on the one hand and non-Muslims on the other within the meaning of Section 153A. Similarly, in my opinion, it may be said that by this petition the petitioners insult or attempt to insult the Muslim religion and the religious belief of the Muslims within the meaning of Section 295A of the Indian Penal Code. It is an affront to Islam's Supreme Scriptural Authority. For this reason the contention of the respondents that this application is motivated cannot be completely ruled out.

38. The learned Attorney General was right in making comments regarding caution to be exercised in entertaining public interest litigation. A Writ petition is a very important proceeding. It is known as a High Prerogative Writ. Article 226 of the Constitution confers a wide power on the High Courts. It is wider than Article 32 itself. The High Court enjoys a jurisdiction which is not enjoyed by an ordinary civil court. In many cases where no remedy is available in an ordinary civil court, the Writ Court is the only forum. It is much more expeditious than an ordinary civil proceeding. However, in my opinion it is the duty of the Court

while entertaining or admitting such application, particularly a public interest litigation, to be very cautious about the same, particularly where it is a matter of great public interest. In this context reference may be made to the judgment of Pathak J. in the case of *Bandhu Mukti Morcha – vs – Union of India* (supra). The present case involves the sentiment and religious feelings of a minority community. The matter involves religious feelings of millions of people not only in India but also outside India. It involves a highly delicate and sensitive issue. The application was entertained and admitted without going into the question of prima facie case and the jurisdiction and power of the Court to entertain this petition. In spite of the same directions were given for filing of affidavits. This by itself amounts to holding that there is a prima facie case though this question was not gone into. The Court should be circumspect in such kind of matters and be very cautious about the same. Otherwise though it might attract cheap publicity but may cause untold misery and disruption of religious harmony. The High Court should have been spared of the embarrassment caused. The petition should have been rejected forthwith and in limine as unworthy of its consideration as soon as it was moved.

39. For the aforesaid reasons I am of the opinion that the Writ Court's jurisdiction has been wrongly sought to be invoked in this case. No prima facie case has been made out. It is clear that this Court has no power of jurisdiction to pass any such order as prayed for in this application.

40. For the aforesaid reasons this applications stands dismissed. No order as to costs.

41. In this connection I record my appreciation of the very frank, fair and sober manner in which this case has been argued by the Attorney General appearing for the Union of India and the Advocate General appearing for the State.

Sd/-
(B.C. Basak)

(7)

The Review Application

MATTER NO. 297 OF 1985
IN THE HIGH COURT AT CALCUTTA
Constitutional Writ Jurisdiction
(ORIGINAL SIDE)

In the Matter of an application for condonation of delay in the submission of the review application.

In the matter of
Chandmal Chopra & Anr.

-Applicant.

Versus

The State of West Bengal

-Respondent.

To

1. The Hon'ble Mr. Satish Chandra, the Chief Justice and His Companion Justices of the said High Court.

The humble petition of the applicant above-named most respectfully

S H E W E T H :

1. That the judgment in the above matter was delivered on 17th May, 1985.

2. That the review petition which has to be moved within 30 days, ought to have been moved by 17th June, 1985, 16th June, 1985, being a Sunday and a holiday.

3. That the applicant got hurt in the palm of his right hand on 13th June, 1985, got a stitch and bandage and was advised not to move his right hand for some days. A medical certificate is enclosed, marked as annexure 'A'.

4. That due to the aforesaid reason the review application has become delayed by a day.

> It is therefore prayed that the delay of one day in the submission of the said application may kindly be condoned.

And for which act of kindness your petitioner as in duty bound shall ever pray.

Sd/-
(Chandmal Chopra)

An application for review of judgement dated 17.5.1985.

Chandmal Chopra of 25, Burtolla Street,
Calcutta - 7.

-Applicant

Petitioner.

Versus

The State of West Bengal, represented by
the Secretary, Department of Home,
Govt. of West Bengal, having his office
at Writers' Building, Calcutta - 1.

-Respondent.

Being aggrieved by some mistakes or errors apparent from the
judgment dated 17.5.85 passed by His Lordship Mr. Justice Bimal
Chandra Basak dismissing in limine the Court Application in
Matter No. 297 of 1985 from which no appeal has been filed and
due to the discovery of new and important matter which inspite of
exercise of due diligence could not be produced by the applicant at
the time when the matter was heard, the applicant above-named
begs to file this memo of review against the aforesaid decision on
the following amongst other

GROUNDS

1. For that the findings in paragraph 28 of the judgment
that the Koran is of divine origin and that the Koran has no earthly
source, based as they are not on any evidence but on mere
religious beliefs, are derogatory to the basic constitutional

principle of secularism and are therefore unconstitutional.

2. For that the finding given in paragraph 34 of the judgment that a court cannot sit in judgment on a holy book is unconstitutional.

3. For that a book, even if it be a book held sacred by any community living in India, loses protection of Sec. 295 if its publication amounts to offences under Section, amongst others, 295A I.P.C. and should have been held accordingly.

4. For that the finding given in paragraph 31 that the Koran does not insult other religions is not correct in view of the various sayings of the book already quoted in para 6 of the Writ application.

5. For that the finding given in paragraph 37 of the judgment that Sec. 153A I.P.C. has no application in this case is not correct as the various sayings of the Koran, already quoted in para 5 of the Writ application, do promote, on grounds of religion, disharmony or feeling of enmity, hatred and ill-will between different religious communities.

6. For that the following submissions are not recorded nor dealt with in the said judgment:

(i)   That Sec. 295 would not protect an object, even if held sacred by any class of persons, if the object happens to be a book and its publication amounts to commission of offences punishable u/s 295 I.P.C. itself apart from Secs. 153A and 295A I.P.C. inasmuch as whoever seeks protection of law must come with clean hands.

Some quotations from the book which exhorts its followers to take the idols (which are also the objects held sacred by other class of persons) to Hell for being burnt in hell-fire, were cited at the time of hearing.

(ii)   In reply to a question which was raised by the ld. Judge, namely, could an object of art, even if somewhat obscene, be proscribed on the ground of obscenity, the following summary of a Supreme Court judgment in A.I.R. 1985 (S.C.) 881 given by Chittaley and Appu Rao, at page 2188 of their book on the Indian Penal Code was relied upon:

"Where obscenity and art are mixed up, art must be so preponderating as to throw the obscenity into a shadow or the obscenity so trivial and insignificant that it can have no effect and may be overlooked."

The volume containing the report of the said judgment of the Supreme Court was also produced before the Judge.

7. For that the finding in paragraph 37 of the judgment that the contention of the respondent that this application is motivated cannot be completely ruled out, is not correct.

8. For that the ld. Judge ought to have held that the petition had been filed with bonafide motives and in the interest of the country and the public good.

I certify that the above are in my opinion good grounds of review.

Sd/-
(Chandmal Chopra)

Chandmal Chopra
– vs –
State of West Bengal

SUBMISSIONS

May It Please Your Lordship

This is an application for review of the judgement delivered in the above matter on the 17th May, 1985, which it is submitted is based, amongst others, on the following premises:

(1) (As) the "Koran' is of divine origin, so are the religion and its tenets and the philosophy and the legal principles which the 'Koran' inculcated. The Koran has no earthly source. (Paragraph 28).

(2) The Court cannot sit in judgment on a holy book... (Paragraph 34).

(3) It cannot be said that Koran offers any insult to any other religion. (Paragraph 31).

(4) Section 153A of the Indian Penal Code has no application. (Paragraph 37).

I now propose to deal with the grounds of review according to the serial in which they appear in my review petition.

GROUND NO. 1

1. The findings that the Koran is of divine origin and that it has no earthly source are based on religious beliefs and not on evidence. Unlike in a theocratic state (where Government is run by priests claiming to rule with divine authority), the courts of law in a secular state, it is respectfully submitted, cannot give their findings based on religious beliefs. Rather, the courts of law in a

secular state, in giving findings and in arriving at conclusions must necessarily act in disbelief, or disregard, of religious faiths and beliefs. The term "secularism" as defined by Webster's New World Dictionary, Second College Edition, 1972, means "a system of doctrines and practices that disregards or rejects any form of religious faith..." and, secondly, secularism "is the belief that religion and ecclesiastical affairs should not enter into the functions of the state..." According to Funk and Wagnalls New Standard Dictionary of the English Language, 1963, a secularist is "one who believes that religion should not be introduced into the management of public affairs." According to Webster's Third New International Dictionary, Unabridged (1971), secularism means "a view of life or of any particular matter based on the premise that religious considerations should be ignored or purposely excluded." According to the Concise Oxford Dictionary, the word 'secular" means "sceptical of religious truth." Accordingly, it is respectfully submitted that in consonance with the principle of secularism, this court should have disbelieved or disregarded, all religious beliefs about Koran.

It is therefore submitted that the findings given about the divine origin of Koran are derogatory to the basic constitutional principle of secularism and are therefore unconstitutional.

GROUND NO. 2

(1) Unlike in theocracy, as already defined above, in a democracy, the people govern themselves according to their own will as expressed through their representatives and not according to any divine book, and if the will so expressed ordains that a book, under certain circumstances, is liable to be forfeited, then any book, whether classic or epic, religious or temporal, old or new, is liable to be so forfeited provided only that those circumstances are present. And if a question arises whether those circumstances are present in the context of a particular book, courts of law, it is respectfully submitted, are the only forum to decide the question. Even otherwise also, under Article 226 of the

Constitution, our High Courts are vested with the power to issue, amongst others, writs of Mandamus to any authority or Government in all appropriate cases. Accordingly, the finding given in para 34 that the courts cannot sit in judgment on holy books, being an abdication of the express constitutional power is, it is respectfully submitted, derogatory to the Constitution, and, in particular, to Article 226 thereof, and is therefore unconstitutional.

GROUND NO. 3

(1) Section 295 I.P.C. no doubt protects objects held sacred by any class of persons from destruction. But this section, in the first place, does not override the provisions of Sections 295A I.P.C. nor of Section 153A I.P.C. In other words, Section 295 I.P.C. does not prevent a Government from acting under Section 95 Criminal Procedure Code, if the Government finds that the publishers of a book have violated the provisions of Sections 295A and 153A I.P.C. This is clear from the language of Section 295 itself inasmuch as the protection of Section 295 is available against those persons who destroy any sacred object "with the intention of insulting the religion of any class of persons." When a Government acts u/s 95 Cr. P.C. it does not act, it is submitted, with any such intention. Rather, the intention is to prevent the publisher of a book from committing offences under Sections 295A and 153A I.P.C., etc.

GROUND NO. 4

1. The finding that Koran does not insult other religions, is not, it is respectfully submitted, correct in view of the various quotations from the book given in para 6 of the Writ Application, in particular the following, none of which, it is respectfully submitted, undergoes any change in its meaning even if read in its context:

(a) "Unbelievers are those who declare, Allah is the Messiah (i.e. the Christ), the son of Mary. Say, 'Who could prevent Allah from destroying the Messiah, the son of Mary, together with his mother?"

(b) "The unbelievers among the people of the Book (i.e. the Christians and the Jews) and the pagans shall burn for ever in the fire of Hell. They are the vilest of all creatures."

(c) "He answered: Would you then worship that, instead of Allah, which can neither help nor harm you? Shame on you and on your idols."

(d) "You and all your idols shall be the fuel of Hell; therein you shall all go down. Were they true Gods, your idols would not go there; but in it they shall abide for ever. They shall groan with pain and be bereft of hearing."

(e) "Then Allah will say, 'Jesus, son of Mary, did you ever say to mankind, worship me and my mother as Gods besides Allah?' 'Glory to You,' he will answer, 'How could I say that to which I have no right? If I had ever said so, You would have surely known it. You know what is in my mind, but I cannot tell what is in Yours. You alone know what is hidden. I spoke to them of nothing except what You bade me. I say, Serve Allah, my Lord. I watched over them whilst living in their midst, and ever since You took me to You, You Yourself have been watching over them. You are the witness of all things. They are Your own bondsmen. It is for You to punish or to forgive them. You are the Mighty, the Wise One'."

(f) "On the day when He assembles them with all their idols, He will say: 'Was it you who misled My servants, or did they wilfully go astray?' They will answer: 'Allah forbid that we should choose other guardians besides You. You gave them and their fathers the good things of life, so that they forgot Your warnings and thus incurred destruction.' Then to the idolaters Allah will say: 'Your idols have denied your charges. Those of you who have done wrong shall be sternly punished'."

GROUND NO. 5

The finding that Section 153A has no application in this case is not, it is respectfully submitted, correct, as the various quotations from Koran already given in paragraph 5 of the Writ Application including the following, none of which, it is respectfully submitted, undergo any change in its meaning even if read in its context, do promote, on grounds of religion, disharmony, or feelings of enmity, hatred and ill-will between different religious communities:

(a) "We renounce you (i.e. idol-worshippers); enmity and hate shall reign between us until you believe in Allah only."

(b) "Believers! do not befriend your fathers or your brothers, if they choose unbelief in preference to faith. Wrong-doers are those that befriend them."

(c) "Therefore, We stirred among them (i.e. the Christians) enmity and hatred, which shall endure till the Day of Resurrection."

(d) "Believers! take neither Jews nor Christians for your friends. They are friends with one another. Whoever of you seeks their friendship shall become one of their number. Allah does not guide the wrong-doers."

GROUND NO. 6

The two submissions, as summarised in ground No. 6, were, it is respectfully submitted, made in course of petitioner's reply, but have not been recorded and may, therefore, it is prayed, be recorded now.

GROUND NO. 7

In paragraph 37 a finding has been recorded that the petitioner may be said to have committed offences under Sections 153A and 295A I.P.C. In this connection, it is respectfully submitted that the petitioner came across a book, the publishers of which, according to the petitioner's humble view, violated the law of the land, in particular, that laid down in Sections 153A and 295A I.P.C. He accordingly requested a responsible Officer of the Government to act under Section 95 Cr. P.C. If the Government so acts under Section 95 Cr. P.C., the Government could not, it is respectfully submitted, be said to commit any offence under Sec. 295 I.P.C. for the reasons already submitted above, and since the petitioner has not requested any street urchins to destroy any sacred object but a responsible Government Officer to act under Section 95 Cr.P.C. his culpability if any, it is respectfully submitted, is co-terminus with that of the Government. Accordingly the conclusion that the application may have been motivated may kindly be reviewed.

GROUND NO. 8

The petition was not filed, it is respectfully submitted, in a sudden fit of religious frenzy. But it was filed after a hard labour of one and a half years. It could thus be said, it is respectfully submitted, to be moved with bonafide motives only unless there is any evidence to the contrary.

Re: Jurisdiction of Writ Court to hear Review Application.

Lastly, in support of my humble plea that this Hon'ble Court has ample jurisdiction to entertain a review application, I may submit that in *Shivdeo Singh* – vs – *State of Punjab* (A.I.R. 196 S C. 1909, 1911) the Supreme Court has held that "the power of review inheres in every court of plenary jurisdiction to prevent miscarriage of justice or to correct grave and palpable errors committed by it."

Sd/-
(Chandmal Chopra)

18th June, 1985

(8)

Review Application Dismissed

MATTER NO. 297 OF 1985
Constitutional Writ
(ORIGINAL SIDE)

BIMAL CHANDRA BASAK
June   21   85.
Chandmal Chopra & Anr.
– Vs –
The State of West Bengal.

Two papers were moved before me. One is an application for condonation of delay in the submission of the review application and another is stated to be an application for review of my Judgment dated 17th May, 1985, but which is actually a memorandum of review. By the said Judgment I have dismissed the Writ petition directed against Koran in limine. Thereafter these two "applications" have been filed.

So far as the condonation of delay is concerned, the time for making an application for review is 30 days. There is only one day's delay. It might be felt that only one day's delay may be condoned but the condonation of delay is not a matter of course. The petitioner must give proper explanation of even one day's delay. In this case in the petition the delay is sought to be explained by making the following averments:

"That the applicant got hurt in the palm of his right hand on 13th June, 1985 , got a stitch and a bandage and was advised not to move his right hand for some days. A medical certificate is enclosed marked as annexure 'A'."

The said annexure 'A' reads as follows:

"Shree Vishudhanand Hospital & Research Institute.

35 & 37, Burtolla Street, Calcutta - 7

General Outdoor Deptt. (EMERGENCY)

Dr. H. Poddar

18 June 1985

No. 20139

Name — Chandmal Chopra, Age — 53 Yrs.

This is to certify that Sri Chandmal Chopra aged 53 yrs. had got injured on 15-6-85 on the right little finger. One stitch and bandage was done on 16.6.85. He is advised to take rest for 4 days from that very day.

Sd/- Illegible."

It will be seen that there are inconsistencies between the averments in the petition and the medical certificate. In the petition it is stated that the applicant got hurt in the palm of his right hand whereas in the medical certificate it has been stated that he had got injured on the right little finger. In the petition the averment is that he is advised not to move his right hand for some days. In the medical certificate it is stated that he is advised to take rest for four days from that very day, i.e, 15th June, 1985. Therefore, I cannot accept such statement. Moreover it is to be seen that from 15th June, 1985, four days mean upto 19th June, 1985. Therefore, according to such alleged advice, he was to take rest upto 19th June, 1985. Accordingly he could not have moved such application before 20th June if such medical advice was correct. But this application was moved on 18th June, 1985, by the petitioner in person. In my opinion, this is not a genuine ground. Further I am not satisfied that such a small injury could have prevented the petitioner from filing the application in Court on 17th i.e., the last day of limitation. On the 18th inst. he appeared in Court and moved the application in person. From my personal observation also, I am satisfied that there was no injury which could disable him from moving any such application on 17th instant.

So far as the "application" for review is concerned actually it is a memorandum of review. It is to be pointed out that there is no application in support of the said memorandum. The only application filed along with the memorandum is that application for condonation of delay. There is no prayer therein for issuing a rule or for any order directing the hearing of the application for review. There is no averment in the said application also so far as review is concerned. Though it is stated in the memorandum of review that it is an application for review, there is in fact no such application.

The power of review is to be exercised very sparingly. This court in its writ jurisdiction has undoubtedly got the power to review its judgment. But there are limits to the exercise of such power.

The petitioner seeks to invoke the power of review based on Order 47 Rule 1 (1) of the Code of Civil Procedure. The said Rule is set out hereinbelow:

"1(1) Any person considering himself aggrieved

(a) by a decision on reference from a Court of Small Causes from which no appeal has been preferred,

(b) by a decree or order from which no appeal is allowed,

(c) by a decision on a reference from a Court of Small Causes, and who, from the discovery of new and important matter or evidence which, after the exercise of due diligence, was not within his knowledge or could not be produced by him at the time when the decree was passed or order made, or on account of some mistake or error apparent on the face of the record, or for any other sufficient reason, desires to obtain a review of the decree passed or order made against him, may apply for a review for a review of judgment to the Court which passed the decree or made the order."

Such power may not be exercised on the ground that the decision was erroneous on merits. That would be the province of a Court of Appeal. A power of review is not to be confused with appellate power which may enable an Appellate Court to correct all manner of errors committed by Trial Court. Reference may be made in this connection to the decision in the case of *A.T. Sharma-vs-A.P. Sharma* reported in A.I.R. 1979 S.C. 1047.

In the case of *Thungabhadra Industries – vs – The Government of Andhra Pradesh* reported in A.I.R. 1964 S.C. 1372 it was pointed out that there was a distinction which is real, though it might not always be capable of exposition, between a mere erroneous decision and a decision which could be characterised as vitiated by error apparent. A review is by no means an appeal in disguise whereby an erroneous decision is reheard and corrected but lies only for patent error. Where without any elaborate argument one could point to the error and say here is a substantial point of law which stared one in the face and there could reasonably be no two opinions entertained about it, a clear case of error apparent on the face of the record would be made out.

It has to be pointed out that in the present case in the memorandum of review altogether eight grounds have been taken. Out of that ground nos. 1 to 5 and ground nos. 7 and 8 are the grounds challenging the correctness of my decision. This may or may not be ground for appeal but not a ground for review. So far as the ground no. 6 is concerned, there is no merit in the same. There is no question of error apparent involved. Further whatever point was raised on behalf of the petitioner was recorded by me and dealt with by me.

In my opinion no case has been made out by the petitioner for exercise of such power. There is no mistake apparent from the judgment for the purpose of review. It is stated that it is also being filed due to the discovery of new and important matter or evidence which, after the exercise of due diligence, was not within the knowledge of the person seeking the review or could not be produced by the applicant at the time when the matter was heard. As I have stated, no application for review has been made stating the alleged new and important matter and alleged exercise of diligence. As I have already stated there is no other application excepting one application for condonation and another being a memorandum of review though described as an application for review.

For the aforesaid reasons these applications/memorandum are misconceived and they are rejected in limine.

It may be recorded that today a written submission has been placed before me which may be kept in the records.

Sd/-
(B.C. Basak)

Bibliography

A Comprehensive History of India, Volume Fifth, *The Saltanat*, edited by Mohammad Habib and K.A. Nizami, New Delhi, 1970, First Reprint, 1982.

Akbar-Nāma of Abul Fazl, translated into English by H. Beveridge, Volume I and II Bound in One, New Delhi reprint, 1993.

Babur-Nāma of Zahiruddin Babur, translated into English by A.S. Beveridge, New Delhi reprint, 1979.

Elliot and Dowson, *History of India as told by its own Historians*, New Delhi reprint, 1990, Volume I, II, III, IV, V, VI, VIII.

Goel, Sita Ram (ed.), *Freedom of Expression: Secular Theocracy Versus Liberal Democracy*, Voice of India, New Delhi, 1998.

Goel, Sita Ram, *Hindu Temples: What Happened to Them*, Volume II (1991), Second Enlarged Edition, Voice of India, New Delhi, 1993.

Goel, Sita Ram, *The Story of Islamic Imperialism in India* (1982), Second Revised Edition, Voice of India, 1994.

Harsh Narain, *Myths of Composite Culture and Equality of Religions*, Voice of India, New Delhi, 1990, reprinted in 1997.

Hedaya, The, of Shykh Burhanuddin Ali, Volume II, translated into English by Charles Hamilton, London, 1791, New Delhi Reprint, 1985.

Hughes, T.P., *Dictionary of Islam* (1885), First Indian Edition (reprint), New Delhi, 1976.

Lal, K.S., *Theory and Practice of Muslim State in India*, Aditya Prakashan, New Delhi, 1999.

Lammens, H., Islam: *Belief and Institutions*, London, 1929, New Impression, 1968.

Machiavelli, Niccolo, *The Prince*, The Translation by Luigi Ricci, revised by E.P.R. Vincent, OUP, 1934, Jaico reprint, Bombay, 1957.

Majumdar, R.C. (ed.), *The History and Culture of the Indian People*, Volume VI, *The Delhi Sultanate*, Bombay, 1960; Volume VII, *The Mughal Empire*, Bombay, 1973.

Malik, Brigadier S.K., *The Quranic Concept of War*, Lahore, 1979, New Delhi reprint, 1986.

Margoliouth, D.S., *Mohammed and the Rise of Islam*, London, 1905, Indian reprint with Introduction by Ram Swarup, Voice of India, New Delhi, 1985.

Muir, Sir William, *The Life of Mahomet*, London, 1894, Indian reprint with Introduction by Ram Swarup, Voice of India, 1992.

Nehru, Jawaharlal, *Glimpses of World History* (1934-35), OUP, New Delhi, Fourth Impression, 1987.

Proceedings of Indian History Congress, New Delhi, 1972.

Qur'ān Majīd, Arabic text with translation in Urdu by Maulana Fath Muhammad and in Hindi by Muhammad Faruq Khān, Maktaba al-Hasnāt, Rampur, U.P., sixth impression, 1976.

Ram Swarup, *Hindu View of Christianity and Islam*, Voice of India, New Delhi, 1992, reprinted in 1993.

Ram Swarup, Introduction, See Margoliouth above.

Ram Swarup, *Understanding Islam through Hadis: Faith or Fanaticism?* U.S. Edition, 1983, Indian reprint, Voice of India, New Delhi, 1984 and 1987.

Rizvi, Saiyid Athar Abbas, *A Hisoty of Sufism in India*, 2 Volumes, New Delhi, 1978 and 1983.

Rodinson, Maxime, *Mohammed*, London, 1971

Sahīh Muslim Sharīf, Arabic text with Urdu translation by Allama Wahid-uz-Zaman, Volume IV, Delhi, 1986.

Sarkar, Jadunath, *History of Aurangzīb*, Volume III, Calcutta, 1928, New Impression, 1972.

Sarkar, Jadunath, *Fall of the Mughal Empire*, Volume II, Fourth Edition, New Delhi, 1991.

Sewell, Robert, *A Forgotten Empire*, New Delhi reprint, 1962.

Shourie, Arun, *Eminent Historians: Their Technology, Their Line, Their Fraud*, New Delhi, 1998.

Sīrat Rasūl Allāh of Ibn Ishaq, translated by A. Gillaume (1955), OUP, Karachi, Eighth Impression, 1987.

Siyar-ul-Awliya of Amir Khurd, translated into Urdu, New Delhi, 1984.

Sunan Ibn Mājah, Arabic text with Urdu translation by Maulana Abdul Hakim Khan Akhtar Shahjahanpuri, Volume I, New Delhi, 1986.

Tārīkh-i-Akbari of Muhammad Arif Qandhari, translated into English by Tanseem Ahmad, Delhi, 1993.

Tārīkh-i-Farishtah, translated into English by John Briggs as *History of the Rise of Mahomedan Power in India*, Volume III, New Delhi reprint, 1981.

Tārīkh-i-Tabari, Volume I, *Sīrat-an-Nabi*, translated into Urdu by Saiyyad Muhammad Ibrahim, Karachi, n.d.

Tuhfat-ul-Mujahideen of Shykh Zeen-ud-deen, translated into English by M.J. Rowlandson, London, 1933.